LIFE IN CHRIST

Register This New Book

Benefits of Registering*

- ✓ FREE **replacements** of lost or damaged books
- ✓ FREE **audiobook** – *Pilgrim's Progress*, audiobook edition
- ✓ FREE information about new titles and other **freebies**

www.anekopress.com/new-book-registration

*See our website for requirements and limitations.

LIFE IN CHRIST

Lessons from Our Lord's
Miracles and Parables

The Miracles of Our Lord
Volume 4

Charles H. Spurgeon

We love hearing from our readers. Please contact us at www.anekopress.com/questions-comments with any questions, comments, or suggestions.

Life in Christ, Vol. 4
© *2022 by Aneko Press*
All rights reserved.
Revised edition 2022

Please do not reproduce, store in a retrieval system, or transmit in any form or by any means – electronic, mechanical, photocopying, recording, or otherwise, without written permission from the publisher. Please contact us via www.AnekoPress.com for reprint and translation permissions.

Scripture quotations are from The Authorized (King James) Version. Rights in the Authorized Version in the United Kingdom are vested in the Crown. Reproduced by permission of the Crown's patentee, Cambridge University Press.

Cover Design: Natalia Hawthorne
Cover Painting: Matt Philleo
Editors: Ruth Clark and J. Martin

Aneko Press
www.anekopress.com
Aneko Press, Life Sentence Publishing, and our logos are trademarks of
Life Sentence Publishing, Inc.
203 E. Birch Street
P.O. Box 652
Abbotsford, WI 54405

RELIGION / Christian Life / Spiritual Growth
Paperback ISBN: 978-1-62245-678-9
eBook ISBN: 978-1-62245-679-6

10 9 8 7 6 5 4 3 2 1

Available where books are sold

Contents

Ch. 1: The Nets of Fishes 1

Ch. 2: At Thy Word 19

Ch. 3: The Chief Physician and the Centurion's Servant 37

Ch. 4: Self Low, but Christ High 55

Ch. 5: A Man Under Authority 73

Ch. 6: A Blessed Wonder 87

Ch. 7: The Centurion or An Exhortation to the Virtuous 103

Ch. 8: The Centurion's Faith and Humility 119

Ch. 9: An Astounding Miracle 135

Ch. 10: How to Meet the Doctrine of Election 153

Ch. 11: The Little Dogs 171

Ch. 12: Children's Bread Given to Dogs 187

Ch. 13: Pleading, Not Contradicting 205

Ch. 14: Little Faith and Great Faith 221

Ch. 15: The Perseverance of Faith 239

Charles H. Spurgeon – A Brief Biography 251

Other Similar Titles 255

Chapter 1

The Nets of Fishes

Now when he had left speaking, he said unto Simon, Launch out into the deep, and let down your nets for a draught. (Luke 5:4)

And he said unto them, Cast the net on the right side of the ship, and ye shall find. They cast therefore, and now they were not able to draw it for the multitude of fishes. (John 21:6)

The whole life of Christ was a sermon. He was a prophet mighty in word and deed, and by his deeds as well as his words he taught the people. It is perfectly true that the miracles of Christ attest to his mission. To those who saw them they must have been evident proof that he was sent of God. But we ought not to overlook that probably a higher reason for the miracles is to be found in the instruction which they convey. To the external world, at the present time, the miracles of Christ are harder to believe than the doctrine which he taught. Skeptics turn them into stones of stumbling, and when they cannot fuss at the marvelous teaching of Jesus, they attack the miracles as monstrous and incredible. I doubt not that even to minds seriously vexed with unbelief, the miracles, instead of being helps to belief, have been trials of faith. Few indeed are there in whom faith is worked by signs and wonders;

nor indeed is this the gospel way of bringing conviction to the soul. The secret force of the living Word is the chosen instrumentality of Christ, and wonders are largely left to be the resort of that Antichrist by whom the nations shall be deceived. We, who by grace have believed, view the miracles of Christ as noble attestations to his mission and divinity, but we confess that we value them even more as instructive sermons than as attesting witnesses; it is our conviction that we should lose much of the benefit which they were meant to convey to us if we were merely to view them as seals to the roll, for they are a part of the writing of the roll itself. The marvels worked by our blessed Lord are acted sermons fraught with holy doctrine, set forth to us more vividly than it could have been in words. We start with this assumption, that Christ's miracles are sermons preached in deeds, visible allegories, truths embodied, and principles incarnated and set in motion. They are, in fact, the pictures in the great Book of Christ's teaching, the illustrations by which he flashed light into dim eyes.

We have heard of some ministers who could say that they had often preached from the same text, but they had never delivered the same discourse. The same may be said of Christ. He often preached upon the same truth, but it was never precisely in the same manner. We have read the narrative of two miracles (Luke 5 and John 21), which seem to the casual observer to be precisely alike; but he who shall read diligently and study carefully will find that although the text is the same in both, the discourse is full of variations. In both descriptions of the miraculous catch of fish, the text is the mission of the saints to preach the gospel – the work of man-catching – the ministry by which souls are caught in the net of the gospel and brought out of the element of sin to their eternal salvation. The preacher is compared to a fisherman. The fisherman's vocation is a toilsome one; woe to that minister who finds his calling to be otherwise. The fisherman must go forth in rough weather and at all hazards; if he should only fish in a calm sea he may often starve. So the Christian minister, whether men will receive the Word with pleasure, or reject it with anger and wrath, must be ready to imperil reputation and risk comfort; yes, he must hate his own life also, or he is not worthy of the heavenly calling.

The fisherman's is a rough occupation; no dainty fingers may come in contact with his nets. It is not a trade for gentlemen, but for rough, strong, and fearless men who can heave a rope, handle a tarbrush, or scour a deck. The ministry is not meant for your dainty souls who would go delicately through this world without a trial, an offense, an insult, or a sneer. Such work is meant for men who know how to do business on great waters, and can go abroad upon the sea, not fearing the spray or the waves. The fisherman's calling, too, must be carried on perseveringly. It is not by one grand haul that a man makes his fortune; he must constantly cast forth his net. One sermon makes not a preacher; he who shall but now and then deliver himself of some carefully prepared oration is no true minister of God. He must be constant in season and out of season; he must cast his net in all waters; he must in the morning be at his work, and in the evening he must not withhold his hand. To be a fisherman, a man must expect disappointments; he will often cast in the net and bring up nothing but weeds. The minister of Christ must reckon upon being disappointed, and he must not be weary in well-doing for all his disappointments, but must in faith continue in prayer and labor, expecting that at the end he shall receive his reward. It needs no great labor for you to work out at leisure the comparison between fishermen and the gospel ministry, for the simile is so aptly chosen.

The two narratives before us have a degree of uniformity; that shall be our first point. *But they have a greater degree of dissimilarity;* we will bring that out in the second place. And then, thirdly, we will suggest *some great lessons which they both combine to teach us.*

First, then, *in these two miracles there are many points of uniformity.* They are both intended to set forth the way in which Christ's kingdom shall increase.

You will perceive, first, that in both miracles we are taught that *the means must be used.* In the first case, the fish did not leap into Simon's boat to be taken; nor, in the second case, did they swarm from the sea and lay themselves down upon the blazing coals that they might be prepared for the fisherman's feast. No, the fishermen must go out in their boat, they must cast the net, and after having cast the net, they must either drag it ashore or fill both boats with its contents. Everything is done here by human agency. It is a miracle, certainly, but yet neither the fisherman, nor his boat, nor his fishing tackle are ignored; they are all used and all employed.

Let us learn that in the saving of souls God works by means, that so long as the present economy of grace shall stand, God will be pleased by the foolishness of preaching to save those who believe. Every now and then there creeps up in the church a sort of striving against God's ordained instrumentality. I marked it with sorrow during the Irish Revival. We constantly saw in some excellent papers remarks which I thought exceedingly injurious, wherein it was made a subject of congratulation that no man was concerned in the work, no eminent preacher, no fervent evangelist; the whole was boasted of as being conducted without human instrumentality. That was the weakness of the revival, not its strength. You say it gave God the more glory. Not so. God gets the most glory through the use of instruments.

When God works without instruments, doubtless he is glorified; but he knows himself in which way he gets the most honor, and he has himself selected the plan of instrumentality as being that by which he is most magnified in the earth. We have this treasure. How? Alone? Without any earthly accompaniment? No, but in earthen vessels. Why? That God may have less glory? No, but in the earthen vessels so that the excellency of the power may be of God and not of us. God makes the infirmity of the creature to be the contrast to the strength of the Creator. He takes men who are nothing in themselves and works by them his splendid victories. Perhaps we would not admire Samson so much if he had dashed the Philistines in pieces with his fist, as we do when we find that with such a weapon, so unadapted to the work, as the jawbone of a donkey, he laid in heaps thousands of his foes.

> The Lord takes ill weapons so that with them he may work great deeds.

The Lord takes ill weapons so that with them he may work great deeds. When he said, *Let there be light: and there was light* without any instrument, he showed his glory; but when instead he takes the apostles and says again, "Let there be light," and sends them forth who were darkness in themselves, and makes them the means of lighting up a dark world, I say there is a greater glory. And if the morning stars sang together when they first saw light upon the newly made earth, surely the angels in heaven rejoiced even more when they saw light thus streaming upon the dark earth through men who, in and of themselves, would only have increased the blackness and made the gloom more dense. God works by means of men whom he specially calls to his work, and not, as a rule, without them.

The Plymouthist strives to get rid of the pastorate, but he never can, for the Lord will ever continue to give pastors after his own heart to feed his people, and all attempts made by the flock to dispense with these pastors will lead to leanness and poverty of soul. The outcry against the "one-man ministry" comes not from God, but from the proud selfconceit of men who are not content to learn, although they have no power to teach. It is the tendency of human nature to exalt itself, which has raised up these disturbers of the peace of God's Israel, for they will not endure to submit themselves to the authorities which God has himself appointed, and they abhor the teachings of the apostle Paul, where he says, by the Spirit of God, *Obey them that have the rule over you, and submit yourselves: for they watch for your souls, as they that must give account, that they may do it with joy, and not with grief: for that is unprofitable for you.*

Brethren, I warn you, there is a spirit abroad which would pull down the men whom God himself has raised up, and that would silence those into whose mouths God has put the tongue of fire, so that foolish men might babble according to their own will to the profit of no one, and to their own shame. As for us, we shall, I trust, never cease to recognize that agency by which the Lord works mightily among us. We should restrain no ministry in the church of God. We should but be too glad to see it more abundantly exercised. I wish to God that all the Lord's servants were prophets! But we enter our solemn protest against that spirit which, under pretense of liberty to all, sets aside the instrumentality by which the Lord especially works. He will have you still keep the fishermen to their nets and to their boats; and your new ways of catching fish without nets, and saving souls without ministers, will never answer, for they are not of God. They have been tried, and what has been the result of the trial? I know not a church in existence that has despised instrumentality, but it has come to an end within a few years either by schism or decay. Where upon the face of the earth is there a single church that has existed fifty years where God's chosen instrumentality of ministry has been despised and rejected? "Ichabod!" is written upon their walls. God rejects them because they reject God's chosen way of working. Their attempts are flashes in the pan, meteoric lights, will-o'-the-wisps, swellings of proud flesh, and bubbles of foam, here today and gone forever tomorrow.

In both our texts there is a second truth equally conspicuous, namely, that *means of themselves are utterly unavailing*. In the first case you hear the confession, *Master, we have toiled all the night, and have taken nothing*. In the last case you hear them answer the question, *Children, have ye any meat?* With a *No* – a sorrowful *No*. What was the reason for this? Were they not fishermen fulfilling their special calling? Truly, they were no raw hands; they understood the work. Had they gone about the toil unskillfully? No. Had they lacked industry? No, they had *toiled*. Had they lacked perseverance? No, they had toiled *all the night*. Was there a deficiency of fish in the sea? Certainly not, for as soon as the Master comes there they are in the shallow waters. What then is the reason? Is it not because there is no power in the means of themselves apart from the presence of Christ? The Great Worker who does not discard the means would still have his people know that he uses instrumentality, not to glorify the instrument, but for the sake of glorifying himself. He takes weakness into his hands and makes it strong, not that weakness may be worshipped, but that the strength may be adored which makes even weakness subservient to his might.

Brethren, let us as a church always keep this in mind, that without Christ we can do nothing. *Not by might, nor by power, but by my Spirit, saith the Lord of hosts*. Put no dependence upon societies, upon committees, upon ministries, or upon anything that we can do. Let us work as if it all depended upon us, but let us come to God depending upon him, knowing most surely that it does not rest with us, but with Him alone. Let us send forth the missionaries to the heathen; let us send forth our men into the dark streets and lanes of London; let us scatter tracts; let us distribute the Word of God; let us send forth preachers by scores from our "School of the Prophets"; but when this is done, let us not sit still and say, "Now it is all accomplished, good must come of it." No, Lord, unless your blessing descends from on high, we might as well have done nothing, for no eternal results can follow.

How often this drives me to my knees. The surprising work which God is doing in connection with this place lifts up my heart with joy, but then the fear lest it all should come to nothing for lack of his blessing casts my spirit to the very earth. One brother was moved some time ago to distribute a volume of the sermons I preached to every student in Oxford and Cambridge. After that had been done, and some two hundred thousand sermons had been distributed, he then gave them to every member of Parliament, to every peer of the realm, and to princes, kings, and emperors of Europe, and having accomplished that work, he still had others in hand of great magnitude. Dear friends, as I think of these books traveling everywhere among high and low, and among the rich and poor in all places of the land, my heart is glad; but then, if God withholds the blessing, they may as well have never been born in the press and circulated by human hands. What good can they do? Let the net be never so broad, never so strong, and let it be never so industriously cast into the sea, yet we shall toil all the night and take nothing unless the Master comes to own the work. Let us then be always in prayer for the blessing. Let us remember that we have done nothing until we have prayed over what we have done. Let us consider that all the seed we have put into the ground is put there for worms to eat unless we have dropped into the soil the preserving grain of prayer to keep that other grain alive. We shall have harvests if we wait on God for them, but after all our sowing, if we look to the soil, the seed, or the sower, we shall see nothing for our pains.

> Let us remember that we have done nothing until we have prayed over what we have done.

There is clearly taught in both these miracles the third fact that it is *Christ's presence that confers success*. Christ sat in Peter's boat. It was his will that by a mysterious influence the fish were drawn to the net, as though he had a hook, a secret hook in each of their jaws, that could stop them in their sportive leapings and hurry them all to one common center. It was his presence on the dry land, when he spoke from off the shore to his toiling disciples out yonder, and said, *Cast the net on the right side of the ship*. It was his presence that drew the fish to the place where they were taken. Oh, brethren, we must learn this: that it is Christ's presence in the midst of the church that is the church's power – the shout of the King in the midst of her. It is the presence of Christ's great representative, the Holy Spirit, that is to give the church force. *I, if I be lifted up from the earth, will draw all men unto me.* There is the attraction. The Spirit gives the power, and we must tarry until we get it; but when we have it, then we cannot preach in vain, for we become a *savour of life unto life* to those who hear.

Christians, Christ's presence with you must be your power. Be much in fellowship with him; catch much of his Spirit; meditate much upon his sufferings; keep close to his person, and then, wherever you go there shall be a power about you which even your adversaries shall be compelled to acknowledge. Oh, that we had more of Christ's presence in us as a church! Lift up your hearts for it. If Christ be here at all, let us not grieve him. *I charge you, O ye daughters of Jerusalem, . . . that ye stir not up, nor awake my love, till he please.* And if he is not here, let us rise from the bed of our sloth and go forth and seek him, crying, "O thou whom my soul loves, tell me where you feed, where you make your flock to rest at noon! And if you find him, I charge you to hold him, and not let him go till you bring him into our mother's house, into the chamber of her that bore us, even the church of Christ; there will we hold him, there will we embrace him, and he shall show to us his loves."

In both instances *the success* which attended the instrumentality through Christ's presence *developed human weakness*. We do not see human weakness more in non-success than in success. In the first instance, in the success you see the weakness of man, for the net breaks and the ships begin to sink, and Simon Peter falls down, saying, *Depart from me, for I am a sinful man, O Lord.* He did not know so much about that until his boat was filled; but the very abundance of God's mercy made him feel his own nothingness. In the second instance, they were scarcely able to draw the net in because of the multitude of fish. Brethren, if you or I would know to the fullest extent what utter nothings we are, if the Lord should give us success in winning souls, then we would soon find it out. As we see first one, and then another, and then scores, and then hundreds brought to the Lord Jesus, we shall say, "Who has brought me these? How can such wonders be worked by me?" And we shall fall prostrate before the footstool of sovereign grace, and confess that we are unworthy of such amazing favors.

Let the church spread, let her conquests be many, let her overrun whole provinces with her heavenly arms, and instead of man becoming more famous, man shall sink lower and lower, and it shall be more and more fully perceived that it is the Lord. Little works, such as have been common in our churches for years, where twos and threes are added, are quite consistent with great self-congratulation, and so is utter barrenness; mark the arrogant sense of many a fruitless preacher and see if it be not so. Let the Lord make bare his arm and the man humbles himself in the dust, for when hundreds are gathered in, this cannot be the minister – this is the finger of God. The man is forgotten, then, in the very abundance of his success, and the Lord alone is magnified in that day.

Oh, that God would do in the churches of England some great and stupendous works by all his ministers! Then would they discover their own weakness, and then would the name of God be glorified. You frequently meet with the observation, if a man be successful in winning souls: "I am afraid he will grow proud; how we ought to pray that he may be kept humble!" Brethren, that is a very necessary prayer for anybody; but it is no more necessary for the man who is successful than for the unsuccessful one; in fact, it is an assumption of pride on any person's part to think that he has less need to pray against pride than any other man. Think not that when the church prospers it becomes necessarily proud. No, the very fullness of the boat makes it sink, and the very abundance of the miracle makes us cry out the more, *It is the Lord*, for we feel that it could not have been of man, for it is out of man's reach to have accomplished such wonders.

So far, then, there is a likeness running through the whole. Means must be used – means alone, unavailing. Christ's presence gives the success; that success develops human weakness and leads to the exclamation, *It is the Lord*.

Having, then, shown the likeness, you will be still more interested in *marking the dissimilarity*. Allow us to say in the commencement that we think the first picture represents the church of God as we see it; the second represents it as it really is. The first pictures to us the visible, the second the invisible. Luke tells us what the crowd saw; John tells us what Christ showed to his disciples alone. The first is common truth which the multitude may receive; the next is special mystery revealed only to spiritual minds. Observe then, carefully, the points of divergence.

First, there is a difference in the orders given. In the first, it is, *Launch out into the deep, and let down your nets for a draught.* In the second, it is, *Cast the net on the right side of the ship.* The first is Christ's order to every minister; the second is the secret work of his Spirit in the word. The first shows us that the ministry is to fish anywhere and everywhere. All the orders that the Christian has, as to his preaching, are, *Launch out into the deep, and let down your nets.* He is not to single out any particular character; he is to preach to everybody – sensible sinners and insensible sinners. He is to preach to the dead, dry bones of the valley as well as to the living souls. He is not to look for where the fish are, but to just throw the net in, doing as his Master tells him. *Go ye into all the world, and preach the gospel to every creature.* Those ministers who preach only to the elect should remember this. Our business is to include all sorts of fish, and not to be particular about where we are, but just splash the net in. What if we be in town, or city, or village? What if we be among the rich or poor, the learned or illiterate? What if we be among the debauched or immoral? We have nothing to do with that. Our duty is the same: to launch out into the deep, and let down the net, and that is all. Christ will find the fish, it is no business of ours.

The secret truth is that when we are doing this, the Lord knows how to guide us so that we *cast the net on the right side of the ship.* That is the secret and invisible work of the Spirit whereby he so adapts our ministry, which is in itself general, that he makes it particular and special. We speak to all, and he speaks to some. We blow the trumpet, but only the bankrupt debtors hear it. Only those who are truly of the Spirit of God know the joyful sound and rejoice therein. *We* cannot single them out, but God can. We thrust in the blessed loadstone of the gospel, and that heavenly magnet has an affinity to some hearts which God has stimulated, so that as many as were ordained unto eternal life believe. The apostles preached to the crowd, but the Lord God the Holy Spirit, who had decreed the salvation of his chosen, sent the word home with power to the chosen and separated ones. What a joy it is to think that we always have a picked congregation here, for the Lord has picked them! Though they are crowded together indiscriminately – here the good and there the bad, all sorts mingled and mixed together – yet God brings them in according to his eternal purpose, and all the while there is a core of chosen souls inside the mass of the congregation to whom God is applying the word. We cast the net, after all, on the right side of the ship, and we do find it full.

In the first account you will clearly see that there is a distinct plurality. The fishermen have nets – in the plural; they have boats – in the plural. There is plurality of agency employed. Each man seems to come out distinctly. In the next case, it is one. There are many men, but they are all in *one boat*. They unitedly drag the net, and it is but *one* net; there is no division, it is all one. Now, this is the visible and the invisible. To us, the means that God makes use of to bring sinners to himself are various. Sometimes we are in one boat trying to catch all the fish we can. There is another boat over yonder, and they are trying to do the same. We ought to consider them as being partners, and whenever our boat gets too full, we should beckon to our partners in the other ship to come and help us. We ought not to look upon those brethren who differ from us as though they were emptying the sea and rivaling us. The more the merrier. The more men to do good, the more will the Lord's name be praised.

I think, in many of our towns where some of our whining brethren say that all good people should go to one chapel, that it is far better to have three or four chapels. I question whether the plurality of agency involved in denominations is not a great benefit and blessing. Instead of, in the slightest degree, standing out against my brethren for carrying out their convictions, I praise them and look upon them as partners in another ship. Our denominational distinctions help to keep us awake, thus we stir one another up and do far more good in the world than would be the case if there were only a nominal church. God would have the agency diverse. There must be several nets, and there must be several fishermen, and these fishermen must be in different boats. So far as we are able to see, there will always be a Paul and a Barnabas who cannot get along together; there will always be outward divisions in the ministry, and I avow myself the advocate and lover of these things. As I stated previously, the thing called sectarianism I do not disown but maintain.

But let us look to the inward. In John they are all in one boat, all fishing together, all dragging one net. And, brethren, this is what is really the fact. We do not see it, but all God's ministers are dragging one net, and all God's church is in one ship. Oh, I bless God for that sweet doctrine! It is no use striving after outward uniformity; we shall never see it. Neither the texture of the human mind nor the will of God require it. It is of no use to contend against the diversities which exist in the great visible church; I do not think that these differences are evils. They are the natural results of man's finite character, and they must and will exist to the end of the chapter. It is the unity of the Spirit, it is unity in Christ Jesus, and it is unity in love for one another that God would have us regard. Let us learn this unity from the fact that, after all, though we may look as if we differed, yet if we are God's ministers, there is only one ministry; if we are God's church, there is only one church in the world; there is only one spouse of the Lord Jesus; there is only one fold and one shepherd. Though to our eyes it will always be so – two boats or twenty boats, two nets or fifty nets – yet to him who sees all things better than we do, there is only one boat and one net, and all who are taken in that one net shall be safely brought to shore.

Thirdly, there is another difference. In the first case, how many fish were caught? The text says, *a great multitude*. In the second case, a great multitude are taken too, but they are all counted and numbered: *an hundred and fifty and three*. Luke does not tell us how many were caught the first time, for there were some of them not worth the counting; but the second time you will perceive that the exact number is recorded: *an hundred and fifty and three*. What was Peter's reason for counting them? We cannot tell. But I think I know why the Lord made him do it. It was to show us that though in the outward instrumentality of gathering the people into the church the number of the saved is to us a matter of which we know nothing definitely, yet secretly and invisibly the Lord has counted them even to the odd one, for he knows well how many the gospel net shall bring in.

See where the Word is preached what a great multitude are brought in! Thousands, tens of thousands, are added to the different churches of Christ, and make a profession of their faith. It is impossible to reckon all over Christendom how many have been taken in the outward net of the visible church of Christ. But, brethren, it is quite possible for it to be known of God how many shall be brought at last, and how many now are in the *invisible* church. He has counted them, foreordained their number, fixed them, and settled them. The number *an hundred and fifty and three* seems to me to represent a large, definite number. They shall be in heaven a number that no man can number, for God's elect are not few; but they shall be a number whom God can number, for *the Lord knoweth them that are his.* They shall be a number certain and fixed, which shall neither be diminished nor increased, but shall be the same according to his purpose and will. Now I, as a preacher, have nothing to do with counting fish. My business is with the great multitude. Splash goes the net again! Oh Master! You who have taught us to throw the net and bring in a multitude, guide into it the hundred and fifty and three!

Yet again, notice another difference. The fish that were taken the first time appear to have been of all sorts. The net was broken, and therefore it's doubtless that some of them got out again; there were some so little that they were not worth eating and doubtless were thrown away. They shall gather *the good into vessels, but cast the bad away.* In the second case, the net was full of great fishes; they were all great fishes, all good for eating, all the one hundred and fifty-three were worth the keeping, and there was not one little fellow to be thrown back into the deep again. The first gives us the outward and visible effect of the ministry. We gather into Christ's church a great number. And there will always be in that number some that are not good, that are not really called of God. Sometimes we have church meetings in which we have to throw the bad away. We have many blissful meetings where there is a gathering in of the fish, and what big hauls of fish has God given to us! Glory be to his name! But at other times we have to sit down and count our fish over, and there are some who must be thrown away; neither God nor man can endure them. Thus is it in the outward and visible church.

Let no man be surprised if the tares grow up with the wheat; it is the order of things, it must be so. Let none of us wonder if there be wolves in sheep's clothing; it always will be so. There was a Judas among the twelve; there will be deceivers among us to the end of the chapter. Not so the invisible church – the church within the church – the holy of holies within the temple. In that, there is none to throw away. No, the Lord who brought them into the net brought the right sort in. He did not bring one hypocrite or apostate, and having brought them in to the exact number of one hundred and fifty and three, they cannot one of them get out again. They are kept in that net, for that net does not break. They are in the secret, invisible church of Christ, and they cannot get out of it, let them do what they may. They may give up their nominal profession and thus get out of the visible church, but they cannot give up their secret possession; they cannot escape from the secret and invisible church, and they shall all be kept there till the net is dragged to land, and the whole hundred and fifty and three are saved.

Yet again, you notice in the first case the net broke, and in the second case it did not. Now, in the first case, in the visible church, the net breaks. My brethren are always calling out, "The net is broken!" No doubt it is a bad thing for nets to break, but you need not wonder at it. We cannot just now, when the net is full, stop to mend it; it will break. It is the necessary consequence of our being what we are that the net will break. What do I mean by this? Why, that instead of having one denomination, we have twenty or thirty? The net is broken. I do not at all grieve over it. I believe it is what must be as long as we are flesh and blood. For until you get a set of perfect men, you never will have anything but these divisions. The net must break and will break. But glory be to God, the net does not break after all in reality, for though the visible church may seem to be torn to pieces, the invisible church is one. God's chosen, God's called, God's revived, God's blood-bought – they are one in heart, and one in soul, and one in spirit. Though they may wear different names among men, yet they still wear before God their Father's name written on their foreheads, and they are and always must be one.

You perceive, brethren, that I do not advise you to strive after a nominal unity. The more you strive after that, the more divisions there will be. Certain brethren left many of our denominations and formed, they said, a church that should not be a sect. All they did was to make a sect the most sectarian of sects, the most narrow and most bitter of cliques, though containing some of the best men, some of the best Christians, and the ablest writers of the times. You cannot make a visible uniformity, it is beyond your power, the net is broken. There now! take care of the fish and leave the net alone, but still maintain the unity of the Spirit in the bond of perfectness. Take care that you are not a schismatic in your heart, that you hold no heresy in your soul, and that you are one with all those who love the Lord Jesus Christ in sincerity. In this you will soon see that the net is not broken, but that the saints are one.

Ah, I bless God that when once we get with God's people it does not matter what they are, because we soon find that the net is not broken. There is many a godly clergyman of the church of England with whom I commune with the greatest joy, and I have found the net was not broken; and in conversing with brethren of all denominations, some who from doctrine, some who from sentiment, stand as wide as the poles asunder, I have still found and known that there was such a real and perfect harmony of heart that the net was not broken. I do not believe that charity would ever have had such perfect work in Christ's church if it had not been for our being divided into tribes, like the twelve tribes of old. It is no charity for me to love a brother who thinks as I think; I cannot very well help it. But for me to love a dear brother who differs from me in some points, there is exercise and room for my charity. And as God has left trials and troubles to exercise faith, I believe he has left us in many doctrinal difficulties on purpose to exercise our love till the day shall come when we shall all grow to the stature of perfect men in Christ Jesus. The net is not broken, brethren; do not believe it, and when you read about this denomination and that, do not be grieved at these names and tribes, but rather thank God for them. Say, that is the visible church, and the net is broken; but there is an invisible church where the net is not broken, where we are one in Christ, and must be one forever.

There are several other points of difference, but I think we have hardly time to enlarge upon them. I will only hint at them. In the first case, which is the visible church, you see that human weakness becomes the strongest point; there is the boat ready to sink, there is the net broken, there are the men all out of heart, frightened, amazed, and begging the Master to go away. In the other case it is not so at all. There is human weakness, but still they are made strong enough. They have no strength to spare, as you perceive, but still they are strong enough, the net does not break, the ship goes slowly to land dragging the fish, and then, lastly, Simon Peter pulls the fish to shore. Strong he must have been. They were just strong enough to get their fish to shore. So in the visible church of Christ you will often have to mourn over human weakness, but in the invisible church, God will make his servants just strong enough to drag their fish to shore. The agencies, means, and instrumentalities shall have just sufficient force to land every elect soul in heaven, so that God may be glorified.

Then notice, in the first case, that in the visible church they launched out into the deep. In the second case, it says they were not far from the shore, but just a little ways out. So today our preaching seems to us to be going out into the great stormy deep after fish. We appear to have a long way to reach before we shall bring these precious souls to land. But in the sight of God we are not far from shore, and when a soul is saved, it is not far from heaven. To us there are years of temptation, and trial, and conflict; but to God, the Most High, it is finished, *it is done*. They are saved: they are not far from shore.

In the first case, the disciples had to forsake all and follow Christ. In the second, they sat down to feast with him at the dainty banquet which he had spread. So in the visible church today we have to bear trials and self-denial for Christ, but glory be to God, the eye of faith perceives that we shall soon drag our net to land, and then the Master will say, *Come and dine*, and we shall sit down and feast in his presence, with Abraham, Isaac, and Jacob in the kingdom of God.

The time is gone, and I close by *noticing one among many lessons which the two narratives in common seem to teach*.

In the first case, Christ was in the ship. Oh, blessed be God, Christ is in his church, though she launches out into the deep. In the second case, Christ was on the shore. Blessed be God, Christ is in heaven. He is not here, but he has risen; he has gone up on high for us. But whether he is in the church or whether he is on the shore in heaven, all our night's waiting shall, by his presence, have a rich reward. That is the lesson. Mother, will you learn it? You have been toiling long for your children. It has been night with you as yet. They give no evidence of grace; rather, they give many signs of sin, and they grieve your spirit. Your night's toiling shall have an end; you shall at last cast the net on the right side of the ship. Sunday school teacher, you have been diligently laboring long and with but little fruit; be not discouraged, for the Master will not let you work in vain. In due season you shall reap if you faint not, and as these disciples had a great sea harvest, so shall you have a harvest of souls. Minister, you have been ploughing some barren rock, and as yet no joyful sheaves have made your heart glad. You shall, doubtless, *come again with rejoicing, bringing [your] sheaves with [you].* And you, O church of God, laboring for souls, meeting daily in prayer, pleading with men that they will come to Christ, what if they are not saved yet? The morning comes, the night is far spent, and the Master himself shall soon appear; and though he may not find faith on the earth, yet his advent shall bring to his church the success for which she has waited – such success that as a woman remembers no more her labor because a child is born into the world, so shall the church remember no more her toils, her efforts, and her prayers, because Christ's kingdom has come, and his will is done on earth even as it is in heaven. Work, dear friends! If there are any of you that are not working, *begin now.* If there are any of you not yet saved, the Lord grant that when the Word is preached, you may be caught in it as in a net. *Believe on the Lord Jesus Christ, and thou shalt be saved,* for *he that believeth and is baptized shall be saved; and he that believeth not shall be damned.* Flee to Christ! Escape from the wrath to come! May the Spirit apply that word to you, and lead you to the place where high on Calvary with bleeding hands and feet the Savior dies! One look at him and you are saved. Look, sinner, and live! God save you, for Christ's sake! Amen.

Chapter 2

At Thy Word

And Simon answering said unto him, Master, we have toiled all the night, and have taken nothing: nevertheless at thy word I will let down the net. (Luke 5:5)

How very much may simple obedience partake of the sublime! Peter went to pull up the net and let it down into the sea, and he said as naturally as possible, *At thy word I will let down the net*, but he was there and then appealing to one of the grandest principles which rules among intelligent beings, and to the strongest force which sways the universe: *At thy word*. Great God, it is *at thy word* that seraphs fly and cherubs bow! Your angels which excel in strength obey your commandments, hearkening to the voice of your word. *At thy word* space and time first came into existence, and all things else that are. *At thy word* – here is the cause of causes, the beginning of the creation of God. *By the word of the* Lord *were the heavens made*, and by that word was the present constitution of this round world settled as it stands. When the earth was formless and dark, your voice, O Lord, was heard, saying, *Let there be light*, and *at thy word* light leaped forth. *At thy word* day and night took up their places, and *at thy word* the waters were divided from the waters by the firmament of heaven. *At thy word* the dry land appeared, and the seas retired to their channels. *At thy word* the globe was mantled over with green, and vegetable life began. *At thy word* appeared the sun and moon and stars, *for signs, and for seasons, and for days, and years. At thy word* the living creatures filled the sea, and air, and land, and man at last appeared. Of all this we are well assured, for by faith we know that the worlds were framed by the word of God. Acting in conformity with the word of our Lord we feel ourselves to be in order with all the forces of the universe, traveling on the main track of all real existence. Is not this a sublime condition, even though it is seen in the common deeds of our everyday life?

It is not in creation alone that the word of the Lord is supreme, but in providence too its majestic power is manifested, for the Lord upholds all things by the word of his power. Snow and vapor and stormy winds are all fulfilling his word. His word runs very swiftly. When frost binds up the lifefloods of the year, the Lord sends forth his word and melts them. Nature abides and moves by the word of the Lord. So too, all matters of fact and history are beneath the supreme word. The Lord stands as the center of all things, as Lord of all he abides at the saluting-point, and all the events of the ages come marching by at his word, bowing to his sovereign will. *At thy word*, O God, kingdoms arise and empires flourish. *At thy word* races of men become dominant and tread down their fellows. *At thy word* dynasties die, kingdoms crumble, mighty cities become a wilderness, and armies of men melt away like the hoarfrost of the morning. Despite the sin of man and the rage of devils, there is a sublime sense in which all things from the beginning, since Adam crossed the threshold of Eden even until now, have happened according to the purpose and will of the Lord of Hosts. Prophecy utters her oracles, and history writes her pages, *at thy word*, O Lord.

It is wonderful to think of the fisherman of Galilee letting down his net in perfect consonance with all the arrangements of the ages. His net obeys the law which regulates the spheres. His hand consciously does what Arcturus and Orion are doing without thought. This little bell on the Galilean lake rings out in harmony with the everlasting chimes. *At thy word*, says Peter, as he promptly obeys, therein repeating the

> The Lord stands as the center of all things, and all the events of the ages come marching by at his word, bowing to his sovereign will.

watchword of seas and stars, of winds and worlds. It is glorious thus to be keeping step with the marchings of the armies of the King of Kings.

There is another way of working out this thought. *At thy word* has been the password of all good men from the beginning until now. Saints have acted upon these three words and found their marching orders in them. An ark is built on dry land, and the crude crowd gathers around the aged patriarch, laughing at him. But he is not ashamed, for lifting his face to heaven he says, "I have built this great vessel, O The Lord, at thy word." Abraham leaves the place of his childhood, leaves his family, and goes with Sarah to a land of which he knows nothing, crossing the broad Euphrates, and entering upon a country possessed by the Canaanite, in which he roams as a stranger and a sojourner all his days. He dwells in tents with Isaac and Jacob. If any scoff at him for thus renouncing the comforts of settled life, he lifts also his calm face to heaven and smilingly answers to the Lord, "It is at thy word." And even when his brow is furrowed, and the hot tear is ready to force itself from beneath the patriarch's eyelid, as he lifts his hand with the knife to stab Isaac to the heart, if any charge him with murder, or think him mad, he lifts the same placid face towards the majesty of the Most High and says, "It is at thy word." At that word he joyfully sheathes the sacrificial knife, for he has proved his willingness to go to the utmost at the word of the Lord his God. If I were to introduce you to a thousand of the faithful ones who have shown the obedience of faith, in every case they would justify their acts by telling you that they did them "at God's word." Moses lifts his rod in the presence of the haughty Pharaoh, *at thy word*, great God! Nor does he lift that rod in vain at the Lord's word, for thick and heavy fall the plagues upon the children of Ham. They are made to know that God's word does not return to him void, but fulfills his purpose, whether it be of threatening or of promise.

See Moses lead the people out of Egypt, the whole host in its myriads! Mark how he has brought them to the Red Sea, where the wilderness shuts them in. The heights frown on either side, and the rattle of Egypt's war-chariots is behind. How did Moses come to so play the fool and bring them here? Were there no graves in Egypt that thus he brought them forth to die on the Red Sea shore? The answer of Moses is the quiet reflection that he did it at the Lord's word, and God justifies that word, for the sea opens wide a highway for the elect of God, and they march joyfully through, and with timbrels and dances on the other side they sing unto the Lord who has triumphed gloriously.

If in afterdays you find Joshua circling Jericho, and not attacking it with battering rams, but only with one great blast of trumpets, his reason is that God has spoken to him by his word. And so right on, for time would fail me to speak of Samson, and Jephthah, and Barak: these men did what they did at God's word, and doing it, the Lord was with them.

Is it bringing things down from the sublime to the ridiculous to talk of Peter and the net which he casts over the side of his little boat? Oh no. We are ourselves ridiculous when we do not make our own lives sublime by the obedience of faith. Certainly there may be as much sublimeness in casting a net as in building an ark, lifting a rod, or sounding a ram's horn; and it is clear that if it is done in faith, then the simplest action of life may be sublimely great. The flash of the wave as it covers Peter's net may be as sublime before the Lord as the glory of the Red Sea billow when it returned in its strength. God who sees a world in a drop sees wonders in the smallest act of faith.

Do not, I pray you, think that sublimeness lies in masses, to be measured by a scale, so that a mile shall be sublime and an inch shall be absurd. We measure not morals and spirituals by rods and chains. The common act of fishing at Christ's word links Peter with all the principalities, and powers, and forces which in all ages have known this as their only law: *He spake, and it was done; he commanded, and it stood fast.* We too shall have fellowship with the sublime if we know how to be perfectly obedient to the Word of the Lord.

This ought to be the rule of all Christians for the whole of their lives: *At thy word.* This should direct us in the church and in the world; it should guide us in our spiritual beliefs and in our secular acts: *At thy word.* I wish it were so. We hear boastings that the Bible, and the Bible alone, is the religion of Protestants. It is a mere boast. Few Protestants can honestly repeat the assertion. They have other books to which they pay deference, and other rules, and other guides, beyond and above, and even in opposition to, the one Word of God. It ought not to be so. The power of the church and the power of the individual to please God shall never be fully known till we get back to the simple yet sublime rule of our text: *At thy word.*

I am just going to hammer upon that phrase as God shall help me. *At thy word.* This rule has many applications. First, I shall somewhat repeat myself by saying that *it ought to apply to the affairs of ordinary life;* secondly, *it should apply to matters of spiritual profiting;* and thirdly, and here I shall enlarge, *it ought to find its chief application in our great life business, which is being fishers of men.*

At thy word should apply *to all the affairs of ordinary life*. I mean, first, as to continuance in honest industry. *Let every man abide in the same calling wherein he was called.* Many a man in the present trying crisis is half ready to throw up his work and run away from his business, because he has toiled all night and taken nothing. Truly, the financial darkness has lasted long, and does not yet yield to the dawning, but yet Christians must not murmur or leave their posts. Oh tried ones, continue to be diligent in your business, still provide things honest in the sight of all men. Labor on in hope. Say just as Peter did, *Nevertheless at thy word I will let down the net. Except the* Lord *build the house, they labour in vain that build it.* You know that truth full well; know this also, that the Lord will not forsake his people. Your best endeavors will not of themselves bring you prosperity; still, do not relax those endeavors. God's Word to you is to conduct yourselves like men, and be strong, gird up the loins of your mind, be sober, and stand fast. Throw not away your shield, cast not away your confidence, but stand steadily in your rank till the tide of battle turns. God has placed you where you are, so move not till his providence calls you. Do not run before the cloud. Take down the shutters tomorrow morning, and display your goods, and let not despondency drive you to anything that is rash or unseemly. Say, *Nevertheless at thy word I will let down the net.*

If I am speaking to those who are out of work just now, searching for some place where they can provide bread for themselves and for their families, as is their duty, let them hear and ponder. If any man does not do his best to provide for his own household, he comes not under a gospel blessing, but he is said to be worse than a heathen man and a publican. It is the duty of us all to labor with our hands at that which is good, that we may have to give to the needy as well as to those dependent on us. If after having gone about this city till your feet are blistered you can find nothing to do, do not sit at home next Monday sulkily saying, "I will not try again." Apply my text to this painful trial, and yet again set out in hope, saying with Peter, *We have toiled all the night, and have taken nothing: nevertheless at thy word I will let down the net.* Let men see that a Christian is not readily driven to despair. No, let them see that when the yoke is made more heavy, the Lord has a secret way of strengthening the backs of his children to bear their burdens. If the Holy Spirit shall make you calmly resolute, you will honor God much more by your happy perseverance than the talkative one will by his fine speeches, or the formalist by his outward show. Common life is the true place in which to prove the truth of godliness and bring glory to God. Not by doing extraordinary works, but by the piety of ordinary life is the Christian known and his religion honored. At God's word hold on even to the end. *Trust in the Lord, and do good; so shalt thou dwell in the land, and verily thou shalt be fed.*

It may be, too, that you have been endeavoring in your daily life to acquire skill in your business and you have not succeeded, or you have tried to acquire more knowledge so that you could better fulfill your vocation, but yet you have not prospered as you could wish. Do not, therefore, cease from your efforts. Christians must never be idlers. Our Lord Jesus would never have it said that his disciples are a sort of cowards who, if they do not succeed the first time, will never try again. We are to be patterns of all the moral virtues as well as of the spiritual graces. Therefore, at the bidding of the Lord, work on with mind and hand, and look to him for the blessing. *At his word* let down the net once more. He may intend largely to bless you when by trials you have been prepared to bear the benediction.

This will apply very closely to those who are laboring hard in the training of children. It may be that with your own children you may not have succeeded yet; the boy's spirit may still be wild and proud, and the girl may not yet have yielded to obedience and submission. Or you may be working in the Sunday school, or in the day-school, trying to impart knowledge and to fashion the youthful mind aright, and you may have been baffled; but if it is your business to teach, do not be overcome. Stand to your work as though you heard Jesus say, *Whatsoever ye do, do it heartily, as to the Lord, and not unto men.* Earnestly, then, at his word again let down the net.

I counsel you, dear friends, in everything to which you set your hands, if it be a good thing, do it with all your might, and if it be not a good thing, have nothing to do with it. It may be possible that you are called to teach the age some moral truth. In most generations individuals have been called to carry out reforms and to promote progress. You are bound to love your neighbor as yourself; therefore, as you have opportunity, do good unto all men. If you have tried, and yet have not won a hearing, do not give up your point. If it is a good thing, and you are a Christian man, never let it be said that you were afraid or ashamed. I admire, in Palissy the potter, not only his Christianity, which could not be overcome by persecution, but also his perseverance in his own business of making pottery. His last farthing and his last breath would have gone in discovering a glaze, or bringing out a color. I love to see such men believers. I should not like to see our Lord followed by a set of cowards who could not fight the common battles of life. How should such as these become worthy of the lordlier chivalry which wrestles with spiritual wickedness in high places? It is for us to be bravest among the brave in the plains of common life, so that when we are summoned to higher fields, where still greater deeds are needed, we may go there trained for the higher service.

Does it seem to you to be a little out of place to be talking thus from the pulpit? I do not think so. I notice how in the Old Testament we are told of the sheep and the cattle, and the fields and the harvests of good men; and these had to do with their religion. I notice how the prudent woman according to Solomon looked well to her household; and I observe that we have in the Bible a book of Proverbs, and another called Ecclesiastes, with little spiritual teaching in them, but a great deal of good, sound, and practical common sense. It is evident to me that the Lord intends that our faith should not be penned up in a pew, but that it should walk the shop, and be seen in every walk of life. The great principle of my text fell from the lips of a working man, and to the working man I return it. It was connected with a net and a boat, the implements of his labor, and with these common things I would link it; and I would say to all who serve the Lord in this present evil world, in the name of God, if you have anything to do, be not so desponding and despairing as to cease from it, but according to his Word, once more go forward in your honest endeavors and, like Peter, say, *I will let down the net.* This may prove a word in season to some who are weary of the hardness of the times. I shall rejoice if it nerves an arm or cheers a heart. Have faith in God, my tested brethren. *Be ye stedfast, unmoveable, always abounding in the work of the Lord.*

In matters of spiritual profiting we must at the word of Christ let down the net again. I put this, first, to those who have been searching for the Lord's blessing a great many times, heartily, if I am to believe them, *hoping to find salvation.* You have prayed that the Lord would really bless you. Now mark, I do not understand you at all. I cannot make you out, because the way of salvation is open to you at this very moment, and it is, *Believe on the Lord Jesus Christ, and thou shalt be saved.* You have nothing to wait for, and all your waiting is sinful. If you say you are waiting for the stirring of the pool, I tell you there is no pool to be stirred, and no angel to stir it. That pool was dried up long ago, and angels never go that way now. Our Lord Jesus Christ shut up Bethesda when he came and said to the man lying there, *Rise, take up thy bed, and walk.* That is what he says to you. You have no business waiting; but I would earnestly invite you at the word of Christ, who has bidden us to preach the gospel to every creature, to believe and live. Let down the net once more, and let it down this way: say, *Lord, I believe; help thou mine unbelief.* Breathe a prayer now to Jesus that he would accept you. Submit yourself to him, and implore him to become now at this moment your Savior. You will be heard. Plenty of fish are waiting to be taken in the net of faith. At the Lord's word, let it down.

But I will now speak to others present who have been letting down their nets in vain, perhaps, in the form of *compelling prayer.* Have you been praying for the conversion of a relative, or pleading for some other good thing which you believe to be according to the will of God, and after long pleading – pleading in the night, for your spirit has been sad – are you tempted never to offer that petition anymore? Now then, at

Christ's word, who said that men ought always to pray and not to faint; at Christ's word, who says, *Pray without ceasing*, let down the net and pray again. Not because the circumstances which surround you are more favorable, but simply because Jesus bids you continue in prayer; and who knows but that this very time you will meet with success!

Or have you been *searching the Scriptures to find a promise* which will suit your case? Do you want to get hold of some good word from God that will cheer you? Shoals of such fish are around your boat; the sea of Scripture is full of them: fish of promise, I mean, but alas! you cannot catch one of them. Nevertheless, try again. Go and search the Scriptures again with prayer, and beg the Holy Spirit to apply a precious portion to your heart, that you may by faith enjoy the sweetness of it; and who knows but you shall this very day obtain your desire and receive a larger blessing than your mind can fully contain, so that in your case also the net shall break through the fullness of the favor.

Or it may be that you have been laboring a long while after *some holy attainment;* you want to conquer a besetting sin, to exercise firmer faith, to exhibit more zeal, or to be more useful, but you have not yet gained your desire. Now then, since it is the Lord's mind that you should be *perfect in every good work to do his will,* do not cease from your purpose, but at his word let down your net again. Never despair. That temper of yours will be conquered yet; that unbelief of yours will give way to holy faith. Let down the net, and all the graces may yet be taken in it, to be yours for the rest of your life. Only at Christ's word still labor for the best things, and he will give them to you.

Or are you seeking just now *the closer presence of Christ* and a nearer fellowship with him? Are you yearning after a sight of his face – that face which outshines the morning? Do you wish to be brought into his banqueting-house to be satiated with his love? And have you cried in vain? Then cry once more, *at his word*, for he bids you come to him; his loving voice invites you to draw near. At his word press forward once again, let down the net once more, and joys await you unspeakable, surpassing all you have yet experienced.

Thus you see that there is a just application of the great principle of the text to our spiritual profiting. God help us by his gracious Spirit to carry it out from day to day.

The great principle of our text should be applied to *our life-business*. And what is the life-business of every Christian here? Is it not soul winning? That we may glorify God by the bringing of others to the faith of Christ is the great object of our remaining here on earth; otherwise we should have been caught up to swell the harmony of the heavenly songs. It is expedient for many wandering sheep here below that we should tarry here till we have brought them home to the great Shepherd and Bishop of souls.

Our way of winning people for Christ, or, to use his own metaphor, our method of catching people, is by letting down the net of the gospel. We have learned no other way of holy fishery. Those with great zeal and little knowledge are inventing ingenious methods for catching others, but for my part I believe in nothing but letting down the gospel net by telling out the story of the love of God for people in Christ Jesus. No new gospel has been committed to us by Jesus, and he has authorized no new way of making it known. Our Lord has called all of us to the work of proclaiming free pardon through his blood to all who believe in him. Each believer has a warrant to seek the conversion of his fellows. May not every person seek to save his brother from the burning? Must not Jesus smile on anyone's endeavor to deliver their neighbor from going down to eternal death? Has he not said, *Let him that heareth say, Come*?

Whosoever hears the gospel is to invite others to come to Christ. The word of the Lord is our warrant for keeping to our one work of making known the gospel. It would be a sorry act of mutiny if we were either to be silent or to preach another gospel which is not another. The word of the Lord is a warrant which justifies the man who obeys it. *Where the word of a king is, there is power*. What higher authority can we need? "Oh, but," they say, "you ought to advance to something higher than the mere elementary doctrine of grace, and give the people something more in keeping with the progress of the period." We shall not do so while Jesus bids us go into all the world and preach the gospel to every creature. If we do what he bids us, the responsibility of the matter rests no longer with us. Whatever comes of it we are clear if we have obeyed orders. A servant is not to justify his master's message, but to deliver it. This makes it a joy to preach, this doing it *at thy word*. Our business is to do what Christ tells us, as Christ tells us, and to do this again and again, so long as we have breath in our bodies. The commanding word cries ever to us, "Preach the gospel, preach the gospel to every creature!" Our justification for setting forth Christ crucified, and incessantly bidding men believe and live, lies in that same word which told Peter to walk on the sea, and told Moses to fetch water out of a rock.

The result of this preaching will justify him who commanded it. No man at the last day will be able to say to the Savior, "You set before your servants an impossible task, and you gave them an instrument to wield which was not at all adapted to produce its end." No, but at the closing up of all things it shall be seen that for the salvation of the elect there was nothing better than a crucified Savior; and to make that crucified Savior known, there was no better means than the simple proclamation of his Word by honest lips in the power of the Spirit of the Lord. The foolishness of preaching will turn out to be the great proof of the wisdom of God.

Brethren, you that teach in the school, or you that preach from the pulpit, or distribute tracts, or speak personally to individuals, you need not be afraid but what wisdom will exonerate herself from all charges, and vindicate her own methods. You may be called a fool today for preaching the gospel, but that accusation, like rust on a sword, will wear off as you use the weapon in the wars of the Lord. The preaching of the Word soon puts down all clamors against itself: those clamors mainly arise because it is not preached. No one calls the gospel decayed where it is striking right and left like a great twohanded sword.

Our reply to the outcry about the failure of the pulpit is to get into it and preach with the Holy Spirit sent down from heaven. Indeed, this word of Christ, whereby he gives us his warrant for letting down the net, is such that it amounts to a command, and it will leave us guilty if we do not obey. Suppose Simon Peter had said, "We have toiled all the night, and have taken nothing; and therefore, notwithstanding thy word, I will not let down the net." Then Simon Peter would have been guilty of disobedience to his Lord, and blasphemy against the Son of God. What shall I say to any of my fellow Christians who profess to be called of God, and to be Christ's disciples, and yet never let down the net? Is it so that you are doing nothing for the truth? that you never disseminate the gospel? Is it so that you call yourselves lights of the world, and yet never shine? that you are sowers of the seed, and yet forget that you have a seed basket? Am I addressing any members of this church who are in this respect wasting their lives? Is it so that it is professedly your life's object to be fishers of men, and yet you have never cast a net, nor even helped to draw one on shore? Are you dwelling among us under false pretenses? Are you mocking God by a fruitless profession which you never try to make fruitful? I have not the strength with which to condemn you, but I wish to God that your own conscience might fulfill that office.

What shall be said of the man to whom the Lord gives it in charge that he shall make known the glad tidings of salvation from eternal misery, and yet he is sinfully silent? The Great Physician has entrusted you with the medicine which heals the sick; you see them die around you, but you never speak of the remedy! The great King has given you the meal with which to feed the hungry, and you lock the storehouse door, while the crowds are starving in your streets. Is not this a crime which may well make a man of God weep over you? This great London of ours is growing heathenish to the very core, and yet our Lord has given the gospel into the hands of his churches; what can be the reason for the indifference of the godly? If we keep this gospel to ourselves, truly, coming ages will condemn us as cruel to our posterity. Succeeding generations will point to our era and say, "What sort of men were these, that had the light, and shut it up in a dark lantern?" In a century to come, when others shall stand in this city and walk these streets, they will say, "A curse upon the memory of the ministers and people who failed in their duty, who came to the kingdom in a solemn time, but never realized their calling, and so missed the end and object of their being!" May we be spared from such a calamity as this. Yes, we have a warrant for laboring to spread the truth of God, and more than a warrant; we have a statute from the throne, a peremptory command, and it is woe to us if we preach not the gospel.

Now, brethren, this warrant from Christ is one which, if we be in the state of heart of Simon Peter, will be omnipotent with us. It was very powerful with Simon Peter. For, observe, he was *under the influence of a great disappointment,* yet he let down the net. *We have toiled all the night.* Some say, "We have had all this gospel preaching, we have had all these revivals, all these stirs, and nothing has come of it." When was that? I hear a good deal of this talk, but what are the facts? "Oh," you say, "you know we had a great deal of revival a little while ago." I do not know anything of the sort. We have had flashes of light here and there, but comparatively so little that it is a pity to make so much of it. Moreover, considering the little that has ever been done for it, the spread of the gospel has been marvelous. Look at gospel-work at the present moment in India! People say that the Christian faith is not spreading. I say that it is spreading wonderfully as compared with the labor expended and the sacrifice made. If in that land you spend a penny and get a thousand pounds, you have no right to say, "What is that? We want a million." If your desires are thus exacting, then prove their sincerity by corresponding action. Increase your outlay. The harvest is wonderful considering the little seed, but if you wish for more sheaves, then sow more.

The church has had an enormous return for what little she has done. In England there have been partial revivals, but to what have they amounted? A flash of light has been seen in a certain district, but darkness has still remained supreme over the length and breadth of the country. The papers have reported a great work in a certain spot, but if the papers had reported the places wherein there has been no revival, we should have had a different view of things! A little corner at the top of a column would have sufficed for the good, and column after column would not have sufficed to make known the black side of the situation. The fact is the church has scarcely ever been in a state of universal revival since the day of Pentecost. There has been a partial moving among Christians every now and then, but the whole mass throughout has never burned and flamed with the earnestness which the grand cause demands. Oh, that the Lord would set the whole church on fire! We have no cause whatever for disappointment. In proportion to the little effort put out, great things have come to us; therefore, let us get to our nets again, and say no more about the night in which we have toiled.

But next, this command to Peter *overcame his love of ease.* Evidently he was tired when he said, *We have toiled all the night.* Fishing is hard work, especially when no fish are caught. It is natural to wish to be excused from further toil when you are already weary with unrewarded labor. I have heard some Christians say, "You know I had my time in the Sunday school years ago, and then I used to work too much for my strength." No doubt their efforts were stupendous in the remote ages of their youthful zeal; we can hardly imagine what they must have been like, for no relic remains to assist our conceptions. At this time they feel authorized to take things easy, for they owe no more to their Lord, or at least they do not intend to pay any more. Is it so that any one of us can cease from service when it is plain that we do not cease from receiving mercy at the Lord's hands? Are we not ashamed of the case when it is plainly put? "Take it easy." Yes, soon, very soon, we shall take it easy, for there will be rest enough in the grave. Just now, while souls of men are perishing, to relax our efforts is wickedness. No, no, Peter. Although you may be now in a dripping sweat through having toiled all night, you must get at it again. He does so. The night's work is nothing; he must work in the day too, if he is to catch fish.

Moreover, the command of Christ was so supreme over Peter that he was *not held back by carnal reason,* for reason would say, "If you could not catch fish in the night, you will certainly not do so in the day." Night was the special time for taking fish on the Gennesaret lake, and by day, when the glaring sun was lighting up the waves and letting the fish see every single mesh of the net, they were not likely to come into it; but when Christ commands, the most unlikely time is likely, and the most unpromising sphere becomes hopeful. No act is out of season when Christ commands it. If he says, "Go," then go at once, without deliberation. Say not, *There are yet four months, and then cometh harvest. [The fields] are white already to harvest.* Peter lets down the net at once, and wisely does he act at Christ's word.

> The command of Christ was so supreme over Peter that he was not held back by carnal reason.

The lesson to you and to me is this: let us do as Peter did, and let down the net *personally,* for the apostle said, *I will let down the net.* Brother, can you not do something yourself with your own heart, lips, and hands? Sister, can you not do something yourself with your own gentle spirit? "I was thinking about getting half a dozen friends to form a committee to relieve the poor around us." Nothing will ever come of it; the poor will not get a basin of soup or a lump of bread. Set about it yourself. "But I think I might get a dozen to come together and organize a society." Yes, and then move resolutions and amendments all day long, and finish up with passing votes of mutual commendation. You had better get to work yourself as Peter did.

And you had better do it *at once,* for Peter immediately let down the net, as soon as ever he had launched out into the deep. You may never have another opportunity; your zeal may have evaporated, or your life may be over. Peter, however, only let down one net, and there was the pity of it. If John and James and all the rest had let down their nets, the results would have been much better. "Why?" you ask. Because through there being only one net, that net was overstrained and it broke. If all the nets had been used, they might have taken more fish, and no net would have been broken. I was reading some time ago of a catch of mackerel at Brighton; when the net was full, the mackerel sticking in all the meshes made it so heavy that the fishermen could not raise it, and the boat itself was in some danger of going down, so that they had to cut away the net and lose the fish. Had there been many nets and boats they might have buoyed up the whole catch of the fish; and so they might have done in this case. As it was, many fish were lost through the breaking of the net. If a church can be so awakened that each individual gets to work in the power of the Holy Spirit, and all the individuals combine, then how many souls will be captured for Jesus! Multitudes of souls are lost to the blessed gospel because of our broken nets, and the net gets broken because we are not well united in the holy service, and by our lack of wisdom bring loss to our Master's cause. Ministers need not become worn out with labor if all would take their share; one boat would not begin to sink if the other boats took a part of the blessed load.

Now, brothers and sisters, I close by saying that if I have accomplished anything by the help of God's Spirit, I hope I have made you ready to accept the following directory of service drawn from the text. The way in which to serve God is to do it at his word. I pray that none of us may sink into serving the Lord as a matter of routine. We must preach, teach, and labor in his name because we hear him bidding us do it. We must act at his word. If this were the case, we would work with much more faith, with much more earnestness, and with much more likelihood of success. It is a blessed thing to see Christ sitting in the boat while you cast out the net. If you catch a glimpse of his approving smile as he watches you, you will work right heartily. We must labor in entire dependence upon him, not preaching or teaching because in our judgment it is the right thing to do – Peter did not think so – but because Jesus gives the word, and his word is law. You may not work because you have any expectation of success from the excellence of your work, or from the nature of the people among whom you labor, but because Jesus has given you the word. You stand there doing a thing which critics sneer at as absurd, but you do it in all confidence, believing that it must be wise, because Jesus bids you do it.

I remember well how some of our brethren used to talk to us. They said, "You preach the gospel to dead sinners; you bid them repent and believe. You might just as well shake a pocket-handkerchief over a grave and bid the corpse come out of it." Exactly so. They spoke the truth, but then I would delight to go and shake a pocket-handkerchief over graves and bid the dead live if Jesus bade me do so. I should expect to see the cemetery crack and heave from end to end if I were sent on such an errand by the Lord. I would accept the duty joyfully. The more absurd the wise men of our age make the gospel out to be, and the more they show that it is powerless to produce the end designed, the more will we persevere in our old method of preaching Jesus crucified. Our resolves are not to be shaken by that mode of reasoning. We never did draw our argument for preaching the gospel from the work itself, but from the orders given us to do it, and we would rather be acting upon the responsibility of Christ than upon our own. I would rather be a fool and do what Christ tells me, than be the wisest man of the modern school, and despise the word of the Lord. I would rather lay the responsibility of my life at the feet of him who bids me live according to his Word, than seek out an object in life for myself, and feel that the responsibility rested on my

> I would rather be a fool and do what Christ tells me, than be the wisest man of the modern school, and despise the word of the Lord.

own shoulders. Let us be willing to be under orders of Christ, willing to persevere under difficulties, and willing to begin anew in his service from this very hour. Amen.

Chapter 3

The Chief Physician and the Centurion's Servant

Jesus saith unto him, I will come and heal him.
(Matthew 8:7)

And Jesus said unto the centurion, Go thy way; and as thou hast believed, so be it done unto thee. (Matthew 8:13)

The centurion of Capernaum is an example to us in a matter which bears upon the collection appointed for today, which, you know, is for the hospitals. This good soldier cared for the sick, and was anxious for the recovery of his paralyzed servant. Every employer should take a sympathetic interest in his servants when they are ill, but in some cases this is not thought of. "If they cannot do their work, they must go." This is too often the language used about them, and they are got out of the house as soon as possible. I do not say that masters and mistresses are often cruel, but I fear that some of them are none too kind. Among religious persons, kindness towards man should be as manifest as devotion to God. The centurion had done what he could to benefit religiously the people among whom he dwelt, for the elders of the Jews said, *He loveth our nation, and he hath built us a synagogue.* But he combined with a desire to benefit the soul a sincere desire for the welfare of the body, and this was apparent in the interest which he took in his "boy," his personal servant, or young valet. God has joined body and soul together, and they ought not to be separated in our deeds of charity.

This captain's sympathy with his suffering valet was shown by practical action. He did not say that he felt for him, and then go off to the guardroom and stay clear of the sick youth; nor did he merely stand and watch him in his pain, to see how he would fare, but he aroused himself, he went abroad, he called together the elders of the city, and he summoned his choice friends to him. In fact, he made the whole circle of his acquaintances feel a sympathy with him concerning the illness of his servant. Then he sent these elders and friends to the best physician of the age, and I think he also followed at their heels himself. He used the nearest means within his reach, and appealed to him to whom none ever appealed in vain. From the centurion I gather that we must not be content with loving our people and building them synagogues, but we must also build them hospitals and dispensaries. Find them preachers by all means, but find them surgeons too. We may not forget the soul, but we must also remember that the soul dwells in a body liable to many disorders. We may become just a little too spiritual, so spiritual as to spirit away the very spirit of Christianity. God grant us grace to be as tenderly considerate of suffering humanity as this centurion was, and we probably shall be so if we have as strong a faith and as deep a humility as he had.

> God grant us grace to be as tenderly considerate of suffering humanity as this centurion was.

Our Lord himself also in our text sets us an example which may plead with us on behalf of hospitals today; for he was here upon the high errand of our redemption, yet did he not consider it at all derogatory to his divine purpose to be continually engaged in healing diseases.

For three years he walked the hospitals: he lived all day long in an infirmary; for all around him at one time they laid the sick in the streets, and at all times physical evil in some form or another came in his way. He put forth his hand, or spoke the word, and healed all sorts of diseases. This our Lord did very readily, for it was part of his lifework. *I will come and heal him,* said he, for he was a physician in constant practice, and would come around at once to see the patient. He *went about doing good,* and in all this he would let his people know that he intended not to bless one part of man alone, but the whole of our nature, taking upon himself not only our sins, but also our sicknesses. Jesus means to bless the body as well as the soul; and though for this present time he has left our bodies very much under the power of sickness – for still *the body is dead because of sin; but the Spirit is life because of righteousness* – yet he foreshadows in his healing miracles the resurrection, when he shall raise us perfectly healed, and the inhabitant shall no more say, "I am sick." Every restored limb, and opened eye, and healed wound is a token that Jesus cares for our flesh and blood, and intends for the body to share the benefits of his death by a glorious resurrection.

As in our Lord's life his teaching was always connected with healing, he would have the church also take a very deep interest in the bodily sorrows of the people as well as in their spiritual needs. It will be a very great pity if ever it should be thought that benevolence is divorced from Christianity, for up to this time the crown of the faith of Jesus has been love for men. It is indeed the glory of Christianity that wherever it comes it erects buildings altogether unknown to heathenism: hospitals, asylums, and other places of charity. The genius of Christianity is pity for the sinful and the suffering. Let the church be a healer like her Lord; or at least if she cannot pour forth virtue from the hem of her garment, nor *say in a word* so that sickness may flee, then let her be among the most prompt to help in everything that can relieve pain or assist in poverty. So it ought to be, for as Jesus was, so are we also to be in this world. Did he not tell us, *As the Father hath sent me, even so send I you*? We cannot too diligently study his character, for he has left us an example that we may follow in his steps. Since we cannot practice the healing art, let us give support to those whose whole time is spent in it, that they may be able without fee or reward to watch over the sick and poor; and let none among us act the rude or stingy person when the blind and the lame cry to us as they did to our Master of old.

This said, I desire to move on to my main subject, which is of a spiritual kind. I want you to mark the development of the faith of the centurion, and side by side with it the growing manifestation of our Lord's power. Both are seen in the narrative.

The centurion had evidently heard about Christ; perhaps the healing of the ruler's child had satisfied him that Jesus was the Messiah. He had attended the synagogue. I cannot doubt that a man who had built a synagogue would be sure to go to it, and there he had learned of the Coming One, foretold by prophets and expected by saints. This Anointed One was to work wonders among mankind, and especially wonders of healing. Thus he had determined that Jesus was the Christ, and he believed in him as having power to heal his sick servant.

The first practical result was that he humbly sent the elders with the urgent request to *come and heal his servant*. He believed that Jesus, if he were present, could restore the dying youth. He had thought it over, and his faith had reached as far as that of Mary and Martha when they said, *Lord, if thou hadst been here, my brother had not died*. In effect he said, "If you will come here, great Master, my servant will not die." He therefore cried, "Come and heal him." Observe that our Lord's answer was exactly proportioned to the measure of faith in the prayer: *I will come and heal him*. "You say, 'come and heal him'; I reply, 'I will come and heal him.'" So far so good, but the captain's faith is to be seen in a still clearer light. He has been considering the matter still further, and his humility leads him to feel that he ought not to expect Jesus to come to his house. Why should he trouble the Master to leave the crowd and to cease preaching, to come and attend to his servant? He is grieved to think that he should have proposed a visit. He feels himself unfit to entertain one so holy and so great, and therefore he sends off his friends posthaste to offer humble apologies and to beg the Master not to come. He has at the same time advanced in his belief in Christ's power, for he says in effect, "There is no need that you should come; only will it, merely say the word, and the healing is done. For I also am a man under authority, deriving authority from being under it, and I have only to say to one soldier go, and to another, come, and my will is done. I have no need to execute my own wishes personally, for my will governs my troop, and each man is eager to do my bidding. So, great Master, stay where you are, go on with your other work, and only will to bless me and it will be enough; your desire will be accomplished without fail. Oh, great Emperor of all the forces of the universe, bid your triumphant eagles fly this way, and the foe will vanish before you." Here was growing faith, and side by side with it was a clearer manifestation of the Master's power. Our Lord Jesus there and then wills that healing power should go forth; he moves no further towards the house where the paralyzed patient lies, but rather he turns around, and in obedience to the wish of the centurion he walks away. Yet he works the miracle, the paralytic child has risen from the bed, the captain's heart is gladdened, and those who came to plead stand in the house to praise the Lord. Awestruck by the finger of God so near and so manifest, what could they do but bless the Lord who had visited his people?

That is the story, and it proves that our Lord Jesus Christ is omnipotent in the physical world. He can do what he wills, and though at this present time we do not as much appeal to him for miraculous cures, it would be well if we trusted him more upon that point; for all the power which dwells in medicine, and all the skill which is found in physicians, is only effective through his tender mercy. We know, however, that our Lord is omnipotent in the moral and spiritual world, and there today he displays his most sublime feats of power and wisdom. We are going to think about this, and may the Holy Spirit make the meditation useful to us.

> We know that our Lord is omnipotent in the moral and spiritual world.

The first thing I invite you to consider is *the perfect readiness of our Lord Jesus* for works of mercy. The centurion was concerned about his servant, just as you and I are, I hope, today concerned about certain poor souls who lie paralyzed by sin. We mourn over them, and if we could heal them we would gladly suffer any self-denial or endure any suffering. If we could bring our neighbors to Christ, it would be the utmost joy to us; their perishing souls are to some of us as a burdensome stone, a load heavy to bear. How can we endure to see them die? The mass of working men around us as well as the majority of our wealthy neighbors are under the power of the wicked one. To them the things which are seen are the only objects of their thoughts. They will not regard the gospel of Christ, or eternity, or judgment, or heaven, or hell. The privileges with which our country is so largely endowed are treated as if they were of no value whatever: Sabbaths, Bibles, the gospel, and the throne of grace are despised. This is mournful indeed! Brethren, we must go to Jesus about this evil thing, and it may help us to do this if we now think of his great willingness to bless servant or child, or any other person whom we may bring before him in prayer.

That willingness we shall see first if we notice that *he did not quibble at the pleas which the Jewish elders urged* on behalf of the centurion, though they could have been distasteful to his mind. They said, "He is worthy for whom you should do this." That was not the right style of pleading with him who came to save the lost and bless the undeserving in the freeness of his grace. The elders said, *He loveth our nation, and he hath built us a synagogue*, and so on. Poor souls, they were doing their best, and using the kind of argument by which their own hopes were sustained. Our Lord regarded the spirit of their intercession rather than the form in which they uttered it; and though the plea, laying so much stress upon human merit, might very well have warranted him in saying, "Hold your peace, for you are damaging rather than helping the case," yet our Lord raised no question. From afar he read the heart of the centurion and he knew that the good man's advocates were misrepresenting his views and feelings. The last thing in the world that the lowly minded soldier would have pleaded would have been personal worthiness. His own words were, *I am not worthy*. Had he known that his advocates would have talked in that fashion he surely would never have allowed them to speak on his behalf. If the centurion could have been there he might have said, "Your words cut me to the heart, for I am not worthy. What little I have been able to do I cannot boast of. I have done no more than I ought to have done. Do not speak to my Lord in such a style." But Jesus was so willing to go that he put up with all the blunders of the elders and responded to their request, *I will come and heal him.*

Beloved, very likely you and I make quite as great mistakes when we pray; we imagine we pray very correctly, but I wonder what our Lord thinks of our prayers. Surely he has often to pick out the meaning of our hearts from among the errors of our lips; but so willing is he to bless us, that if there be first a willing mind it shall still be accepted, for he rejoices to hear every prayer which seeks healing for sin-sick souls.

His willingness is seen, next, in the fact of his so cheerfully *granting the first prayer in the form in which it was put*. They begged him to *come and heal* his servant. Now, that was not exactly the best form in which to put it, and certainly it was not that which commended itself to the more mature thoughts of the centurion. Why should Jesus go? He could heal the patient without moving from the spot. Was there not a considerable measure of unbelief about the elders' prayer? Yet our blessed Master took the prayer just as it was, and he seemed to say, "I see the measure of your faith, and I will give you the blessing as you are able to receive it." The Lord is very generous to come down to our capacities; if he were always to act according to his own divine standard, we would be greatly dazzled, but we would be afraid to draw near to him. He condescendingly lays aside the splendor of his majesty in order to act as well as to speak to us after the manner of men, and then we see the sweet voluntariness of his grace, and the cheerful willingness of his spirit to do us good. If we cannot receive a blessing in any other than a second-class way, we shall have it in the way in which we can take it; as our faith can get no further, he will do the wonder according to the manner in which our scanty thought is able to conceive and ask and receive. Oh, what a willing friend we have in Christ. He bows the heavens and comes down, meeting the weak in his weakness and the fainting in his faintness; answering prayers not only according to the riches of his glory, but also according to the poverty of our infirmity.

Notice further, that when the centurion sent a fresh deputation of his choice friends to say to the Master, *Trouble not thyself: for I am not worthy that thou shouldest enter under my roof,* our Lord did not quarrel with the change of this prayer. Some people would have said, "What is it that you want? First, I am to come, and when I am almost there I am met with a request not to come; what do you mean? This is not respectful, and I will not come." Our gentle Jesus spoke not so. Oh no. Such talk might come from you, and from me, who are so great in our own esteem, but never from him, because he is so much greater than we are. He thought not of himself, nor his own dignity. Let us imitate his meek and quiet spirit. When you are trying to do good you will often be put about by the whims of those whom you would benefit. You will find that when you do what people ask of you they are not satisfied: many adults are like sick children who are always cross and fretful. We must humor these poor hearts, as our Lord did. He was so willing to bless that he seemed to give *carte blanche* to those who asked of him: "Yes, you shall have the blessing in the way you like, so that you are but able to receive it. It shall be given to you according to your faith." Our Lord shifted his movements without pressure and would go to the house or not, just as the centurion's faith might lead him to pray. Blessed, forever blessed, be our most gracious Savior who never wearies of us, nor takes offense at our childish changes.

The Savior's willingness to bless this centurion's servant was very manifest from the fact that *he did not impute an ill motive to the centurion* when he bade him refrain from visiting the house. There was no mistrust about our Lord. He knew too much both of man's evil and of the sincerity of those in whom his grace was placed to suspect and to interpret harshly. Ignorance and selfishness are mistrustful, but love thinks no evil. If there are two ways of understanding a sentence, my brothers, and one is better than the other, always read it in the kindest way, if you can. Never put hard constructions upon words and actions. You and I might have said in the case before us, "You see he does not want me in his fine house. He is a centurion and thinks much of himself, and I am wearing a poor garment, and therefore he does not want me in his villa to disgrace his halls. He is a captain, a man in authority, having soldiers under him, his pride forbids my approach, and therefore I will have nothing to do with him." But no, it was not in the Master's heart to think thus bitterly, but as at the first he had said, *I will come and heal him*, so now when genuine humility requests him not to come, he turns about, but works the miracle all the same.

> Our Savior must be very willing to bless men, since he takes the true meaning prayers where others write a harsh interpretation.

Brothers and sisters, our condescending Savior must be very willing to bless men, since he takes the true meaning of their prayers where others would write a harsh interpretation. Be not afraid to approach him however unworthy you are, for he will put the best construction upon your broken petitions, and interpret them always to your gain. His disciples may severely criticize one another and may criticize you, but they have learned no hard words in his company.

Nor did he at all object to the comparison which the centurion made. *I also*, said the centurion, *am a man set under authority*. If you were to read that expression with dark glasses, you might make a great deal of mischief out of it. A nitpicker might say, "How dare he even for a moment compare himself to the Son of God! How can he draw a parallel of which he is one side and the blessed Lord the other? What impertinence!" Brethren, our Lord was no critic. No, among the brotherhood of faultfinders you never see the Christ of God. When he has to deal with sincere people, he picks no holes, imputes no motives, and dwells on no mistakes. The centurion did not wish to make his metaphor go down on all fours, and our Lord did not treat him as if he did. Many a time have some of us had to suffer from this mode of attack, but never from our Master, nor from those who imitate him. He took the meaning of the centurion's illustration, and he admired it; for indeed it was a grand and beautiful idea, to set forth our Lord Jesus as the great Emperor of the universe to whom all things are under rule, and to whose faintest word each form of force, whether good or evil, is sure to render obedience. He showed that he had rightly estimated Christ, and had enthroned him as he should be enthroned in the place of unlimited sovereignty and power. The Master did not, therefore, for a moment object to anything he said. No, but the prayer had been offered that the servant might be healed, and the prayer was granted. The faith had been exercised which believed that Christ could heal, and that faith was honored. Our Lord did exactly as the prayer requested him to do. He came when he was asked to come; he stayed when he was asked to stay. He spoke the word when he was requested to speak the word; he healed when he was asked to heal. In all things he yielded himself entirely to the centurion's wish, to show his cheerful willingness in benefiting the suffering boy and in answering the master's prayer.

Come then, dear friends, we may be quite sure of our Lord's sympathy, though we are not praying about a sick boy, but pleading for our sinful neighbors. He loves sinners better than we do, for they have cost him more than they have ever cost us, even if we have spent nights in watching and praying on their behalf. To him it is committed of the Father to save the lost, and his zeal to accomplish the work never droops; therefore, we may be sure that our pleadings and efforts will touch a kindred chord in his heart.

Secondly, an equally interesting topic is before us in *the conscious ability of our Lord.* You have seen his perfect willingness, now behold his boundless power. I do not know how it affects your minds, but that sentence from the lips of Jesus, *I will come and heal him,* has a strange majesty about it to my soul. It is the word of a king wherein there is power. Perhaps the most majestic word that was ever uttered was, *Let there be light.* No sooner was it heard than the eternal darkness fled, and light was. But surely this is scarcely second in grandeur, if second at all, for its sound is as much the voice of the Lord as that which scattered the primeval shades: *I will come and heal him.* Yet this royal and powerful word was spoken as a matter of course; our Lord Jesus did not deliberate, but the healing word flowed from him as naturally as the perfume from the flowers. *I will come and heal him.* It is an utterance resolute, true, clear, comprehensible, unconditional, and *to him* natural and commonplace, though to us divine.

It shows, dear friends, our Lord's conscious ability to deal with all manner of evil, since he was not at all puzzled by this intricate case. Almost any other physician would have felt some measure of perplexity. The case is described as that of a man sick with paralysis and yet *grievously tormented.* How could that be? Paralysis can hardly be connected with acute pain. It brings numbness and so ends sensation, at least such is my impression. Some interpreters think the disease must have been a form of tetanus, but there is no mention of tetanus in either account. It was paralysis, and yet he was *grievously tormented.* I know nothing about it, but I have read that there is a period in which paralysis may turn into a stroke, and the patient may suffer extreme agony. If so, this may explain the mystery. However, though the case perplexed many, it did not perplex the Lord Jesus, for he said, *I will come and heal him.*

Now, my brother ministers, have not you and I a great many cases coming our way which tax our experience and make us feel at a loss? I have had during this week to deal with several tempted ones whose difficulties have put me in a quandary, or would have done so if I had not borrowed from my Lord. Some experiences are a tangled skein, we cannot follow the thread, and so far as we do follow it, knots and snarls are our chief reward. See how Jesus sweeps away all debates with, *I will come and heal him.* All the complicated phenomena of human disease he comprehends, and along the dark labyrinth of human experience his mighty word makes a way for itself: undisturbed, and even undelayed, the eternal energy enters the soul, for Jesus says, *I will come and heal him.*

Neither did the extremity of the case at all dishearten him, for this poor man was ready to die, so Luke tells us, just on the verge of expiring, yet Jesus says, *I will come and heal him.* It does not matter to Jesus what the stage of the disease may be. A common physician would shake his head and say, "Ah, you should have sent for me before. I might have done something at an earlier date, but the sufferer is now beyond all human help." Poor souls are never beyond the reach of the divine healer, and so he says without a word of doubt, *I will come and heal him.* Had he been dead, Jesus could have said and could have done the same. *I will come and heal him* is a word for all emergencies. Beloved, let us never hesitate to hope in prayer because the persons for whom we plead are such great and horrible sinners, and so very far gone in crime. So long as they are not actually in hell, let us firmly believe that Christ can save them; and, verily, if we can believe in our great Savior with mighty faith, we shall yet hear him say of many a reprobate and outcast, *I will come and heal him.*

I again remark that *our Lord speaks of this healing as quite a matter of course,* for his language is after the manner of speech which men use when they know that they are *au fait* at their work, and can do it as soon as they have it before them. A person asks a workman to repair a lock or a window, and he answers, "Yes, I will come and attend to it." He means that he can do it, it is quite in his line, and it is as easy for him to do it as to come there. So can our blessed Master save a sinner as easily as his Spirit can come to that sinner, and we all know that his Spirit is a free Spirit, and like the wind, he blows where he lists. Jesus could come to the centurion's house, and he could as easily heal as he could come. *I will come and heal him.* The work is simple enough to the divine Redeemer, to whom nothing is impossible. No disease of sin can baffle the Savior or even cost him special effort to eject it. Look to him, you ends of the earth, and prove for yourselves that none are beyond his mercy's reach. Oh, that all who hear me this day would make a like trial of his healing power.

> No disease of sin can baffle the Savior or even cost him special effort to eject it.

As for the method of procedure, our Lord in his conscious power *treats the modus operandi as a matter of indifference.* He grants the first petition as it was presented to him, and will come and heal him; but when he is requested not to come, he quite as willingly says, "According to your faith, so be it unto you." He could heal as well at a distance as near at hand. Present or absent, it was all the same to him. A touch, a word, or a thought could do all that was wanted. It was so, and it is so still, for our blessed Lord saves sinners in all sorts of ways. He can save them in their pews, under the preaching which they have heard so constantly, or he can meet with them in their lonely chamber, reading some godly book, or he can wound their hearts by a loving word spoken during a walk with a friend. We have known him call men by his grace right out of the paths of sin, wounding them with secret arrows when they were at ease and secure in the service of the devil. Where no churches or preachers were present, yet have sinners been smitten at heart and have been turned to God by that heavenly influence of the Spirit, which remains the supreme miracle of the present dispensation. Saul of Tarsus was not on his knees in prayer, but was hastening to shed innocent blood, and yet the Lord brought him down and made him seek salvation. Beloved, our Lord knows how to reach inaccessible persons; they may shut *us* out, but they cannot shut *him* out. This should much encourage us in pleading for souls who are out of our usual line of action. When we plead with Jesus, let us never bind him down to ways and means of our own choosing, but let us leave to him the method of salvation.

Jesus was so conscious of his power that *you neither find him uttering an expression of wonder, or manifesting the slightest surprise when his will is done, and a notable miracle is worked.* No, but he did wonder at the centurion's faith, and on another occasion he marveled at the people's unbelief. It is no wonder to Christ that he saves sinners, for he is so in the habit of doing it, and he is so able to do it. You and I will wonder, and throughout eternity we will declare that wonder, singing with rapture and surprise the loving-kindness and pardoning power of Christ Jesus; but *he* does not wonder. Virtue goes out of him almost unconsciously, for he is so full of power that he can bless on all sides and scarcely know it. Even as the sun shines north, south, east, and west, and never wonders at its own shining; or as a fountain sends forth its sparkling drops and never stops to admire itself, or to marvel at its own flashing flow, so does Jesus readily, easily, and out of his very nature scatter pardon and salvation on all sides. He marvels at our faith, and he marvels more often at our unbelief, but to him his own power is not a thing of wonder at all.

Beloved, I want you to get fast hold of this thought if you can, and I beg you to hide it away in your hearts – that Jesus Christ is beyond measure able to save. We do not half believe it; we think we do, but we do not even a tenth believe it, for when we meet with a rather hard case we are ready to give it up in despair. Despairing persons we too soon leave in their gloom, and even melancholy men and women we are shy of; we wish we had never seen them, instead of believing up to their point, and believingly interceding until we see them happy in Christ. If we meet with a horrible blasphemer, or one who lives a foul life, or a bloated drinker, we feel quite out of our latitude and in the land of monsters, whereas it is with such cases that our Lord is much at home, and we ought to pray for such persons, and to be most confident that the gospel was meant to meet their grievous ills. Is there not a great Savior for great sinners?

We shall close by noting a third equally interesting point of great practical value. I have spoken of our Lord's willingness and power; now we will note *the abiding method of our Lord Jesus.*

The first method mentioned here was, *Come and heal him.* Jesus then went about doing good, but he does not now vouchsafe his bodily presence, or give physical tokens of his being near to anyone. If any say to us, "Lo here," or "Lo there," let us not believe them, for Jesus is not new upon the earth; he has gone up on high. We do not now pray, *Come and heal him,* in the sense of expecting a vision or a revelation of Christ after the flesh to those whom we love. We hope that he will come one day a second time, and heal the sicknesses of this poor world, but till then we know him not after the flesh, neither do we seek any personal coming.

The other and permanent mode of our Lord's action was that he should speak the word and so perform the cure. *Say in a word, and my servant shall be healed.* That is the style of our Lord today and throughout the whole of this dispensation. The healing energy of Jesus is now seen not by his personal presence, but by the power of his word in answer to the prayer of faith. This is henceforth his fixed and abiding method of cure: the word rendered effectual by believing prayer.

Now, I want you to notice that this mode of operation is outwardly similar to the Lord's usual and natural way of exercising his power in nature and in providence. Though clearly it is one of the highest forms of supernatural action, it may not at first seem to be so. Look at this: when Jesus stands at a bedside, bows over the sick child, and touches his little hand, and he is healed, the deed is notable, and is a great miracle; but will it not seem to you to be even a greater display of power, if possible, that Jesus should remain at a distance, and not see the suffering one, nor even speak so as to be heard in the darkened chamber, and yet his mere will shall be able to revive life and restore health? It is a very clear display of supernatural power, is it not – this healing by volition, or by a single word? Yet it does not seem so striking, somehow, to half-opened eyes when you look at it from the bigger point of view; for this is just how the good God is working every day in nature and in providence, achieving his purposes by his silent will, and by those echoes of his creating voice which linger among us still.

When but a little while ago your fields were bare, and your gardens desolate, if the Lord had suddenly come forth in awful glory, and caused snow and ice to fly before him, and had then graciously touched the valleys and the hills, and covered them with grass and corn, you would have exclaimed, "This is a great miracle!" But in truth it is an equally great display of power that the deed is done, though by less glaring processes. The will of the Lord transforms the clods of the valley into an army of wheat ears and clover balls; his quiet wish reddens the clusters of the vineyard and ripens the fruit of the garden; is not this also a marvel of power? Though the Lord has not come forth riding upon cherub wings, nor has he spoken audibly in commanding sentences, yet the secret energy of the eternal Word is evermore going forth to give us seedtime and harvest, cold and heat. What more divine form of miracle is to be desired?

I believe that when we rise to the possession of a fully developed faith, we shall see ourselves to be daily compassed about with the omnipotence of God, and shall look on every tiny blade of grass, and upon the insect which balances itself thereon, and the dewdrop that decorates it, as being quite as manifestly the finger of God as when the Nile River turns to blood, or the dust of Egypt becomes flies. To the believer, miracles have not ceased, but the common course of nature teems with them.

The power of the Word in answer to the prayer of faith is now our Lord's way of blessing, and this method exactly suits the wish of true humility. Humility says, "I am not worthy that God should do anything for me which would attract attention to me or make me seem honored above others." The lowly soul hears of one who was saved through a dream or a vision, and he feels that he is not worthy to be thus favored. No, my friend, and you need not wish for it, for the Word of the Lord is enough, and that Word is near you at this moment, in your mouth and in your heart. You have but to hear and your soul shall live. If I were pleading for the conversion of a sinner, I should feel hampered by my own unworthiness if I believed that salvation necessitated a bodily manifestation of my Lord or some extraordinary display of power before men's eyes; but if my Lord will save by his Word only, then do I venture to ask with confidence. Here is no parade of power, but rather quiet, divine energy, and this the meek of the earth delight in.

> The power of the Word in answer to the prayer of faith is now our Lord's way of blessing.

I am sure that it pleases *faith* better than any other way. Oh, that the power of the word might be displayed at this time. Oh, my Lord, how I desire of you that you would save thousands, and I would be glad if it were done without me, without any of your servants, if you would only say in a word, and by your Holy Spirit cause a nation to be born in a day!

Certain professing Christians eagerly pine for a great stir: they will not believe that the kingdom of God prospers unless thousands crowd into our assemblies, and unless great excitement reigns, and all the papers are ringing with the names of famous preachers. They like it all the better if they hear of persons being thrown into fits during the meetings, or read of men and women falling down, or screaming under excitement, and I know not what else besides. They can believe in Christ's power if there are signs and wonders, but nothing else. That is going back to, *Come and heal him*. But we are content to abide by the second mode. Can you not believe that by each one of us making the gospel of God to have free course, our Lord can effectually save men by his Word? Quietly, without observation, without sign or wonder, Jesus will bless believing testimonies and answer believing prayers. Strong faith is well content with the Lord's settled and usual mode of action, and it rejoices to see him save men by his Word in answer to the prayer of faith.

It is perfectly reasonable that we should expect our Lord to display his healing power in this way. What the centurion said was full of forcible argument. He said, "I am a captain of a troop. I do not have to go about from place to place to do everything personally. No, I remain in my quarters and issue orders, and I am sure of their being carried out. I say to this one, 'Go,' and he goes, and to my servant, 'Do this,' and he does it." Is it not clear that the far greater Captain of our salvation does not need to come forth bodily in order to save any, and that his Word will suffice? Give your order, O Immanuel. Speak to the powers of darkness, and the captive sinner shall be free. Speak, and the human will must yield to you, and the human heart must receive you. Is it not so? My brethren, we do not believe enough in our Lord. I come back to that: we do not believe enough in what is so perfectly reasonable. If we will but speak our Master's Word, and let it go forth, and bear sway, with less and less of our own word to cripple and hinder it, then souls must be saved. Do you not believe in the plain preaching of the glad tidings? Do you not believe in the rams' horns? O children of Israel, do you despise the rams' horns, and do you long for horses and chariots and battering rams and mighty engines of war? Remember Jericho, and how by God's own appointed, though simple, means, the huge walls rocked to their fall. Will not the Lord's own means suffice you still? Oh believers, do you want anything this day except the simple preaching of the gospel? If so, you are departing from the point wherein your faith ought to remain, since still it pleases God by the foolishness of preaching to save them who believe. *The world by wisdom knew not God*, and never will know God. Trust not philosophy, but stand by the old, old story, and pray the Master to work by it as in former ages. You want no new word to be spoken, only let the living Word be filled with power, and souls will be healed.

Now, if anyone here will try in his own case this divine method of healing, it will succeed in his instance as in that of the centurion's servant. If you, dear hearer, will believe the power of Christ and trust him to save you, you shall certainly obtain eternal life, and that at once. Can you heartily believe in Jesus as you find him revealed in Scripture? Can you be content without strange feelings, without remarkable terrors, without dreams or visions? Can you be content simply to trust your Savior? You shall be healed immediately; yes, this very moment, before this shower has ceased, the showers of everlasting grace shall have fallen upon you. You must not ask the Lord to come by some singular feeling within you, but just to speak while you are hearing, and the miracle of grace will be worked.

> If you will believe the power of Christ and trust him to save you, you shall certainly obtain eternal life.

Let me add once more: if you who are converted long to see others saved, you will be wise to keep to the established method. Pray, believe, and then expect the Lord to work by his own word in answer to your prayer. The centurion rose to this method; he began lower by desiring a personal visit, but he grew up to this plain, simple, yet glorious way. Can you not do the same? Seek no marvels, but test the power of the gospel upon your friend. Do not ask the Lord to go out of his way, but implore him to apply his Word with power to those whose eternal welfare lies near your heart. Bring your loved ones under the sound of the gospel and entreat the healing Lord to put forth his power thereby, and your desire shall be accomplished. Alas, if the Son of Man comes, shall he find faith on the earth? If he were to come now, and ask us all to put into the collection box what faith we have, when he opened it, would it come to the eighth part of a farthing? Yet every man among us that is a believer ought to have an inexhaustible treasure of golden faith. Lord, we believe; help our unbelief! Lord, increase our faith. Amen.

Chapter 4

Self Low, but Christ High

The centurion answered and said, Lord, I am not worthy that thou shouldest come under my roof: but speak the word only, and my servant shall be healed. (Matthew 8:8)

This centurion was a worthy man from the human point of view, but he called himself unworthy when he turned towards our Lord. He was so excellent a man that the elders of the Jews, who were by no means partial to Roman soldiers, pleaded with Jesus that he was worthy. Had he been personally there, he would have repudiated their plea; and he did so by the second party of friends whom he sent to our Lord. As one set of friends had said, "He is worthy," another set of friends was bidden to say, in his name, "Lord, I am not worthy." The worthiest men in the world do not think themselves worthy, while the most unworthy people are generally those who boast of their own worthiness and, possibly, of their own perfection. We should not have wondered had this man been proud; for he was one of the conquering race, and the representative of a tyrannical power. If he was not a very great officer, but only the captain of a hundred men, yet it is not unusual for petty officers to be more haughty than their superiors. If a man is placed in a very high and responsible position, he is frequently sobered by his responsibilities; but a mere jack-in-office is usually greater than the emperor himself. However, this centurion was a man of gentle mold, and said of himself, *I am not worthy.*

He might have been proud of his popularity among the Jews. Few can bear to be surrounded by an atmosphere of esteem without beginning to esteem themselves much too highly. He had built for the Jews a synagogue. That is a good thing to do, but it is very possible to build a synagogue, and to become a great man in one's own opinion, and stand several courses of bricks higher in pride. Not so, however, this good man, who had built a synagogue, but did not presume upon the greatness of his own generosity. He never mentioned it, but said, *I am not worthy that thou shouldest enter under my roof.*

He was a man used to command. He says to this man, *Go, and he goeth; and to another, Come, and he cometh.* Those who are accustomed to being obeyed are apt to hold themselves at a high valuation; but this centurion had not fallen into that very common fault. He watched carefully over the sickness of his young servant, and was earnest that he might be healed: he was a tender master as well as a liberal neighbor. If we wished to pick out a truly worthy man, we need not go further than this Roman soldier, or we might fare worse; and yet he said, *Lord, I am not worthy.*

Further, note that he did not say, "Lord, the room in which my servant sleeps is not worthy of you, and it is not suitable that you should climb to the loft where the boy lies sick"; but he said, "*I am not worthy that thou shouldest come under my roof* – not even into the best parlor, or the drawing room. It is my house, and being such, it is the abode of one who has not dared to seek a personal interview with you, and I judge it to be altogether unfit for your entertainment." He was fearful of troubling the Lord, and felt that to bring him through the street to his door was more than he could think of for a moment, when a word would suffice to work the miracle he sought.

Beloved friends, my point is this: I would call your attention to the happy blending of this beautiful humbleness with an extraordinary degree of faith. In his confession of sin he is unsparing – *Lord, I am not worthy that thou shouldest come under my roof*; but in his confession of faith he is equally clear – *Speak the word only, and my servant shall be healed.* It is a kind of vulgar error that a lowly esteem of ourselves must be connected with a very great distrustfulness towards Christ. I call it a vulgar error, for it is an error both common and baseless. The fact is that high thoughts of self go with low thoughts of Christ; and well they may, for they are birds of a feather. But low thoughts of self should always be associated with high thoughts of Christ, for they are both products of the Spirit of God, and they help each other. Our unworthiness is a foil to the brightness of our Lord's infinite grace. We sink deep in humility, but soar high in assurance. As we decrease, Christ increases.

To make this point clear, I shall say, first of all, that *a sense of unworthiness is very desirable and commendable*; but, secondly, that *a sense of unworthiness can be very wrongly used,* and can even be made the occasion of grave sin; and then, thirdly, I shall add that *a sense of unworthiness finds a fit companion in a strong faith in Christ.* Of this the text supplies us with an instance. May the Holy Spirit help our meditations and make them truly profitable!

First, then, *a sense of unworthiness is very desirable and commendable.* Some of you are destitute of it. I dare say you think it a mean and miserable thing. You suppose it would injure your manliness, lower your self-respect, and dampen your courage. Dear friends, the manliness which feeds on sin is a poisonous fungus which grows out of the rottenness of a corrupt heart. May it be taken away from us! Any condition of mind which is founded on a falsehood must be an evil one: it is a bubble blown by ignorant conceit. Let us not desire more self-respect, manliness, or courage than will be consistent with the truth of things.

> We sink deep in humility, but soar high in assurance. As we decrease, Christ increases.

I commend a sense of our unworthiness because *it is a sense of what is true.* When a man thinks himself unworthy before the Lord, his thoughts are right. When he feels that he could not be saved by the merit of his own works, for his works are faulty and defiled, then he judges according to fact. Whatever result a thought may have upon us, whether it makes us happy or makes us sad, this is a secondary matter; the main point with an honest mind must always be: Is it true? If it be a truthful thought, I ought at once to entertain it, cost me what it may. Should the truth create devastation within my soul, and destroy all my fair hopes and promising fancies, it must be so; for the most painful effect of truth is better for me than the most flattering results of falsehood. Better the strikes of truth than the kisses of deceit. The arrow which pierces the heart of self-conceit is a blessing. If you take a very lowly view of yourself, some may call you morbid, but they know not what spirit you are of. Humility is healthy: lowliness is no disease. When we think worse and worse of ourselves, we are getting nearer and nearer to the truth. We are by nature depraved, degraded, guilty, and worthy of the wrath of God. If any hard thing can be imagined against fallen man, it is assuredly true of him. What worse character can be given to human nature than that which is drawn by the pen of inspiration in the third chapter of the epistle to the Romans! Oh, that God would make us lowly in spirit and fill us with a deep feeling of our own unworthiness! For this will only be revealing to us the truth and delivering us from the way of falsehood.

In the next place, note that *a deep sense of unworthiness is no proof that a man has grossly sinned.* It may be viewed in quite the opposite light: if the man had been heinously wicked, his conscience would have lost its sensitiveness, and he would not in all probability have felt his unworthiness so keenly. He that has high thoughts of himself is not necessarily a man of clean life; and on the other hand, he that has very depreciative thoughts of himself is not thereby proven to be worse than others. He that feels himself unworthy has something about him that God esteems. We are sure of this; for when the Lord seeks a lodging among men, though he might have his choice of palaces, he nevertheless condescends to say, *I dwell in the high and holy place, with him also that is of a contrite and humble spirit, to revive the spirit of the humble, and to revive the heart of the contrite ones.* Do not judge men by their estimates of themselves; or if you do, take this as your guide: that he that humbles himself is to be exalted, and he that exalts himself is to be abased. He that is great, is little; let him that is little to himself be all the greater with you. God loves not those who boast: he has filled the hungry with good things, but the rich he has sent empty away.

I commend this sense of unworthiness, because *it has a tendency to make a man kind to others.* He who thinks himself everybody, thinks another man nobody. Pride has no bowels, and will rather turn a sick servant out of doors than seek a physician for him. If a man be proud, he will say, "I am a man under authority, having soldiers under me; and I am not to be worried by having sick boys to look after." Sympathy, tenderness, and the valuation of others are strangers in the house of the proud; but they take up their abode with those who think themselves unworthy. Beloved, it is well to think little of yourselves, for then you will have more thought to spare for the sorrows of others. If you know yourself to be unworthy, you will cheerfully recognize the claims of others, and you will feel that it is not beneath you to care for the poorest and most obscure. There is some trace of a work of grace in your heart when you have a love for your neighbor because you feel that you are no better than him. This is infinitely better than to be so great that you can trample down the crowd in your imperial and domineering dignity, and look down with contempt upon the many who have not attained to that eminent degree of honor which you suppose yourself to be enjoying. The great man, the very great man, the highly deserving man, the person who is a right honorable and worshipful personage, rides roughshod over his fellows and crushes them without misgiving, if they lie in his way and may hinder his plan; but the consciously unworthy man, the man who feels that he owes everything to the mercy of God, and must still depend upon that mercy and that mercy only, will be tender and gentle towards his fellow sinners, and speak comfortably unto them.

We commend again this sense of unworthiness, because *it makes a man lowly towards the Savior.* Of all things that are contemptible, a proud demeanor towards the Lord Jesus is the most hateful, yet it is by no means unusual. Some seem to fancy that Jesus is their servant, at their beck and call, and they talk about his salvation as though he ought to give it, and they could claim it for themselves and all mankind. If we speak about the sovereign choice of some unto eternal life, they begin chattering about injustice and partiality, as if any guilty man had a right to anything from the Lord of glory except the dreadful right to be punished for his sins. I think I hear the Master say, "May I not do as I will with my own?" Many of those who pretend to be the advocates of grace are the betrayers of it, and they snatch from its hand the silver scepter of its sovereignty. Beloved, it is well in prayer to come to our Lord not as creditors seeking a debt, but as condemned criminals begging for a free pardon. We have no claim on God. If he chooses to save us, it must be of his own free grace. Let us come humbly, saying, "Lord, I am not worthy that you should come under my roof. That you should die for me remains the greatest of all miracles in my esteem. That you should choose me, and call me, and pardon me, and save me is a world of wonders at which my soul stands gratefully amazed. What is this to me? How could you look on such a dead dog as I am?" Our right state of heart, when dealing with our Lord Jesus, is that of the penitent washing his feet with tears, or of the leper who fell at his feet and worshipped him. If we would come to the Savior of sinners, we must come as sinners. We must come as humble petitioners, and not as those who proudly fancy that they have a claim upon the grace of God.

A sense of unworthiness is exceedingly useful, because *it puts man where God can bless him*. "Oh," you say, "where is that?" The Lord will only act in conformity with his own attributes. God will always be God, and as he will be God alone in creation, so he will certainly be God alone in the new creation. Our only right position before God is to know that we are undeserving and unworthy while he is holy and glorious. We must hear him say, "I am God, and beside me there is none else," or we shall never look unto him to be saved. If I am somebody, and I stand up with my rights and my claims, God cannot bless me without conceding to me that which he never will concede. How dare I claim that which he calls a free gift? How often have I made this place ring with that voice of the Lord, *I will have mercy on whom I will have mercy, and I will have compassion on whom I will have compassion*. Depend upon it, God will be God; and if you will not be saved without his leaving the throne of his sovereignty, then you will perish without hope. He will be King and Lord in the work of salvation; you must take it as his free gift, or die without it. If it be of grace, it cannot be of right – those things are contradictory. Unutterably great is his pity, immeasurable is his mercy; but still he will have no pity for those whose proud selfwill stands out against his sovereign grace.

O sinner, if you would be pardoned, you must confess that the Lord is King. Your touch of Jesus himself must be like that of Thomas when he put his finger to the wound and cried, *My Lord and my God*. You must have Jesus to be Lord and God to you, or he will be nothing to you. Beloved, no man will yield to this till he has a thorough conviction of his own unworthiness. We are not worthy to be saved; if we were, it would be of debt, and not of grace. We are not worthy to receive any good from the hand of an offended God; if we were, we should make our appeal to justice, and mercy would not be needed. Come, dear hearers, let us bow before the Lord, and own that he alone is King. Let us confess that we deserve nothing but his wrath.

> If sudden vengeance seize my breath,
>   I must pronounce thee just in death;
> And if my soul were sent to hell,
>   Thy righteous law approves it well.

It is assuredly so, and therefore we put in no claim, but simply cry, "O God, be merciful to me."

This state of mind, once more, *makes a man in love with the simple Word of God.* This man, because he was not worthy, did not ask of Christ any mystic words or imposing ceremonies, nor even so much as a visit to his house. No, he was content that the Lord should speak the word. It is our proud human nature that so much yearns for finery and pomp: we would readily go to heaven by some royal road or glittering way; we want to be saved by music and perfected by paraphernalia. We would like to be forgiven, but we must have a visible priest in full robed garments, and we must have a decorated altar and a show of candles in the daylight. Trinkets are needed to conceal the humiliation of being saved by pure grace. But a soul that feels its own unworthiness cries, "Lord, save me in your own way. Your word is enough for me. Speak the word of command, and it suffices me." We read, *He sent his word, and healed them*; and a sense of unworthiness will make us content to be saved in that most simple manner.

Humble souls love a plain gospel. I know what some are: they read a book which contains the gospel, and because it is very simple, they say, "This will do for my servant-girl, or for the laborer in my field"; but for themselves they seek something more difficult to understand, and consequently more flattering to their pride. Many people like a preacher who can confound the gospel for them: plain speech offends them. We are overwhelmed with such folk in this generation. Certain people, when they hear what they cannot comprehend, say fervently, "What a wonderful discourse! I delight in a man of culture who raises the tone of preaching above what the lower classes can understand." Fools that they are to talk so! The plainer the word, the more likely it is to be the word of God. Did not Paul say, *Seeing then that we have such hope, we use great plainness of speech*? The gospel is not sent into the world for the *elite,* or for the few choice souls that read the reviews. The gospel is sent into the world for *every creature*; and if it be meant for *every creature,* then it must be made so plain that even nonreaders may be able to comprehend it, and persons with the most meager education, or none at all, may be able to grasp it. You, learned sir, may like a highly finished gospel which only a half dozen gentlemen like yourself can comprehend; but I like the common salvation, the good news for the crowd, the writing which he that runs can read. Does not your candor and humanity admit that it is well that the gospel should be simple enough for the poor and the illiterate, since they need salvation as well as the educated? I wish to God that a sense of unworthiness brought us all down from those pinnacles of the temple of vanity where we stand in mutual admiration, but in awful danger of a fall. Oh, that the heavenly wisdom would make us willing to be saved like commonplace sinners, willing for Christ not to come to our house, but to give the word of command by which the miracle of grace would be worked!

Now, beloved friends, I leave that point, only putting it thus: Do you know your own unworthiness? I do not ask you whether you have been racked with terrors, nor whether you have been tormented with doubts, nor whether you have been drowned in despair – that may be, or may not be. But are you willing to subscribe to this: that you are not worthy, that sentence of condemnation may fitly be passed upon you, and if you are saved it must be of free grace alone?

But now, secondly, I have to show you that *this sense of unworthiness can be wrongly used*, and is often perverted to ruinous ends.

Yonder is a person who cries, "I hear the gospel, but *I cannot believe that it is intended for me.* I cannot think I am aimed at in the proclamation of free forgiveness and gracious acceptance." Friend, why not? "Well,

I am unworthy." Listen! Is there a man on earth who is not unworthy? Hear the words of Jesus: *Go ye into all the world, and preach the gospel to every creature. He that believeth and is baptized shall be saved; but he that believeth not shall be damned.* We are not sent to every *worthy* creature, but to *every* creature, worthy or unworthy. Are you not a creature? Well, then, the gospel is to be preached to you. And do you think God means it to be preached to you as a mere form, or a grim farce? Has it no relation to you? Your believing and being baptized according to the divine command, will God say, "I never meant that promise for you"? It is atrocious that you should think so. It is a new and grievous sin to imagine that the Lord would run back from his Word. You are unworthy, we grant it; but does that make God false? You are unworthy, more unworthy than you know of; but does that prove the Lord to be untrue? Will he tantalize men by sending them a gospel which is not intended for them? Will he put salvation before them, and bid them believe in Jesus for it, when he never means to give it to them if they do comply with the conditions he has laid down? Come, come! I will go with you as far as you like in your confession of your own unworthiness, but I cannot tolerate your making God unworthy because you are unworthy. He will keep his word, however false you may be, and every soul that believes in Christ Jesus has everlasting life.

> The Lord delights in mercy, and do you doubt it? Do you dare to say that he cannot have mercy on whom he will have mercy?

I have seen this same evil come up in the form of *doubt as to the mercy of God.* When a man's sin appears very great, he is apt to say, "God cannot have mercy upon me." Now, sir, you shall be allowed to be the chief of sinners if you feel yourself to be so, but you cannot be allowed to deny the omnipotence of God. You are sadly unworthy, but it is in the unworthy that grace finds its sphere of operation, and you must not limit the power of that grace which comes to men through Christ Jesus. The Lord delights in mercy, and do you doubt it? Do you dare to say that he cannot have mercy on whom he will have mercy? Why, that denies the whole body of Scripture, throughout which he declares to us that *all manner of sin and blasphemy shall be forgiven unto men.* He testifies that *the blood of Jesus Christ his Son cleanseth us from all sin.*

Do you deny this? He puts it expressly: *Though your sins be as scarlet, they shall be as white as snow; though they be red like crimson, they shall be as wool.* You know these promises; will you give them the lie, and so make God a liar? Your unworthiness must not be allowed to be used as an argument for the denial of God's glorious attribute of mercy. Does he not say, *Let the wicked forsake his way, and the unrighteous man his thoughts: and let him return unto the* L{\smaller ORD}*, and he will have mercy upon him; and to our God, for he will abundantly pardon*? Which is true, you or God? Depend upon it that the lie is not with him. Oh, let it not be with you either; but now, even now, believe that his mercy endures forever, and that where sin abounded, grace did much more abound.

Poor creatures have even gone the length of *doubting the power of the blood of Jesus to cleanse them.* If you talk so, I must put my hand on your mouth; you must not say another word of that sort. Is it not enough that you have spattered yourself with sin? Must you now malign your Savior? Will you trample on the blood of Christ? Will you deny its cleansing power? As he was God as well as man, our Lord's sacrifice has an infinite virtue in it, and we cannot endure that you, guilty as you are, should add to all your former crimes this highest and most ungenerous iniquity of charging the blood of Christ with a lack of cleansing power. Will you give God the lie about his own Son? O sirs, if you perish, it will not be because the blood has too little efficacy, but it will be because you have not believed on the name of the Son of God, and will not come unto him that you might have life.

We have known persons under deep distress *doubt the promise of God.* A great and sure promise, which obviously belonged to them, they have set aside, saying, "It is too good to be true. I cannot believe it, because I am so unworthy." Again I follow the same mode of reply: *you* may be a liar, but do not make God one. You may have made many promises which you have broken, but do not charge God with doing so. You have vowed that you would do this and that, and you have forgotten your pledges and thrown your promises into forgetfulness; but dream not that God will do so. He is not a man that he should lie. O man, I pray you, if you feel as if you were on the brink of hell, do not doubt God's faithfulness to his promise; do not cast a doubt upon his truthfulness, for that would be an excess of naughtiness. I feel sometimes that even if I were lost, I must still believe God to be true. *Though he slay me, yet will I trust in him.* Here, put the killing sword to my bare neck, and let me die the death I deserve, but I will still believe that God is good and true. O Lord, you keep your word! Such faith is not one jot greater than the Lord deserves of us; for he has never deceived us, and he never will. Dear heart, do take the promise of God to mean what it says, and believe it. Suppose somebody were to trust himself with Christ for salvation, and were to believe that God would therefore save him, and yet he does not get saved; what then? I will not suppose such a case; but I will wait till you find me an actual instance, and then I will consider how to answer you.

If a soul that trusted in the promise of God, and fled to Christ for refuge, could be sent down to hell, then the legions of the infernal pit would exhibit him as a trophy of their victory over God. They would carry him on their shoulders and shout, "Here is a proof that God can lie. Here is a proof that Christ's blood has failed to save a believer. Here is a sinner that trusted God, and, after all, was lost in the teeth of God's covenant and oath!" Do you think that such a thing will ever happen? Let not such a blasphemous idea be tolerated in your mind for a moment. Take the promise as coming from God, and therefore as assuredly true; simply believe it, and be happy.

Some, because they are unworthy, *would deny the Lord Jesus the pleasure of saving them.* When Cato committed suicide, Caesar was sad that Cato would envy him the glory of saving his life. Perhaps if Cato had known what Caesar would have said, he would not have been so swift with his sword. Beloved, will you deny Christ the pleasure of forgiving you? Will you go to hell so that you may spite the Savior by not permitting him to save you? Will you look the eternal Father in the face and express a hate so malignant that you venture to say, "I would rather be condemned forever than be saved by the grace of God"? I cannot believe it. Surely you are not such a madman! Come, come, man! I will let you use the blackest language about yourself: you may paint yourself as almost a fiend, and little better than the devil, if this will please you; you shall sweep up hell itself for epithets, if you will, with which to set forth your own sin and misery; but, I pray you, touch not God, deny not his mercy, doubt not his faithfulness, refuse not his love, but submit yourself to his saving grace. Remember how the Syrian messengers diligently observed whether anything would come from the king of Israel; and when Ahab said, *He is my brother*, they *did hastily catch it: and they said, Thy brother Benhadad*. Oh, that you would hastily catch the word of grace, for one word may be enough to bring you consolation! Remember how the Ninevites, when Jonah preached to them, repented on the bare hope of, *Who can tell?* They had not a word of promise to back them up in their confidence, but they ventured upon, *Who can tell if God will turn and repent, and turn away from his fierce anger, that we perish not?* Come, dear heart, catch the smallest hopeful thing. Have a trap for sunbeams as well as for hailstones. Take fast hold upon the sweet words which God has said, believe them to be true, and risk all upon them. You will never believe better of God than you shall find him to be.

Alas! there are some whose sense of unworthiness *turns to sullen rebellion*. I will not speak harshly of them, but I do know some few who frequent these courts of whom I must say that they are their own jailors and tormenters. Like one of old, they must confess, *My soul refused to be comforted*. There is another passage in the psalm which says, *Their soul abhorreth all manner of meat*. Who were these? David says they were fools. I do not say so much as that, dear friends, of any of you, but I am solemnly afraid it would be true if I did say it. He that refuses all manner of meat is likely to be starved, and who is to be blamed for it? If you refuse the Bread of Life, can we pity you if you die of hunger? To put away from you the one and only salvation out of sullen hopelessness is as suicidal as if you stabbed yourself. Will you do so? Will you cry out, "I shall be lost; I know I shall. It is of no use preaching to me; it is of no use praying for me!"

My dear friend, are you really going to give yourself up in such an absurd way while you are yet in the land of hope? Here you sit in the dungeon, and I stand before you with a free pardon; will you not have it? It is to be had for the asking; will you not ask for it? It is to be had by the willing receiver; will you not receive it? Then I solemnly tell you that if you remain obstinate, there will soon be the rope around your

> You will never believe better of God than you shall find him to be.

neck, and you will reap the due reward of your sin and folly. What! You still cry you are so unworthy! We know you are, yet a free pardon is granted you if you will accept it. "Oh, but I feel my unworthiness so terribly!" Would a man be hanged out of spite to the mercy of our gracious queen? Would he choose to be executed because he felt unworthy to be pardoned? Will you be lost because you do not feel worthy to be saved?

If I were you, I would say nothing against the grace which would save me, but I would gratefully accept the loving pardon and the tender mercy of my Lord. I feel that it is no business of mine to plead for my own damnation. The devil and I have had many a skirmish; and if there is anything to be said against my being saved, I have no doubt whatever that he will be particularly sure to say it. Therefore I do not go into that line of business, for there is no room for me; Satan will do all that can be done in that direction. I find it far more profitable to be picking up all the crumbs of comfort that I can find, in the form of reasons why I should be saved. In reading the Word of God I find these reasons are as plentiful as blackberries in autumn. God has said it, and I believe it: *He that . . . believeth on him . . . hath everlasting life.* I believe in Jesus, and I have everlasting life. Hallelujah! Bless the Lord!

Yes, we can all of us join in that shout, and bless God for his free love which has abounded towards us, which love we have seen and known, and tasted, and handled. Well might we all join in one long hallelujah and make the streets ring with, *Blessed be the name of the* LORD. But the poor folk I am thinking of sit down, and bite their nails, and chew their lips, and weep their eyes away, and never move an inch towards the one blessing which they need above all things. Let me warn them. Remember, a man may commit suicide as truly by refusing to eat as by taking poison; and you may destroy your own souls by refusing Christ quite as surely and guiltily as if you plunged into open rebellion against the Lord God and ran to an excess of riot. Think of this, I pray you.

But now, thirdly – and I am glad to proceed to this much more pleasing subject – *a sense of unworthiness finds a fit companion in strong faith in Christ.*

For, look you first, *when you have no faith in yourself, there is more room in the soul for faith in Jesus.* If you have confidence in yourself, that bit of self is filled; but if you have no confidence in yourself, your soul is one great vacuum, and you can hold more of Christ. The greater the emptiness, the more room for that which is to be the fullness. If you have no reason whatever why you should be saved, except for the free grace of God in Christ, then take that free grace here and now. God help you to do so, and may nothing hinder you! Believe more in Christ, because you cannot, in any degree, believe in yourself.

Again, he that has low thoughts of himself is on a vantage ground as to receiving saving truth. He who has true views of himself is likely also to discover the truth with regard to the Lord Jesus and the covenant blessings which come to us in him. Everything depends, you know, upon the measure with which we calculate. If your yard is too short, or too long, everything will be inaccurate in proportion to the faultiness of your standard of measurement. When you have the right measure as to your own lost, ruined, and undone condition, you will soon receive the right measure as to the grace and ability of the Son of God, who is able to save unto the uttermost those who come unto God by him. Jesus is an almighty Savior: there is no horrible crime, no unmentionable offense, or no damnable sin which he cannot forgive. There is no criminality or baseness of character which he cannot overcome and remove. *All power is given unto [him],* and in the salvation realm he is King of Kings, and Lord of Lords, and nothing can resist his sway. Do you believe this? If so, trust yourself to him now, and the moment you do it, you will pass from death unto life.

This man, again, through his being so lowly, had not the conceit to question and doubt. Doubt is, in most cases, the daughter of pride. Think of a man criticizing God! Job might possibly have done that while he heard of God by the hearing of the ear, but when his eye saw him he abhorred himself in dust and ashes. How dare we fuss at God's way of saving the guilty! It is impertinence! It is insanity! Let us have none of it.

This lowly estimate of himself brought the centurion away from dictating to Jesus how the blessing should come. A great many persons we meet with are always mapping out courses for the Holy Spirit. They are willing to be saved if they can be saved by a certain mode. They will believe if they see signs and wonders, but not otherwise. Their peace must come in the way they have selected, and in no other: their mind is made up as to how it ought to be. The centurion might have said,

"Lord, come under my roof, and then I will believe. The token of your presence shall make me sure." He did not ask for signs, or wonders, or comforts. Lots of you here are waiting till you feel some singular feeling, or see some strange vision, or undergo a special experience; you cannot believe Christ's bare word, you are too proud to be saved by that only. O my hearers, if the Lord shows you your utter unworthiness, you will be willing to be saved in the simplest manner. You will then ask nothing but this one thing: "Lord, save me, or I will perish." If Christ had come to the centurion's house, he would have had a very remarkable experience. It would be strange for a Roman soldier to entertain the Savior of the world, but he did not ask for that remarkable experience and peculiar honor. You read biographies, or you hear Christian people tell how they were saved, and you put your finger on certain memorable points, and you say, "If ever I feel that, or see that, I will believe in Christ, but not otherwise." Thus it seems that the Lord must bow to your will and not do as he thinks fit. Truly, the wind blows where it lists, and none of our dictation will have weight with the free Spirit or with the sovereign Savior.

If Christ had come to the man's house, there would have been great joy in it; but he did not ask for that joy. Some will not believe in the Lord Jesus unless they feel great ecstasy; but, dear friend, is it right to resolve that if you feel no joy you will not believe in him? No, rather, if you walk in darkness, and see no light, trust in the Lord. If all within seems to be contrary to the fact of your salvation, believe in Christ, and you are saved; and if every power and passion of your nature should vote you lost, you are not lost if you are simply hanging on to the bare word of the Lord Jesus Christ.

This man was so brought down that he was content with but a word. *Speak the word only, and my servant shall be healed.* This is the point to come to. Are you content to believe God's bare Word, and to be saved by God's Word alone? You would believe at once if I could work you a miracle, would you not? What would you believe? You would believe in me; and as I do not want you to believe in me, but in Christ, I will not work any miracle. Oh, but if you could feel some very singular emotion, you would believe. What would you believe in? Why, in the singular emotion, that is all. You would not believe in God's Word. He that cannot believe God's Word without wonders, really fixes his belief in the wonders and not in God's Word. Take the naked word of God, which is this: *Believe on the Lord Jesus Christ, and thou shalt be saved.* Though you neither sigh nor sing, though you neither have dream nor doubt, though you have neither great comfort nor sharp conviction, believe in Jesus! Sinful, unworthy as you are, say, "This is all my salvation, and all my desire. I accept the Lord Jesus as my all in all!"

After all, such faith is the greatest of faith, for the Lord Jesus said, *I have not found so great faith, no, not in Israel.* One man stands up and tells you the ground of his confidence, and you learn that at such a time he heard a voice, or in such a night he dreamed such a dream, or during certain months he had an awful experience of fear of hell, or at another period he felt such joy that he was carried clean away. Do not think less of the believer who says, "My experience is only this:

> I'm a poor sinner, and nothing at all,
> But Jesus Christ is my all in all."

This last man's experience has the least chaff in it. I find written in the infallible Book that if I trust the Lord Jesus he will perform his office of Savior upon me. I have trusted him, and he has saved me. "Is that all the witness you have?" says one. What more witness do I want? I may be able to mention certain incidents which attended my conversion, but these are not my hope. I place no reliance upon what I have thought, or seen, or felt. If anybody could prove that I never saw, and never felt, and never heard anything of the kind, I should not be troubled about it, for one thing I know: I know that I heard that text, *Look unto me, and be ye saved, all the ends of the earth*, and I did look, and I was saved. What is more, if I did not *then* look, and was not *then* saved, I do not care twopence to contest the point, for I am looking *now*, and therefore I am saved. That is the comfort: we have not to rely on a past faith, but still to go on believing. Looking unto Jesus ever, coming to him always: that is the true position for peace. If I rest in Christ every day, the fruit of that believing will be seen every day. I must not only believe in Jesus,

> **Looking unto Jesus ever, coming to him always: that is the true position for peace.**

but also keep right on believing. God help you to do so! Set side by side with a deep sense of unworthiness a high appreciation of the power of Christ to cleanse you from sin, and to make you holy, even as God is holy. Make progress in these two things. They will not be like the legs of the lame, which are not equal; but they will be much alike in their happy effect upon your life. Down with self, and up with Christ.

> Thus while I sink my joys shall rise
> Immeasurably high.

Chapter 5

A Man Under Authority

The centurion answered and said, Lord, I am not worthy that thou shouldest come under my roof: but speak the word only, and my servant shall be healed. For I am a man under authority, having soldiers under me: and I say to this man, Go, and he goeth; and to another, Come, and he cometh; and to my servant, Do this, and he doeth it. (Matthew 8:8-9)

Without any introduction, as we have just been reading Matthew's record of this notable miracle of our Lord, I shall come at once to the text, and first of all, work out the incident itself, and then secondly, make use of its lessons for our own practical purposes. There is much to be learned from this narrative for our guidance at the present time.

First, let me work out the incident itself.

A centurion, the commander of the detachment of Roman forces then placed at Capernaum, had a servant exceedingly ill. He was paralyzed, or palsied, but it was with that kind of paralysis which still leaves room for great pain. He was *grievously tormented*, and yet paralyzed. This man of war was evidently a good master, thoughtful of his servants; and when he heard that the great prophet, Jesus of Nazareth, had come to the town, he made the best of his way to him, and begged him to heal his servant. The centurion did not ask Jesus to come down and heal him, but the Savior at once replied, *I will come and heal him.*

This was more than the centurion had asked; he had pleaded for the healing of his slave, but he had not expected the personal presence of the glorious Master.

You remember that, on another occasion, a certain nobleman went to Jesus and begged him, saying, *Sir, come down [before] my child die[s].* Jesus did not go down to the nobleman's child, but he sent his powerful word and healed him.

In this case, it was a servant, not a child, who was suffering; and, as if the Savior would pay the greater attention where the rank was lower, he showed the condescension of his spirit by saying in this instance, "I will come and heal him. I myself will come and undertake the cure that you request of me." See how the Savior grants more than we ask, and also how very tender and considerate he is to the poor and needy. He would not have them think that he despises them; and therefore, while to the nobleman's son a gracious word is sent, to the centurion's servant the Lord offers a gracious visit: *I will come and heal him.* Jesus is very tender and pitiful. He knows the soreness of human hearts in poverty and sickness, and he will not inflict upon them any unnecessary wound. No, he will, as it were, go out of his way by a superior gentleness to those who are of the lowest rank that he may show that he is no respecter of persons after the manner of men.

Now see what the centurion does. He had requested the Lord to heal his servant; he is very grateful for the kindness of the Savior in offering to come and heal him; but he is a true gentleman, so he will not put the Savior to any personal inconvenience. He feels that it is not at all necessary that the Great Physician should take a journey to his house, so he says to him, *Lord, I am not worthy that thou shouldest come under my roof: but speak the word only, and my servant shall be healed.* The refining power of faith upon the manners of men is very wonderful. Roman centurions were usually rough, snippy fellows who cared for nobody. On many a hard-fought field they received their training for future service, and they forced their way up from the ranks, not by competitive examinations, but by blows, and cuffs, and bruises, and wounds. Yet this officer, being a believer in Jesus Christ, is evidently softened, more or less civilized, and cultivated by that very fact. You can notice it often, that the roughest men, the least educated of women, will have about them some of the gentlest and sweetest traits of character when they come to believe in the Lord Jesus Christ. So the centurion says, "My Lord, glad enough would I be with a visit from your dignified Majesty, but I am not worthy that you should come under my roof, and it is not needful for you to do so. You can heal my servant with a single word. Therefore, I pray you, speak the word only, and my servant shall be healed." It was this beautiful, thoughtful, and gentlemanly feeling, which I cannot too highly recommend, which led him to speak in this way; and what he said is remarkably instructive.

Let me, then, work out the incident in detail.

Notice, first, that *the centurion drew a parallel between himself and the Lord Jesus Christ.* He said, *I am a man under authority, having soldiers under me*, or, as the Revised Version better renders it, *For I also am a man under authority*. Some have tried to shift the meaning here and to teach that the centurion meant to say, "I am under authority, only a subordinate officer, and yet I can do so-and-so. You are not under authority, but great and powerful, and therefore you can do much more." But that is not the sense at all. The centurion meant that he was himself a man under authority, not merely a private individual, but a servant of Caesar. The uniform that he wore marked him out as belonging to one of the legions of the Roman empire; the insignia upon his regimental uniform denoted that he was a centurion, a commander who derived his position and power from the great emperor at Rome. He was *a man under authority*.

It is not to our great Master's dishonor, but quite the opposite, that this centurion meant to say, "I recognize in you also a man under authority," for this blessed Christ of ours had come into the world commissioned by God. He was not here merely in his private capacity as the Son of David, or as the Son of Mary, or even as the Son of God; but he was here as the One whom the Father had chosen, anointed, qualified, and sent to carry out a divine commission. This officer could see in the person of Christ the marks of his being commissioned by God. By some means, I know not how, he had arrived at this very safe and true conclusion, that Jesus Christ was acting under the authority of the great God who made heaven and earth; and he looked at him, therefore, under that aspect, as duly authorized and commissioned for his work.

Now go a step further. He who is commissioned to perform any work is also *provided by the superior authority with the power to carry out that work*. A centurion, therefore, has soldiers under him: "I am a man under authority, having soldiers under me; men put under me for the carrying out of my commands, because my commands are authorized by the superior authority of Caesar." So this man seems to say to Christ, "I believe that you are provided with due assistance for the carrying out of all the purposes for which you have come into the world. If I have an order to send," says he, "I say to my servant, 'Go,' and he goes. If I want another to come, I say, 'Come,' and he comes. If there is something to be done, I summon one of the men under my authority, and I say to him, 'Do this,' and he does it." He seems to say to the Savior, "You also, commissioned and appointed of the great God, must have had servants appointed to wait upon you. You are not sent to a warfare at your own charges. You are not left to do this work alone. There must be, somewhere about, though I perceive them not, soldiers under you, and servants under you, who wait to do your bidding." You catch that idea, do you not? The parallel is very clear, and I do not wonder that the Savior greatly admired the man's faith which had enabled him to perceive this great truth.

The centurion went, therefore, a step further in his argument. "I, a man duly commissioned, have under me servants to carry out my will, and these servants of mine I keep well in hand." You know that there are masters who have servants to whom they say, "Go," and they do not go, or to whom they say, "Come," and they do not come, or at least they do not come very quickly. They must say "Come" or "Go" several times before the servants actually do come or go; and there are masters who may say, "Do this," and they may again say, "Do this," and they may yet again say, "Do this," but it is not done. But this centurion was a man who knew how to manage men. He was a master, a real master, not in name only, but also in fact. He did not, within his domain, tolerate anything like delay. He said to Christ, "I say, 'Go,' and they go, or 'Come,' and they come." He did not allow anything like mutiny or the resistance of his will; he had his whole household so well in hand that when he said to his servant, "Do this," he did it. This is the right kind of master, and servants in the long run like a master who will be obeyed.

The centurion was a disciplinarian of that sort, as kind as the sunlight, for he sought Christ's aid for his sick servant; but he was also as true and firm as steel, so that what he said was to be done *was* to be done, and done at once. He transfers that characteristic to the Savior. He does not, he cannot, do to Christ the discredit of supposing that he has not his household well in hand, that he has servants who dare to trifle with his commands, or that there are agencies which have broken loose from beneath his rule and will go whichever way they please. "No," says he, "Savior, commissioned of the Father, you have your soldiers and your servants, and I believe that you have them under such control and subject to such discipline that you have but to speak, and the act that you order is done, or you have but to command, and it stands fast forever."

I trust that none of us would dishonor the Savior by questioning the truth of this parallel which the centurion so thoughtfully drew.

Once more, the centurion went a little further and implied that, as Christ had the power to perform the divine will, and had that power well in hand, he believed he was willing to direct all that power to the one object of healing his servant. I believe that many of you know that the Lord Jesus Christ is almighty; you do not doubt that fact, but the question is, Is he almighty to save you? You do not doubt that if the Savior wills it, he can make your spirit whole, but you ask, Will he will it? Will he turn that power in our direction? It does not enter into the centurion's head that there will be any difficulty in his case. "No," he seems to say, "King of Kings, omnipotent Master and Lord, you can at once direct an angel to fly to my servant, or you can bid the disease leave my dwelling, or you can speak to the paralysis and the paralysis itself will be your servant and will fly away at once at your command. You have only to put forth your power upon my servant, and he will at once be healed."

> I trust that none of us would dishonor the Savior by questioning the truth of this parallel which the centurion so thoughtfully drew.

I want you to believe, dear hearts, that our Lord Jesus Christ, no longer here in the flesh, but risen from the dead, is clothed with power equal to that which he had in the centurion's day; no, that he is clothed with even greater power, for after his resurrection he said, *All power is given unto me in heaven and in earth.* And then I want you to believe that he is prepared to turn all that power in your direction, so as to work for your deliverance from spiritual death, your rescue from the power of sin, your help in the way of providence, your guidance in the way of wisdom, or whatsoever – out of ten thousand things – may happen to be the need of this present moment. Oh, that he who gave such faith as this to the centurion at Capernaum would give the same precious faith to many of you, that you also may glorify and bless his holy name!

Now observe that there was only one thing further which was on this centurion's mind, and that was this: he looked upon Christ as a master over all kinds of powers, powers sufficient for all his purposes; he looked at him as having them all well in hand, so that he could have his own bidding done in a moment; and he was anxious to maintain his own position. You ask me how I know this. I am sure it was so, because, when the Savior was willing to come down to his house, he shrank from having such an honor conferred upon him; he seemed to feel that he was being put into a wrong position. He was himself only a servant, and he felt that, in the particular character which he was then bearing, he was not worthy that his Master should come under his roof, so he said, *Speak the word only, and my servant shall be healed.*

I think that this is the principal thing you and I have to do. When we think about our Lord Jesus Christ, we need not worry ourselves about how he will effect his purposes, how the decrees of God will be carried out, or how his promises will be fulfilled. The principal thing we have to do is this: be ourselves the Lord's servants, and when he says to any one of us, "Go," we be sure to go, and when he says, "Come," we be sure to come, and when he says, "Do this," we be sure that we do it. You would rule the seas? You had better rule yourself. You would purge the church? You had better see to it that your own heart is purged. You would reform the world? Get that out of you! What have you to do with reforming the world till you have first washed your own hands in innocence? Get you to your right place, and do your own work, and it shall be well with you. What are you, after all, but a tiny worker on a little anthill? You have your one grain of wheat to carry, and that is enough for you; but do not worry yourself about all the concerns of the anthill;

if you do, at least do not fret yourself about the whole planet on which you live, still less about the complete solar system, for what can you do with it if you worry your poor antship even unto death? No, but do your little share of work upon your own anthill, and carry your own grain of wheat to the general store so you shall have answered the purpose of your being, and it shall be well with you. May God, even our Lord Jesus Christ, give us the grace to set him up very high as Lord and Master, full of power, and wisdom, and love; and then to set ourselves down very low, and to ask that, as his servants, we may serve him faithfully all the days of our life!

Thus have I, as best I could, worked out the incident itself.

Now, secondly, I want to make use of its lessons for our own practical purposes. First then, dear friends, it seems to me that this little narrative should be used to urge us to believe in the power of the Lord Jesus Christ, even if he does not speedily come in the glory of the second advent. I am frequently talking with Christian friends about these evil days in which we live, and of the mischief of the times in which our lot is cast. Certainly, it is not a very cheering subject, and generally I find that friends wind up with some such remark as this: "Well, the comfort is that the Lord Jesus Christ will come very soon. The defections in the professing church, the blasphemies of the world – are they not among the special tokens that the end is hastening on? When our Lord comes, then all these difficult problems will be solved, and all that grieves us will come to an end."

Yes, yes, all that I fully believe, and I look upon the second glorious advent of our Lord Jesus Christ as the brightest hope of his church; but still, do you not think that a more practical and a more God-honoring faith would say without putting aside the blessed hope of the second advent, "Yet the Lord Jesus Christ can deal with the present evils of the church and of the world without actually coming into our midst"? He can say a word while yet remaining in the highest heavens, amid the splendors of the sacred worship of the new Jerusalem; he can speak a word there, and so effect his purpose here. Does not that truth seem to flow naturally out of the faith of this centurion? Our blessed Lord, there is no need that you should at present tear the heavens and in majesty come down; there is no need that you should literally touch the hills and make them smoke, and that the glory of your divine presence should consume your adversaries. If it so pleases you, you can do your bidding where you are, without disturbing this dispensation, without even working a miracle, allowing things to take their usual course, and yet accomplishing your supreme purposes.

Beloved, I want you to exercise this faith continually. You are, perhaps, in a little church, and when that goes to the bad, you say, "Oh well, we cannot make it better! We must wait till the Lord comes." Not a bit of it. Begin to stir up his strength now, for he can work before that second advent, and work right gloriously too. You turn over the newspaper and you say, "I am weary and nearly sick unto death of all this evil." Yes, and so am I; but what then? "Oh!" you answer, "we had better go upstairs to bed, and wait till the Lord comes." Not at all. Let us go and sharpen our swords, and attack the enemies of our Lord more earnestly than ever. We will have another battle or two yet before he does come. Who knows how long he may tarry? But whether he tarries or whether he comes soon, let us not be at all uneasy, as though his power could not be seen apart from his second advent. The power is given to him in heaven and in earth. Even now the name of Jesus is *high over all*. He is now the great attraction to men, the great destroyer of Satan.

Let us not begin, then, to think little of our absent Lord's present power, and to hang all our hopes upon his literal presence among us. I say again, that I am not devaluing that glorious coming of his; God forbid that I should do so! It still is our grandest hope; but let us not put it out of its place so as to make us at all despondent or distrustful about what our risen Lord is able to do for us even now. He still can do *exceeding abundantly above all that we ask or think.*

I want you next, dear friends, to believe in the Lord Jesus Christ's unseen servants. You look around, or you look abroad, and try to find men who will proclaim the gospel vigorously during the next twenty years, and you say you do not perceive them; no, nor do I. Now think a moment. When this centurion saw Jesus of Nazareth standing in the midst of his disciples, what did he see? He saw a lowly looking man, in appearance very much like other men, but certainly not attended by any court, or guarded by any soldiers; yet he believed, concerning this man, that he was surrounded by invisible bands who, in a moment, would do his bidding. I want you to think thus of your Lord. At this day, the Christ of God on earth is attended by all the servants that he needs for his great cause. The scoffers say, "Ah, the old truth is dying out! Where can they find men of mind to preach it?" But our eyes, enlightened by faith, can see a great multitude who shall publish the same old truth until Christ comes again. The mountain is full of horses and chariots of fire round about Elisha, and there shall still be found myriads of burning spirits to proclaim the gospel of Jesus Christ until he comes again. I like that couplet:

> Remember that Omnipotence
> Has servants everywhere.

You cannot see them, but they are waiting for their Lord's orders, and he can see them. He knows where he has put them, and when he will call them to himself, and bid them do his work. Therefore, let us not be in the least disheartened or discouraged because of what we see, or what we do not see. Let us rely upon the invisible; let us expect the unexpected; alas, I was going to say, let us expect the unexpectable. That which we cannot dream of as possible or probable, let us nevertheless believe shall be done; for God must be true, Christ cannot be defeated, and Calvary never will and never can become, in any measure, a defeat. The death of Jesus Christ, the Son of God, must accomplish the purposes for which it was worked out. Let us rest assured, then, that he has his servants waiting to do his bidding.

> Let us rely upon the invisible; let us expect the unexpected.

Now apply this subject a little more closely still. I wish that some poor soul would even now *believe that the Lord Jesus Christ could save him at once with a single word.* I know you are apt to think that the conversion of men must be brought about in some very particular and special way. Pictorial and descriptive accounts of striking conversions have been repeated so often that many people get the idea that the scenery is necessary to the effect; but I want you to put all such ideas away from your thoughts. If you needed any scenery, it is here before your eyes, but you do not want it. Otherwise, for a preacher to stand in this dense heat in the midst of six thousand immortal souls is scenery enough for anyone who wants something striking. And if the Lord shall come to you, and in a moment save you, there will be quite enough of the special and the particular just in the mere fact that you are the subject of the Lord's mighty working. But I want you to believe that this work of divine grace upon the soul does not have to do with any particular position in which a man is found. The Lord Jesus Christ can save a man when he is in bed, when he is putting on his clothes, when he is walking in the street, when he is at his business, or when he is not at his business but is indulging in sin. I could give many instances to show that there is nothing lacking in the way of peculiarity of position in order for Christ to save.

When you are at home, you say to your servant, "Mary, go to such and such a place," and Mary goes. Or you say, "Sarah, come here," and Sarah comes. If there is anything to be done, you say, "Jane, do this," and she does it; yet you do not put a paragraph in the newspaper saying, "Here, on the second day of October 1887, Jane So-and-so made a cup of tea for her mistress." It is such a usual and ordinary thing in connection with the duties of the household, is it not? Very well, just so is the work of conversion in connection with the church of Christ. He himself has but to speak the word, and the great work is straightway done. The surroundings of the sinner do not matter at all to him. He can now, under the present circumstances in which you are, come to you, and pluck you out of death into life, out of darkness into light. Out of all your wanderings he can bring you home at once.

If you truly believe in the Lord Jesus Christ, you are born of God. If you do now, at this very moment, trust Christ with your soul, you have passed from death unto life. If, at this instant, you will have no further concern with every other hope, and just come and rest yourself upon the finished work of Jesus Christ the Savior, you – John, Thomas, Mary, Jane, Sarah, whoever you may be – are saved. I put it in a very simple way just now intentionally, for I want to bring it down to this point, that just as the centurion said, "I have only to say to my servant, 'Do this,' and he does it," so has Christ only to speak the effectual word of his grace, and the devil will fly, sin will be removed, grace will be infused, and the soul will be saved. Oh, what a mercy this is!

To you who are the people of God I would apply this subject in this way. If it be as I have said concerning the sinner, that he must trust in Christ if he is to be saved, it is also true that you should believe for your servants, your friends, and your acquaintances. Your children are still unconverted. Have you ever prayed for them, believing in the power of Jesus Christ to convert them? One said, the other day, of a certain person, "It seems no use praying for such a fellow as that." Of course, it is no use to pray such prayers as you would be likely to present if you talk like that. When you have given a person up, and you have no further hope concerning him, what prayer can you offer for him? I want you, my brother, my sister, to believe concerning your child, your brother, your friend, your unconverted neighbor, just as this centurion believed concerning his sick servant, that Jesus had but to speak the word, and his sick servant would be healed. "Oh, but the doctor says that this is a case of paralysis! He says that he will never get over it; it is impossible for him to be cured; the disease is complicated in such a peculiar way that we must give up all hope." Ah, but this centurion does not look at the patient! He looks at the Physician, and he says, and says rightly, "Jesus can as easily bid this disease depart as I can bid my servant go when I wish him to start upon an errand."

Think not of the sinner, or of the greatness of his sin, but think of the greatness of the Savior. I am sure that if we preached with more faith in Christ, we would see more results. Perhaps you do not see conversions in your work because you keep looking to the people, looking to the sinners, or looking to the hardness of their hearts. What has all that to do with Christ's power to save? If this man, in addition to having paralysis, could have had fever, and leprosy, and dropsy, and all other diseases at once, it would not have mattered in the least to the Great Physician, for when Christ comes on the scene, if you have one impossibility, he can meet it, and if you had fifty impossibilities, he could meet them all just as easily. Granted an almighty Savior, what room is there for doubt as to what he can do?

I wish I could drive this truth home to some who have been praying for others but who have never prayed the prayer of faith. It is the prayer of faith that saves the sick; it is the prayer of faith that saves the sinful; it is the prayer of faith that makes everything of Christ, and takes him at his right valuation as being a master of every situation. That is what you should do; make Jesus Christ master of the situation, and plead with him in that capacity, and you shall not plead in vain, and your child, your friend, your servant shall yet be saved.

Let the practical close of this meditation be that we believe in Jesus a great deal more than we have ever believed before. If we have believed in Jesus, let us have still more confidence in him. I think it is a sad pity when a man preaches the gospel with a doubt at the back of his throat. What good can come of his preaching? They sometimes charge us with dogmatism. We would be more dogmatic if we could be, for we speak what we do know, and testify to what we have seen; and if men receive not our witness, we cannot help that. We must not change our witness because some men do not care to receive it. Go forth, minister of God, and preach the gospel as a certainty, and you shall prove it to be a certainty. If you preach it as something which may or may not be true, it will paralyze you, and it will not profit your hearers. In the name of Jesus Christ of Nazareth, I claim from every man to whom I preach that he should believe in him, accept his great salvation, and bow before him. If you do so, dear friends, you shall be saved; but if you will not, it is not left as a matter of choice with you, but the Lord Jesus has himself declared, *He that believeth not shall be damned.* He will not allow us to trifle with him. He is a Sovereign, he is the King of Kings, and Lord of Lords, and he calls upon us to kiss his feet, bow down before him, and own him as our Lord and God.

Our chief business just now is not so much to think of what Christ can do in the great battle of the present, or what he will do in the dread conflict of the future, but rather of what we have to do, and I think that what we have to do is believe in Christ to be his obedient servants. If he says, "Go," let us go. If he says, *Come unto me, all ye that labour and are heavy-laden,* let us come unto him. If he says concerning any service, "Do this," let us do it; and if, instead of bidding us do anything, he bids us believe him, let us come and believe him, for this will be our wisdom, this will be our happiness, and this will be our heaven, to be the obedient servants of him who must be Ruler over all. God has decreed that this shall be his glory; he has set him on his throne expectantly, till his foes be made his footstool. If you choose to be his enemies, you shall choose it to your own destruction; but if you will come and bow before him, and be his servants, you shall find that heaven and earth are waiting at his back to bless you, and you shall go from strength to strength beneath his loving and unfailing care.

The Lord bless you, dear friends, for Jesus' sake! Amen.

Chapter 6

A Blessed Wonder

When Jesus heard it, he marvelled, and said to them that followed, Verily I say unto you, I have not found so great faith, no, not in Israel. (Matthew 8:10)

You remember that we observed previously that Jesus is not reported to have marveled either at the gigantic architecture of the temple, or at the wonderful discipline of the Roman army, or at the profound knowledge of the rabbis. He only marveled twice, according to the record, and on both of those occasions he marveled concerning faith: once at the absence of it, and once at its presence. In the case which we spoke of earlier, he marveled at the unbelief of his fellow townsmen; in the narrative before us now, he marveled at the faith of the centurion. From this we learn that we ought not to be so engrossed with the wonders of science and of art, or even with the wonders of creation and of providence, as to become indifferent to the marvels of grace. These should occupy the very highest place in our estimation. The seven wonders of the world are nothing when compared with the countless wonders of grace. That man must be foolish who does not admire the works of God in nature; he is frivolous who does not trace with awe the hand of God in history; and he is even more unwise who despises the masterpieces of divine skill and wisdom which are to be seen in the empire of grace.

The museum of grace is richer than that of nature. A heart broken on account of sin is a far greater wonder than the rarest fossil, whatever it may tell of ancient floods of the sea or convulsions of the land. An eye that glistens with the tears of penitence is a greater marvel than the waterfalls of Niagara, or the fountains of the Nile. Faith that humbly links itself to Christ has in it as great a beauty as the rainbow; and the confidence which looks alone to Jesus, and so irradiates the soul, is as much an object for admiration as is the sun when it shines in its strength. Talk not of the pyramids, the Colossus, the golden house of Nero, or the temple of Ephesus, for the living temple of God's church is fairer by far. Let others glory in the marvels they have seen, but be it mine to say unto my Lord, *I will praise thee. Thou hast done wonderful things. Thy love to me was wonderful. Surely I will remember thy wonders of old.*

Consider well the work of God within the human heart. Consider well the faith which lies at the beginning and foundation of spiritual life, and you will have as good a point for wonder as the Savior had when he marveled at the centurion's faith. The peculiar point for admiration may not be the same, but all faith has in it admirable elements, and like its divine Author, it may be called *wonderful.*

I shall speak upon what there was that was so remarkable in the centurion's faith, making practical remarks in a kind of running comment as we move along; and then if there should be any fragments that remain to be gathered up, we shall try again to apply them in the same style of personal application.

What was there, then, about the centurion's faith that was so remarkable that Christ wondered at it? I think the first point was that there was such faith found in such a person.

The Lord seemed to imply this when he said, *I have not found so great faith, no, not in Israel,* as if he might have expected to find it in Israel, among an instructed people, among a people to whom the oracles had been committed, but that he could not have expected to find it in a Gentile, in a Roman, in a soldier, or in one who was apparently an unlikely subject for spiritual influences. From this I gather that the most astonishing and acceptable faith may be exercised by the most unlikely persons. Here was a Gentile believing – a Gentile believing far better than one of the seed of Israel. Rich grace thus brought the far-off one into the full blessing of the kingdom. Here was a soldier believing, a Roman soldier believing, in the Lord. Roman soldiers in Judea were not as our armies are, a guard protecting their native hearths and homes, but they were the servants of tyrants, treading down the liberties of the Jewish people, and obnoxious, of course, in the highest degree to the Jews. And yet for all that, though the soldier's trade in those days was oppression, and his wages were plunder, here was a soldier believing in Jesus Christ; and, to increase the wonder, this believing legionary was not a common soldier merely, but one who occupied a position of responsibility, bringing to him no small degree of honor and of respect. Alas! the honors of this world are seldom helpful to belief. When a man receives honor of men, he too often finds it impossible to receive the gospel as a little child. All these things met in the centurion, and yet he was not only a believer, but also a surpassing believer, even to a marvel, so that Christ wondered at his faith.

My dear friend, though you should happen to be in the most unlikely circumstances of body and of mind for you to be converted and to become a Christian, yet I see not what hinders your being so converted if the Lord blesses the word. If you have been brought up altogether apart from the influences of religion, remember that so also was this centurion, and he became a master-believer. Why should not you? Though the ground of your heart has as yet never been tilled, and remains like the virgin soil of the primeval forest, yet my Lord may get a gracious crop out of your heart not many days hence, when the tillage of the law and the sowing of the gospel shall have been tested upon you, for by his gracious touch he can turn a barren wasteland into a fruitful field. Though you feel as the waste of the moorland, yet you need not despair. Though now dewless as Gilboa, he can water you as plentifully as Hermon itself. The barren woman shall yet keep house, and the desolate shall rejoice in her children. Nature's death may yet yield to the Spirit's life.

Perhaps you follow a calling which is supposed to be unfriendly to religion, but even then despair not. Why should not the Master call you by his grace, and constrain you to leave the calling, as Matthew left the tax collector's booth; or else through the power of grace within you, enable you to exercise your calling without sin? You have, perhaps, never read the Bible, so why should you not begin? It is possible that you have been a disbeliever in it, yet there are such arguments in its favor. I am not about to trouble you with them just now, but there are among them living arguments which may convince you before you are quite aware that your prejudice is being removed, for some of us have tasted and handled of the Word of Life, and are witnesses of the power which comes with the gospel. We are ourselves living witnesses of what it can do in breathing peace into the soul, and in putting sin away, and I don't see why you also should not prove it and rejoice in it, yes, and even outdistance others in the race of grace.

That tinker playing tip-cat on Sundays on Elstow Green did not look a likely man to write *The Pilgrim's Progress*, and yet John Bunyan did it. That blaspheming sailor cast ashore on a slave-trade settlement on the coast of Africa, and there made a slave himself, did not look as though he would become a minister of evangelical godliness, whose name should be sweet and full of savor to later generations, and yet such was John Newton. There is no reason, because of the darkness of the past, why the future should not be bright, for there is One who can blot out sin and pass by transgression and iniquity. However hostile your nature may be to the gospel and to spiritual truth, there is power in Jesus Christ to change that nature, and to cause you, the most unlikely person, to become a leader in his camp, a mighty trophy of his sovereign grace.

Is it not written, *I was found of them that sought me not; I was made manifest unto them that asked not after me? I will call them my people, which were not my people; and her beloved, which was not beloved*? Surely angels rejoiced when they heard the Roman legionary say, *Speak the word only, and my servant shall be healed*. Surely the disciples, as they clustered around the Master, said one to another, "What strange work of grace is this, that this soldier should stand here and speak better than any of us concerning the truth and the power of the Lord Jesus!" I do pray to see some in this place become equally remarkable trophies of Christ's power. I do expect to see throughout this our country the most unlikely persons converted. The great trumpet shall be blown, and great sinners shall find that the day of their redemption has come. From the east and from the west, the far-off ones shall gather to the feast of love, while the astonished church shall cry, *These, where [have] they been?*

The church could not have thought that Saul of Tarsus who once persecuted the church would have become her chief apostle, and yet so it was, and so it shall be still while the King sits on his throne. He will yet come down again and take out of the ranks of the Enemy the most stouthearted men, and make them bow their knees before his majesty, and afterwards he will enlist them beneath his own standard, and send them forth conquering and to conquer. The prey shall be taken from the mighty, and the lawful captive shall be delivered. Grace shall yet more abound where sin abounded. As in the present case, the marvel of grace shall be the more memorable because of the singularity of the person enjoying it. May God make you such a person, and such a wonder too!

The next point concerning which our Lord may have marveled was *the subject of the centurion's confidence.*

He had a servant who was struck with palsy. This was a disease which at that time, at any rate, if not at present, was reckoned to be utterly incurable. In the case of this servant the disease was of the most aggravated kind, for he was *grievously tormented.* The strength of his constitution battling with the paralysis caused an unusual agony. It had come to a climax, for he was at the point of death; yet, though a cure of the palsy had never been heard of, and would be a most astounding miracle if ever wrought, this man believed that Christ could heal the palsy and could at once restore his servant to perfect health. Yes, here was a faith which took an impossibility into its hand, and threw it aside; faith which knew that all things were possible with an omnipotent Savior; faith which saw in Christ that omnipotent Savior, and therefore raised no question as to his ability or willingness.

Dear hearers, this is the kind of faith I wish that we all exercised. I will suppose, dear friend, that your case, your sinful case, is like that of the centurion's servant's physical case. You believe your sin to be incurable, that is to say, unpardonable. You think also that if it were pardoned as to the past, you would be sure to go back to it again, as a dog returns to his vomit. You therefore look upon your case as being an utterly hopeless one. O do not do so; do not do so! He who can heal the drunkenness that lies in one, or the tendency to lust that lurks in another, can cast out any and every sort of sin, and cast it out with a word. There is no transgression too black for his blood to wash out the stain, and there is no propensity to sin too strong for his Spirit to control and at last destroy it. Cures of all cases of spiritual disease are possible with him. The blackest sinner may yet become the brightest saint. At the gates of hell you may sit in your moral filthiness, and yet not only at the gates of heaven may you yet stand in the brightness of holiness, but within those gates you may yet be enclosed in the perfection of spotlessness with all the rest who have washed their robes and made them white in the blood of the Lamb.

The centurion's faith was this: he believed that there were no impossibilities with Christ, and he left his paralyzed servant in those gracious and mighty hands. And, my friend, your faith, if it is to save you, must do the same. It must take your case at its worst, and yet believe that Christ can save even to the uttermost. Your sin has been aggravated – confess it. Your sin is in its own self unpardonable; justice writes it with a pen of iron, and no tears of repentance or endeavors for reformation can blot it out. Only sovereign grace, fresh from the altar of atoning sacrifice, can make an end of sin.

Confess all this. You are far gone from hope – confess it. Your natural state is perilous, no, deadly – confess it. Make out your case to be as bad as you can conceive it to be – because it is so – and when you have done so, say, "But for all that, I believe that God in Christ Jesus can forgive me, and I rest my guilty soul at the foot of the cross where atonement was made for sin. I believe that Jesus put my guilt away there, and thus I have peace with God." If you believe that you are a little sinner, and that therefore, because of the moderate degree of your guilt, Christ can save you, you know nothing about it; but if knowing your sin to be great, heinous, aggravated, and damnable you can still come to Jesus, you glorify his name. If you profess yourself to be the chief of sinners, and yet believe that he can save you, and rely upon him to do it, you have a marvelous faith, a faith that will bring you to heaven. Not to forget the guilt of our sin, and then trust Jesus, but to remember our sin with more shame and grief than ever, and yet to trust in the cleansing blood of Jesus – this is faith, this is the wonder of the skies.

Be of good cheer, O sinner, if all your reliance leans on the Mediator, despite ten thousand times ten thousand accusing sins, you are a saved man. O that others like you would place their dependence upon the same sin-forgiving Savior! May the Eternal Spirit draw them now to Jesus, and give them immediate salvation by precious faith in a precious Christ. Faith is the vital point, the one needful matter, and may it be worked in you now. Faith can soon remove the difficulties which stand in your path, and make you a straight road to glory, for it is a wonder-worker, and all things are possible to it.

> It says to the mountains, Depart,
>   That stand betwixt God and the soul;
> It binds up the broken in heart,
>   And makes wounded consciences whole;
> Bids sins of a crimson-like dye
>   Be spotless as snow, and as white,
> And makes such a sinner as I
>   As pure as an angel of light.

Thirdly, another wonder was *the realizing energy* of this man's faith which led him to deal with the case in such a businesslike way.

Alas, alas, the hackneyed form which most men's religion assumes! They take it up as secondhand, or they cut and shape it after somebody else's fashion. Not so this man. I do not know that he had ever had a religious acquaintance, but falling in probably with some of the books of Scripture, he read them, and he discovered that Jesus Christ was what he professed to be: the Son of God and the Savior of men. Having come to this conclusion, he at once trusted in him as a matter of fact, not as a matter of profession merely; and having trusted in the Savior, he acted upon the trust in a businesslike, commonsense manner. He sat down and thought about this to himself: "I am a captain. I say to a soldier, 'Go,' and he goes; I say to another, 'Come,' and he comes; I appoint my servant who waits upon me to do certain business, and he does it. Now, this Jesus Christ is a far greater commander than I am;

all the powers of nature must therefore be under his check and control. He will only have to say a thing, and it will be done; if he were to bid the heavens be clothed in blackness, they would don the sackcloth, and if he were to command the clouds to disappear, and the sun to shine or to stand still, the obedient sun would know its Master and yield a willing homage to him."

The centurion, according to the best rules of argument, was led to this conclusion, and his practical mind made immediate use of the inference. That Jesus can accomplish his will with a word is only what you and I ought also to infer from his nature and office, and that he is ready to exercise that power is clear from his character and his promises. "Well then," said the centurion, "I have but to go and ask him, and if his heart be moved with my pitiful story, he will only have to say it in one single word, and, bad as my servant's case is, he will be cured at once, and I shall be the happy master of a healthy servant." Now, that was fine reasoning. That was treating fact as fact, and not as we too often do, as if it were pious fiction. This godly soldier was no mere theorist, no superficial holder of an unpractical creed, but a doer of the word, a genuine matter-of-fact believer in what he held to be true.

Now, I do pray that each one here may be able to treat the gospel as a matter of business; treat it as a matter of fact, and may none of you trifle and toy with it, nor think it to be a mere subtlety for the consideration of doctrinaires, a theme of dispute for theorists and men who merely think and talk. I pray you make the one thing needful the first and truest business of your lives. If anything be real, surely eternal salvation must be.

Your condition before God is not a subject for cloud-land; it belongs to the commonsense, practical, and everyday life-business of men. See, now, how it stands. You have broken God's law. You are guilty. God must punish you; eternal justice demands it. But the Lord Jesus came into the world to provide a way by which, without dishonor to God's justice, sin may be forgiven. That way was substitution. Christ stood in the sinner's stead, was punished with the sinner's punishment, and bore the wrath of God for sinners. But for what sinners? For all sinners? No, but for such as will trust him. I, then, being guilty, come and trust him. I see good reason to do so. He is God, and he was appointed by God to be a propitiation for sin. What God appoints, and God delights in, I may truthfully and confidently accept. I do accept him. I do now trust my soul to Jesus. Then I am saved. My sin has gone; my iniquity has ceased to be; I am a saved soul. Come and reason thus with yourself.

Oh! I pray the Holy Spirit to help you to do so. Let this be the subject of your soliloquy: "If I were omnipotent, as Christ is, it would be as easy for me to move a mountain as a molehill; and therefore it is as easy for him to take away my great sins as another's little sins. If there be a universal cleansing fluid, it will take out great spots as well as little spots, and therefore the blood of Christ can wash out my great sins as well as the lesser sins of other people. One stroke of the hand, and the bill is paid; it is as easy to write a receipt for a bill of fifty thousand pounds as for a bill for tenpence; so if Jesus Christ, who has already paid believers' debts, calls me pardoned and absolved, it is done. He has the power to do it, and I rely upon the merit of his atoning blood." O that you would now do so! and I will add, O that you would do so now!

These Sabbath days, how they are flying! Your time, how it is passing away, and with your time, your opportunities for finding mercy! It does not seem long ago since we were in the depth of winter, and now we are getting near the longest day in summer, and the wings of time will soon bear us again into months of frost and snow. How long do you waver between two opinions? Are these delays to continue forever? Will you always go on hearing about these things but never attending to them? I do pray you, by the flight of time, by the certainty of death for each of you, and your ignorance of its appointed hour, seek the Lord while he may be found, call upon him while he is near. Lay hold of eternal life, and, like the centurion, come and put your trust in Jesus to save you; and though your faith will be marvelous, yet the honor shall be all to him, and the glory to his blessed name.

> Lay hold of eternal life, and, like the centurion, come and put your trust in Jesus to save you.

I will move on. Fourthly, another point of wonder in the centurion's faith was this, *that he did not ask for a sign.*

Many of the great ones of old, when God was about to fulfill a promise, needed to be strengthened for service by a sign. Gideon was a man of great faith, yet he needed first to have the fleece wet when all was dry around, and then to have the fleece dry while the threshing floor was wet. He needed to hear the soldiers' dream of the barley cake that tumbled upon the tent of Midian. He wanted signs and wonders or his heart would have fainted. With many others the desire for signs and wonders has been a great barrier to simple faith. Now the centurion did not say as Naaman did, "I thought he would surely come and put his hand over the place and recover the paralytic." No, he did not need Jesus to come to the house and say a word, or offer prayer, or even touch the sick with his hand. "No, Master," said he, "there is no need for you to come. My servant is far away, lying sick and near to death; you don't need to stir an inch; say in a word, and he will be healed. Distance is nothing to you; your word at a mile's distance can cure as well as your touch." Oh, but this was grand faith! He wants no visible sign; his spiritual eye sees the invisible, and his heart is fixed, trusting in the Lord. His unstaggering faith requires no crutch. He wants nothing, but only prays that the Master will say the word. I do not think he expected to *hear* the Lord speak that word aloud, for in Luke he is described as praying that Jesus not so much *say* a word as say *in* a word. Perhaps he remembered the language of the psalmist when he sang, *He sent his word, and healed them, and delivered them from their destructions*, and he looked to that same creating and almighty word for the restoration of his servant.

Now, brethren, transfer this to yourselves. I pray the Holy Spirit that many here may have the faith which does not crave for signs and wonders. "I could believe," says one, "that I was saved, if I felt some terrible work of the law within my heart. I have heard of others who have been ready to despair, and have been tempted to commit suicide, and if I felt as they felt I could then think that there was grace for me." Ah! poor simpleton. You know not what you say. Be glad to be delivered from such dreadful things as these, for if some have come out of them to Christ, I am afraid that some have been brought by them to the noose or to some other suicidal death. Do not desire the terrors of hell, but accept the tender mercy of our God whereby the Dayspring from on high has visited us. Horrors and dreads, if you felt them, would not help you; believe me, they would do the very reverse. "No," says another, "I should like to feel an extraordinary sensation. If I should be struck down while preaching, as I have heard some have been in the Irish revivals; if I felt some remarkable physical, mental, or spiritual emotion, such as I have never experienced before, then I should say that this was the finger of God." My dear hearer, why be so foolish? God's Word tells you that if you trust Jesus Christ you are saved. Is not God's Word enough? Will you not take the assurance of God without laying down this and that as a condition for your Savior? Some of you talk and act as if the great God must do what you like, or else you will not believe him.

I have known persons who were once in the habit of giving away roast beef and other gifts to the poor at Christmastime, but who have given up doing it because of the picking and choosing of those who come to receive the gifts. One woman actually took back her joint of beef because she wanted a piece of beef that could be boiled, and she would have a boiling piece or none at all. I have not wondered when persons who have been charitable have not been allowed to do as they will with their own, that they have ceased to distribute their charitable donations as formerly. Reason teaches us that when we receive benefits we are not to dictate to our benefactors. And is God, when he saves your soul, to let a beggar like you be a chooser about the way in which it is to be done? Are you to exact this and exact that, or else you will not condescend to be saved? This is disgraceful pride. Be ashamed, I pray you, be ashamed to indulge in it any longer. No longer demand new proof of God's truthfulness in the form of feelings and excitements. God's Word is worthy of your trust. If you had these remarkable feelings, what would their evidence amount to if you looked at them as a sane man and not as a fanatic?

If you were to meet an angel, and he were to tell you that you would go to heaven, you would have no reason to believe him unless you believe in Jesus Christ. An angel who gave you any comfort while you remain an unbeliever would be a devil, even though he shined like an angel of light. But if you believe in the Lord Jesus Christ, and are baptized, you have God's word for it that you are saved, and what do you want an angel's word for? Is not the word of the Lord sufficient; is a creature's testimony necessary to make the Lord's word worthy of credence? No, say others, but we should be comforted if we could dream remarkable dreams. Now, what could there be to assure the soul as to its salvation in the vain and frolicsome motions of the mind when they are free from the bridle of reason? Dreams may sometimes happen to come true, but nine times out of ten they are nonsense. If good doctrine and wise warning be brought home to the heart by a dream, it should have nonetheless our most earnest attention; but if presumption should have a thousand visions to back it, it would be nonetheless dangerous. It would be a dreadful thing to hang one's confidence upon such a fragile thing as a dream. No, no, sir; you have God's Word, and will not believe it because you pretend that a dream would help you, and confirm your confidence, as if God were not to be trusted so well as your dreams!

O be not so foolish, but like this centurion, say, *Speak the word only*. Brethren, we must accept the bare word of God in Christ Jesus as the basis of faith, for no other foundation is to be depended on for a moment. Not *your* feeling but *his* promise must sustain you. Can you not consent to this? If you will do so you shall have peace. If you will come to God like that, you shall see many signs and many wonders before long of a better sort than you have ever dreamed of. Your joy shall be like a river, and your peace shall overflow. But you must first come without these things. Come, and take God at his word, and do Christ the honor to believe in him without anything to corroborate what he says, and you shall find the blessing coming to you afterwards. This was a remarkable point in the centurion's faith, that he believed without demanding a sign.

Fifthly, one very remarkable point in this good man's faith was *his conviction that Christ could cure his servant at once: Say in a word, and my servant shall be healed.*

Ordinarily, a successful combat with disease requires time. The surgeon must drive out from his strong entrenchments the fiend of disease, must chase him from one defense to another, and perhaps even then he may fail to dislodge his foe. It may be weary months or even years before some forms of disease can be eradicated. But the centurion believed that the word of Christ could remove the paralysis, and could do so at once. And why not? Omnipotence knows nothing of time any more than of any other of the hindrances which impede mortal progress.

To the eternal God time is nothing; to him a thousand years are as one day, and on the other hand, one day is as a thousand years. The faith that saves lays hold on this truth that Christ Jesus who is now at the right hand of God can in a moment save the soul. The dying thief did not imagine that his salvation would take a month. He simply said, *Lord, remember me when thou comest into thy kingdom*, and the answer was, *Today shalt thou be with me in paradise* – saved that day, saved at once. The pardon of sin is not the result of weeks of fasting, and months of repentance, and years of shame and humiliation. The sinner's eyes look to Christ and the sinner's sin is gone at once.

> The moment a sinner believes,
>   And trusts in his crucified God,
> His pardon at once he receives,
>   Salvation in full through Christ's blood.

The new birth of the soul, the regeneration of our nature by the Holy Spirit, is not a work requiring a long period of time. It is in a moment that the Spirit of God visits our hearts and turns the stone to flesh. It may seem as though I talked without consideration, but yet I speak the words of truth and soberness when I say that if the Lord puts forth the fullness of his power, sinners sitting in these galleries or in this area might be saved before that clock ticks again. Who shall restrain the Lord and say what he can do or cannot do? All things are possible with him, and we will therefore add, that if each one of you were led to put his trust in Jesus, what I said was possible would be literally done; you would all retire, each one saved, and say, "Blessed be the name of the Lord who has taken us out of the horrible pit and out of the miry clay, and set our feet upon a rock, and put a new song into our mouths, and established our actions!" O that you would do this, good Lord, that your name might have praise!

Once more, one other point of wonder. *Throughout the whole, the centurion's deep humility was conspicuous, but that deep humility, instead of weakening his faith, only strengthened it.*

Pride is the associate of presumption, but humility is the companion of assurance. He who thinks that he needs but little grace and power to save him, that he is, in fact, better than most, and as good as any, cannot believe at all. He may be able to presume, but he is unable to believe. Doubtless presumption would grow well in the soil of his heart, but a broken heart alone becomes a believing heart, and an assured heart must first be a humble heart.

The centurion had done good service for the Jews. He loved their nation and had built them a synagogue. They thought a great deal of him, but he thought very little of himself. He said, *"Lord, I am not worthy that thou shouldst come under my roof.* I am not only not worthy of the blessing I ask, but also not worthy that you should come into such communion with me as to tread my floor." Deeply humbled was the man, and in a humbled spirit you also must become a believer.

I have met with a great many who, when they have felt a sense of their sin, have said directly, "I cannot believe in Christ." Then you imagine, do you, that if you had less sin you could believe? No, I tell you, it is not so. If your sense of sin be a hindrance to faith, your sense of righteousness would be infinitely more a barrier. To believe that I shall be saved because I am not a sinner is not faith; but to know that I am one of the very worst of sinners, and very guilty and very vile, and yet I place my trust in Jesus – this is faith. I do love when I look at my sins to look at the cross too. If I have been of service to God, and the Holy Spirit has helped me to do some good thing for the church, it is scarcely faith to say that I am then at peace. Why, that is seeing, not believing. But when I see my imperfections, and bemoan my follies, and lay my mouth in the very dust, and then say, "Notwithstanding all this, I know whom I have believed, and I am persuaded that he is able to keep that which I have committed to him" – that is faith, and I pray God that you may exercise it every day. If my sins were worse than they are, or if I could have a deeper dread of them, I would nevertheless rejoice that he is able to save to the uttermost them that come unto God by him, and from that pimple of confidence my soul should not remove.

My brethren, do not imagine that to have faith in Christ you have to work yourselves up into the idea that there is some good thing in you which can commend you to Christ. You are sailing on the wrong tack altogether when your trust leans on self. Faith is to come to Christ blind, and believe that he can open your eyes; it is to come to him poor, and believe that he will make you rich; it is to come to him as having nothing of your own, and take what he has to be yours forever and ever; it is, in fact, to see death written on the creature, and to find life in him; to see corruption written on your best righteousness, and to count it to be as dross and dung, and then to take Jesus Christ to be your wisdom, your righteousness, your sanctification, your redemption, and your all.

I have thus, I trust, set forth what faith is in as simple a way as I know how to speak, and yet, simple as this statement is, if any of you do so believe, there will be glory brought to God by it, for no man ever did believe except the Holy Spirit led him to believe. "What!" says one, "It's such a simple thing as that?" Permit me to observe that it is the simplicity of faith that makes it difficult. If it were difficult, there would be many who would attempt it; but because it is nothing but "Believe and live," therefore proud hearts will not yield to it. It is as simple as the first elements of spelling, and because it is so, men cannot understand it, for their pride must needs surround it with mystery. Men would rather be wise, and therefore they puzzle themselves with that which a child may understand.

> It is the simplicity of faith that makes it difficult.

What is necessary for a man to know Christ is for him to get his conceit of education winnowed out of him; I mean that what he thinks to be education must be all pulled away, that he may be made like a little child, to sit down at Jesus' feet and trust Jesus as a child believes its father's word. It is not going up that most of you want, but pulling down. It is not getting good, it is feeling you are not good, which is the main matter for most of you to look to. It is not being better in your own esteem, it is being utterly undone in your own esteem, which will make you ready for Christ. This you need, and when you have it I believe you will then come and cheerfully lay hold on this blessed, this simple way of salvation, suitable to the vilest, and yet suitable to the most moral; fitted, as one said once, to poor old women who are on their dying beds, and equally fitted to the profoundest philosophers; fitted for the poor, fitted for the rich; fitted for me, fitted for you. O that you would have my Lord to be your strong refuge. My Lord and Master, grant that he may also marvel at your faith, dear friends; and, though you had none earlier, it is my hope that you now go rejoicing because the Lord has visited you and helped you to believe in his name.

Chapter 7

The Centurion or An Exhortation to the Virtuous

And when they came to Jesus, they besought him instantly, saying, That he was worthy for whom he should do this: for he loveth our nation, and he hath built us a synagogue. Then Jesus went with them. And when he was now not far from the house, the centurion sent friends to him, saying unto him, Lord, trouble not thyself: for I am not worthy that thou shouldest enter under my roof: wherefore neither thought I myself worthy to come unto thee: but say in a word, and my servant shall be healed. For I also am a man set under authority, having under me soldiers, and I say unto one, Go, and he goeth; and to another, Come, and he cometh; and to my servant, Do this, and he doeth it. When Jesus heard these things, he marvelled at him, and turned him about, and said unto the people that followed him, I say unto you, I have not found so great faith, no, not in Israel. (Luke 7:4-9)

This centurion certainly had a high reputation. Two features of character blend in him which do not often meet in such graceful harmony. He won the high opinion of others, and yet he held a low estimation of himself. There are some who think little of themselves, and they are quite correct in their feelings, as all the world would endorse the estimate of their littleness. Others there are who think great things of themselves, but the more they are known, the less they are praised; and the higher they shall carry their heads, the more shall the world laugh them to scorn. Nor is it unusual for men to think great things of themselves because the world commends or flatters them, so they robe themselves with pride and cloak themselves with vanity because they have by some means, either rightly or wrongly, won the good opinion of others. There are very few who have the happy combination of the text. The elders say of the centurion that he is worthy, but he says of himself, "Lord, I am not worthy!" They commend him for building God a house, but he thinks that he is not worthy that Christ should come under the roof of his house. They plead his merit, but he pleads his demerit. Thus he appeals to the power of Christ, apart from anything that he felt in himself or thought of himself. O that you and I might have this blessed combination in ourselves: to win the high opinion of others, so far as it can be gained by integrity, by uprightness, and by decision of character, and yet at the same time to walk humbly with our God!

Now, there are three things I shall speak about, and may God make them profitable. First, *here is a high character*; secondly, *here is deep humility*; and thirdly, here is, notwithstanding that deep humility, *a very mighty faith*.

To begin then, dear friends, here is *a high character*. Let us thoroughly appreciate it, and give it a full measure of commendation.

When preaching Jesus Christ to the chief of sinners, we have sometimes half dreamed that some who are moral and upright might think themselves excluded, but they ought not to think so, nor is it fair for them to draw such an inference. We have heard the whisper of some who have said they could almost wish that they had been more abandoned and corrupt in the days of their unregeneracy so that they might have a deeper repentance, and be witnesses of a more palpable and thorough change so that they might never have cause to doubt the triumph of grace in their experience. We have heard some even say, "I could have wished that I had groveled in the very mire of sin, not that I love it; on the contrary, I loathe it, but because had I then to be rescued from such a course of life, the change would be so manifest and apparent that I should never dare to ask myself whether I was a changed man or not. I would feel it and see it in my everyday course and conversation."

Dear friends, if anything we have ever said should have led you into this mistake, we are sorry for it; it was never our intention. While we would open the gates of mercy so wide that the greatest blasphemer, the most unchaste and the most debauched, may not be without hope, yet we never want to shut those gates in the face of such as have been brought up in a godly manner, and through the providence of God and the checks of education, have been kept from the grosser vices. On the contrary, we thought that when we opened it for the worst there would be room for the best; and if Noah's ark took in the unclean, certainly the clean would not be afraid to enter.

If Jesus Christ was able to cure those who were far gone in sickness, you might infer that he would certainly be able to heal those who, though they were sick, might not be so far advanced in disease. Besides, a little reflection may suggest to you that the repentance of remorseful believers is not regulated by the extent of their crimes against what you call the moral code. It is one thing to estimate sin by its apparent depravity, and another and an infinitely better thing to have the eyes of the understanding enlightened to see sin in its infinite malignity as it appears in the light of heavenly purity and perfection, which proceeds from the throne of God, or as it is reflected from Mount Calvary where the amazing sacrifice of Christ was offered. What! do you think the whitewashed sepulchre of a Pharisee's heart is less loathsome to the Almighty than the open pollution of a Magdalene's life? Or, in the matter of experience, could the recollection of a thousand debaucheries give such a melting sense of remorse as a sight of the Crucified One?

O friends, let me remind you of the words of Jesus: *When he, the Spirit of truth, is come, he will reprove the world of sin, and of righteousness, and of judgment: of sin, because they believe not on me.* That one sin of unbelief is such a concentration of all wickedness that it could outweigh the crimes of Sodom and Gomorrah, and make them more excusable in the day of judgment than the men of Capernaum who saw the mighty works of Christ and repented not. That one sin of unbelief is so heinous that the groanings of the whole creation were but pitiful sighs to deplore it; and rivers of tears were but a weak tribute to lament it. However, as mistakes do arise, and misapprehensions will take place, let us have a few words concerning a high character *in the sight of men*.

Such a character among your fellow creatures may be gained in any situation. The centurion was a soldier – a profession of life not altogether the most promising for moral excellence, though there have been in the army some of the brightest saints that ever lived. He was a soldier moreover in a foreign country – not the place where he was likely to win esteem. He was there as one of the representatives of a power which had conquered Judea, and had treated it with great cruelty; yet, notwithstanding the prejudices of race and nationality, this man's kindness of disposition and goodness of conduct had won for him the esteem of others. Moreover, being a commander of soldiers, naturally every act of violence would be set down to him. Whatever might be done by his hundred men would be laid to the captain, so that his was a condition of peculiar difficulty, and yet, notwithstanding this, the elders said, "He is worthy."

Let none of you despair! Wherever you may be placed, a noble character may be earned. You may serve God in the most menial capacity; you may compel your very foes to own your excellence; you may stand so blameless before men, and you may walk so uprightly before God, that those who watch for your faltering may bite their lips with disappointment, while they shall not have a single word to lay against you except it be regarding the religion of your God and King. Let no man, wherever he may be thrown – though he be surrounded by those who tempt him – despair, especially if the grace of God be in him. Let him pray like Joab that he may have favor in the eyes of his Master, and expect to win it.

This centurion must have been a man of sterling worth. He was not merely quiet and inoffensive like some men who are as unsavory as they are harmless. Though a high character may be won, it cannot be won without being earned. Men do not get character among their fellows by slothfulness and listlessness, or by pretensions and talk. Action! action! this is what the world wants; and there is more truth than we have dreamed of in Nelson's aphorism: "England expects every man to do his duty." Certainly, men will not speak well of you unless you do well. This centurion did so, for you will observe that they said he was worthy, which must have signified that he was just in his dealings and generous in his habits, or they would not have thought him worthy.

It would appear, too, that his private temperament as well as his public spirit contributed to the estimation in which he was held. You will notice in the circumstances which bring him before us, how his tender feelings and his intense anxiety were drawn out on behalf of not a child, but a servant, perhaps a slave! And then we might have thought it had been enough to have said that the man was highly valued by his master, but the expression is one of fondness – he was *dear unto him.* The fidelity of the servant may be implied, but it is the amiability of the master which is most prominent, and chiefly arrests our attention. Nor need we overlook the fact that Matthew lays an emphasis upon the servant being *at home* under his master's roof.

We know that the Romans were not remarkable for the kindness they showed to their dependents; often they were merely looked upon as slaves. In our own days, and in the midst of our boasted civilization, when Christianity has exerted a favorable influence upon all our social relations, I suppose it is not uncommon for a domestic servant to go home to her parents' house in the case of sickness. It is not every good man among us, I fear, whose gentleness would equal that of the centurion in the love which he bears to his servant, and the comfort he provided for him in his own house.

Next to this, you will observe his generosity. It is not, my dear friends, by occasional deeds of showy luster, but by the habitual practice of comely virtues that a worthy character is built up. A thousand kindnesses may be nestling beneath the soil, like the manyfibered root of a gigantic tree, when it is said, *He loveth our nation,* and then the conspicuous fruit appears in its season: *He hath built us a synagogue.* This example of liberality is spoken of as a mere supplement. The Jewish elders do not say, *He loveth our nation **for*** (emphasis added), but *He loveth our nation, **and** he hath built us a synagogue* (emphasis added). This last was a visible token of innumerable good offices which had already won their secret esteem before it bloomed in an open reputation. I have heard all sorts of men praised, and I have noted the qualities which win the applauses of the crowd. Even the high and haughty have some to praise them; but I think I never heard a stingy man praised, or one who was perpetually guilty of meanness. Let him have whatever virtues he may, but if he lacks liberality, then few, if any, will speak well of him. Let me commend to the Christian liberality in all his actions, and benevolence in all his thoughts.

This may sound commonplace, but I am persuaded that the little tricks in trade, those little savings of the pence, those sharp dealings, are just the things which bring religion into disrepute. It were infinitely better that the Christian should pay too much than too little. He had better be blamed for an excess of generosity than take credit to himself for a rigid miserliness. Rather let him become now and then the fool of an imposter, than shut up the bowels of his compassion against his fellow man. I would seek, Christian man, to win a noble character. I cannot see how you can do so, except you should put generosity into the scale, and enroll it in the list of your virtues.

A high character, when earned, is very useful. I am saying this because some might imagine that in the preaching of the gospel we put the base and the wicked before those who have walked uprightly. A good character, when earned, a good reputation in the esteem of men, may win for us, as it did for this centurion, kind thoughts, kind words, kind acts, and kind prayers. There is many a man who will pray for you if he sees you walk uprightly; and your very adversary, who would otherwise have cursed you, will find the curse trembling on his tongue. Though he would rather rail against you, yet he restrains his breath, abashed at your excellencies. Let the Christian labor so to live that he shall not lack a friend. *Make to yourselves friends of the mammon of unrighteousness* is one of Christ's own precepts. If to stoop, to cringe, or to lie wins you friends, scorn to do it; but if with uprightness before God you can still mingle such affection and such generosity towards men that you shall win their votes, do it, I pray you. The time may come when their sympathy shall befriend you.

But remember, and here I close this point, that however good your character, or however excellent your reputation, not one word of this is ever to be mentioned before the throne of the Most High. Job could say when he was talking with his adversaries, "I am not wicked," and he could boast in his excellencies, as he did; but in the presence of God how he changed his note: *Now mine eye seeth thee. Wherefore I abhor myself, and repent in dust and ashes.* Coming before the Lord, we must all come as sinners. When on your knees, you have nothing to boast of more than the same rogue, or the man who has sinned against his country's laws. There, at the foot of the cross, one needs the cleansing blood as much as the other. At mercy's gate we must alike knock, and we must be fed by the same generous hand. There are no degrees here: we enter by the same door; we come to the same Savior; and we shall ultimately – glory be to his name! – sit together in the same heaven whether we have earned a good reputation or not; whether we have crept into heaven, as the thief did at the eleventh hour, or through forty-five years of public service earned the applause of men, as did Caleb the son of Jephunneh.

> Nothing in my hand I bring,
> Simply to thy cross I cling

must be the common footing, and the same confession of all before the God of mercy.

Secondly, in the centurion we see coupled with this high and noble repute *deep humiliation of soul. I am not worthy that thou shouldest come under my roof.*

Humility, then, it appears, may exist in any condition. There are some men who are too mean to be humble. Do you understand me? They are too crouching, crawling, sneaky, and spiritless to be humble. When they use humble words, they disgrace the words they use. You perceive at once that it is more a rise than a stoop for them to be humble. How could it be otherwise? It certainly is not for the littlest vermin that creep on the earth to talk about humility. They must be low: it is their proper place. Such are the creatures who cringe and fawn: "Whatever you please, sir"; "Yes"; "No"; in the same breath. They have not a soul within them that would be worth the notice of a sparrow hawk. They are too little to be worthy of observation, yet they say they are humble.

But for a man to be humble, he needs to have a soul: to stoop, you must have some elevation to stoop from; you must have some real excellence within you before you can really understand what it is to renounce merit. Had he been unworthy, had he been ungenerous and an oppressor, he would have spoken the truth when he said, *I am not worthy that thou shouldest come under my roof*; but there would have been no true humility in what he said. It was because of his excellence, as acknowledged by others, that he could be humble in the modesty of his opinion of himself.

We have heard of a certain monk, who, professing to be humble, said he had broken all God's commandments; he was the greatest sinner in the world; he was as bad as Judas. Somebody said, "Why tell us that? We have all of us thought that for a long time!" Immediately the holy man grew red in the face, and struck the accuser, and asked him what he had ever done to deserve such a speech. We know some of that kind. They will use the words of humility and appear very contrite, and perhaps even at prayer meetings you would think them the meekest and most brokenhearted of men; but if you were to take them at their word, right away they would tell you they use the language, as some ecclesiastical persons do, in an unnatural sense; they do not quite mean what they were supposed to mean, but something very different. That is not humility; it is a kind of mock-modesty which yearns for applause, and holds out deceptive worms as a bait for the trap of praise.

Our centurion was truly humble. This a man may be, though possessing the highest excellence, and standing in the most eminent position. I believe, in my soul, that no man had truer humility in him than John Knox, and yet John Knox never cringed, and never bowed. When Luther dared the thunders of the Vatican, no doubt many said how self-conceited, egotistical, and proud he was; but for all that, God knew how humbly Martin Luther walked with him. When Athanasius stood up and said, "I, Athanasius, against the world," it had the ring of pride about it, but there was true and sound humility before God in it, because he seemed to say, "What am I? not worthy of taking care of; and therefore I do not use the subterfuges of cowardice for my own personal safety. Let the world do what it will to me. God's truth is infinitely more precious than I am, and so I give myself up as an offering upon its altar." True humility will harmonize with the highest chivalry in maintaining divine truth, and with the boldest assertion of what one knows in his own conscience to be true. Though it may be the lot of Christians to be *thought* proud, let it never be true or capable of being substantiated concerning them.

The centurion, though worthy, was still humble; his friends and neighbors found him out by what he said and what he did. He asked them to go for him, seeing he was not worthy; then, finding that they asked for too great a help, he comes to stop them: *I am not worthy that thou shouldest come under my roof.* You need not tell people that you are humble. You have no occasion to advertise that you have genuine humility. Let it discover itself as spice does by its perfume, or as fire by its burning. If you live near to God, and if your humility is of the right kind, it will tell its own tale before long. But the place where humility does speak out is at the throne of grace.

Beloved, there are some things we would confess of ourselves before God which we would not confess before men. There is an attitude of prostration at the throne of the Most High which will never be so gracefully or graciously taken as by that man who would refuse to prostrate himself before his fellows. That is no true humility which bends the knee at the tyrant's throne. That is true humility which, having confronted the tyrant to his face, goes down on its knees before the God of heaven, bold as a lion before men, but meek as a lamb before The Lord.

The true man, whom God approves, will not, dares not, swerve from the love he bears for his sovereign Lord when he faces men; but when he is alone with his Maker, he veils his face with something better than the wings of angels. Wrapped all over with the blood and righteousness of Jesus Christ, he rejoices with fear and trembling that he is justified from all things now; yet, conscious of the total defilement of his nature, with deep prostration of soul he uses the leper's cry, "Unclean! unclean! unclean!" Thus does he fix all his hope upon that cleansing flood, and depends only on that meritorious obedience of Jesus, upon which *every* sanctified believer exclusively relies. Seek, then, as much as it lies in you, that high character which the Christian should maintain among men; but with it always blend that true humility which comes from the Spirit of God, and ever beloves us in the presence of the Lord.

The main thing I am aiming at – because, after all, it is the most practical – lies in my third point. However deep our humility, however conscious we may be of our own undeservedness, we should never diminish our faith in God.

Observe the confession: *I am not worthy that thou shouldest come under my roof.* What, then, will be the inference? "I fear, therefore, my servant will not be healed"? No, no; but rather, *Say in a word, and my servant shall be healed.* It is all a mistake that great faith implies pride. Beloved, the greater the faith, the deeper the humility. These are brothers, not foes. The more the glories of God strike your eyes, the humbler you will lie in conscious depravity, but yet the higher you will rise in urgent prayer. Let us take this principle and endeavor to apply it to a few cases. I say that a deep sense of our own nothingness is not to prevent our having strong faith. We will take a few instances.

> The greater the faith, the deeper the humility.

There is a minister here who has been preaching the Word of God. He has so proclaimed it that God has been pleased to own it in some degree; but it may be that he has stirred up strife; he has caused I know not what amount of turmoil and noise, as the faithful servant of God will in his measure. And now, coming before God, he is asking that a greater blessing than ever may rest upon his labors, but something checks his tongue. He remembers his many infirmities; he recollects, perhaps, how slack he is in his private devotions, and how cold he is in his pleading with the sons of men. He has before him the promise, *My word . . . shall not return unto me void*; but for all that, so conscious is he that he does not deserve the honor of being useful, that he is half afraid to pray as he should pray, and to believe as he should believe.

Dear brother, may I press upon you the case of the centurion? It is right for you, it is right for me, to say, "Lord, I am not worthy to be made the spiritual parent of one immortal soul." It is right for me to feel that it is too great an honor to be permitted to preach the truth at all, and almost too high a thing for such a sinner to have any jewels to present to the Redeemer to fix in his crown. But oh! we must not from this infer that he will not fulfill his promise to us and hear our prayer, "Lord, speak in a word, and feeble though the instrument may be, the congregation shall be blessed. Say but the word, and the marvelous testimony, though marred with a thousand imperfections, shall yet be quick and powerful, and sharper than any two-edged sword." Let this comfort and cheer any despondent pastor. Let him take heart from this and learn that it is not himself to whom he is to look, but that he is to look to God; and that it is not his own arm upon which he is to depend, but upon the promise of God and the strong arm of the Most High. Or, am I addressing some brother or sister in somewhat similar perplexity of mind?

In your private life, dear friend, you have laid upon your heart some of your relatives and neighbors who are very dear to you; or, perhaps, you teach a class in the Sunday school, or possibly you have a larger class of adults, and sometimes Satan will be very busy with you. The more useful you are, the more busy he will be; and he will say to you, "What are you, that you should ever hope to see conversions? Other men and women have had them, but they were better than you are: they had more talent, they had more ability, they served God better, and God gave them a greater reward. You must not hope to see your children saved; you cannot expect it. How should such teaching as yours ever be useful?"

Friend, you are right in saying, *Lord, I am not worthy that thou shouldest come under my roof.* The more you can feel that, the more hopeful shall I be of your success. You are right in feeling that David is not fit to meet the giant, and that the stones out of the brook are scarcely fit weapons for such a warfare; but oh! do not push the right into a wrong; do not, therefore, mistrust your God. No matter what a fool you may be, God has confounded wise things by the foolish, long before now. No matter how weak you are, God has brought down the mighty by weak instrumentalities often enough before this time. Have hope in him, and in your prayer, when you have made your confessions, do not let your faith fail you, but say, "Lord, say in a word, and my class shall be blessed; say in a word, and those stubborn boys and girls, those to whom I have talked so often, who seem to be none the better, shall be saved." Have faith in God, beloved fellow workers! The result of all, under God, must rest with your faith. If you believe for little success, you shall have little success; but if you can believe for great things, and expect great things, you shall certainly find your Master's words fulfilling your desire.

Do I now also address parents here who have been praying for their children? or a husband who has been pleading for his wife? or a wife who has been making intercession for her husband? God only knows what heart-rending prayers are often heard in families, where only some are saved! Ah! what grief is it to a truly godly father to see his sons and daughters still heirs of wrath! And what a pang is it to know that a beloved spouse may be separated from you forever by the stroke of death! I marvel not that you pray for your friends. Should I not marvel at you if you did not?

And now, when you have been praying lately, a sense of your unworthiness has almost stopped you. Though, perhaps, there has been no public sin around you; though before others you could have defended yourself, yet you have said in private, "Lord, I am not worthy of this blessing." You have said, "Lord, my children are not saved, because my example is not as good as it should be; my conversation is not as upright as it should be." You have felt, as I have sometimes, that there was no creature in the whole world so little, and no man loved of God in all the world that was so great a wonder of ingratitude as you are. I say it is right that you should feel this, but do not let this stop your prayers. Offer your request, depend upon the blood of Christ for its plea, and upon the intercession of Christ for its prevalence.

Do not be afraid. A black hand drops a letter into the post office, but the blackness of that hand will not hinder the dispatch of it; there is a stamp upon it, and it will go. And your black hand drops a prayer before Christ's feet, but that black hand will not stop its being heard, for there is a stamp upon it: the Lord Jesus' blood. It may be blotted and misspelled, and there may be many blurs all over it; but do not be afraid, for God knows his Son's signature, and that will give worth to your prayers. It is the bloody signature of him whose hand was nailed to the cross that will carry the day with God. Therefore do not, I pray you, give place to fear; your prayers shall return into your bosom with an answer of peace.

"Well, but," says one, "I have prayed so long." Ah! brother, do not limit the Holy One of Israel. Sister, do not let your doubts prevail. Renew your appeal to Jesus: "Say in a word; only say one word." It is all done if he shall speak. Darkness fled before him in the primeval chaos, and order followed confusion. Do you think, if he shall say, *Let there be light* in a dark heart, that there shall not be light there? Angels fly at his bidding. At his presence the rocks melt, and the hills dissolve. Sinai is all in smoke. And when he comes forth, dressed in the robes of salvation, there are no impossibilities with him. He can win and conquer to your heart's best desire. Therefore be humble, but be not unbelieving.

By your leave, I shall now turn the principle of my text to an account in another way. Concerning yourselves, friends, what are the mercies that you want? If every man could write down his own peculiar prayer, what a variety we should have upon the paper as it just went around the front row of that gallery. If it went around to all, it would not be like Jeremiah's roll, written within and without with lamentations, but it would be filled within and without with diverse petitions. But now just imagine what your own case is, and the case of others, and let us apply this principle to it: we are utterly unworthy to obtain the temporal or spiritual mercy which, it may be, we are now seeking. We may feel this, but in asking anything for ourselves, we must still ask in faith in God, in his promise, and in his grace, and we shall prevail. This blessed principle may be turned to all sorts of uses.

Whatever your desire may be, only believe, and it shall be granted unto you if it be a desire in accordance with his will, and in accordance with the promises of his Word, or else God's Word is not true. Be humble about it, but do not be doubtful about it. The case I have in my mind's eye is this: there may be an unsaved soul reading this. It happens to be one whose character has been morally admirable. Nobody finds any fault with you, and, as I said before, you almost wish they could, for you cannot feel, as some do, the terrors of the Lord. Your heart is not broken with conviction as the hearts of some are, but there is this desire in it: "Lord, save me, or I perish!"

Now, dear friend, it is well that you should feel that there is nothing in you to commend you to Christ. I am glad that you do feel this. Though before the eyes of men, and even of your own parents, there is nothing which can cause you to blush, I am glad that you feel that before God you have nothing whatever to boast of. I think I see you now. You are saying, "My church attendance, my chapel attendance, I do not trust in them. I would not give up attendance at church, but sir, I have no reliance upon all this. As for my baptism, or my confirmation, or my taking the sacrament, I know that all this has nothing whatever in it which can save my soul, and though I *love* God's ordinances, yet I cannot *trust* in them. Sir, I have fed the poor, I have taught the ignorant. In my measure I would do anything to assist those who need my aid, but I do solemnly renounce all this as a ground of trust. I have nothing to glory in."

Well now, dear friend, there remains only one thing to give you perfect peace, and may the Master give you that one thing! Lift up this prayer to him: "Say in a word, and I shall be made whole." Christ can do it; the offering is made; the precious blood is spilled; there is an almighty efficacy in it: he *can* put away your sin. Christ lives to intercede before the throne, and *is able also to save them to the uttermost that come unto God by him*. Doubt not, then, but now, trusting yourself with Jesus Christ, remember you are saved.

> No mountains of sin, nor height of vileness, can shut a man out of heaven if he believes in Jesus.

I am not now looking after the vilest of the vile. How many times have we said from this place that none are excluded from this place except those who exclude themselves? No mountains of sin, nor height of vileness, can shut a man out of heaven if he believes in Jesus, but just now we are after *you*. I know you are a numerous class. You are, in some respects, our dear friends; and though not of us, you hover around us. If there is anything to be done for the cause of God, you are, perhaps, first in it; and yet you yourselves are not saved. I cannot bear the thought of your being cast away – to be so near the gates of heaven and yet to be shut out after all. Why should it be?

The voice speaks to you now: the spirit of the living God speaks through that voice. There is life in a look for *you* as well as for the chief of sinners. Without the strong convictions, without the terrors of conscience, without a sense of any aggravated crimes, if you rest on Jesus, you are saved. There is no amount of sin specified there. You are lost in the fall – wholly lost – even if you had no sin of your own; but your own actual sin has irretrievably ruined you apart from the grace of Christ. You know this, and to an extent you feel it. You will feel it all the more when you have believed in Jesus. But now the one message of mercy is, "Believe, and you shall live." I feel as if I cannot get at you. My soul will not go out as I desire, and yet you know that I am talking about you and about your case. When we are firing our shots at sin, we hardly ever strike you. You have become so used to our appeals that there seems no likelihood of our getting at you. Oh! there are some of you whom I would not find fault with if I could. You make your mother glad with your industry, you make your sister's heart rejoice at your many virtues, but yet there is *one thing* which you lack. Remember that when the strength of a chain is to be measured, it is measured at its one weakest link. If you have that one weak link, the vital union is snapped.

You may have anything and everything else, but you will be only a child of nature and not a living son. I am only telling you over and over truths which you have known for many years. You will not dispute these things; and sometimes you feel an earnestness about your eternal portion, though, like so many others, you are putting off and putting off. But death will not put off; the judgment day will not be postponed for you. O may you be brought in now! What a happy church we should be if such as you should be brought in. We rejoice over the chief of sinners; we make the place ring when the prodigals come in; but elder brother, why will not you come in? You who have not been standing all the day idle in the market, but only for the first hour, do not say that no man has hired you. O come in, that the house of mercy may be filled! God grant the desire of our hearts, and to his name shall be the praise. Amen and Amen.

Chapter 8

The Centurion's Faith and Humility

Then Jesus went with them. And when he was now not far from the house, the centurion sent friends to him, saying unto him, Lord, trouble not thyself: for I am not worthy that thou shouldest enter under my roof: Wherefore neither thought I myself worthy to come unto thee: but say in a word, and my servant shall be healed. For I also am a man set under authority, having under me soldiers, and I say unto one, Go, and he goeth; and to another, Come, and he cometh; and to my servant, Do this, and he doeth it. (Luke 7:6-8)

The greatest light may enter into the darkest places. We may find the choicest flowers blooming where we least expected them. Here was a Gentile, a Roman, a soldier – a soldier clothed with absolute power – and yet a tender master, a considerate citizen, and a lover of God! Let no man, therefore, be despised because of his calling, and let not the proverb, *Can there any good thing come out of Nazareth?* be ever heard from the wise man's lips. The best of pearls have been found in the darkest caves of oceans. Why should it not be so still, that God should have even in Sardis a few that have not defiled their garments, who shall walk with Christ in white, for they are worthy? Let no man think that because of his position in society he cannot excel in virtue.

It is not the place which is to blame, but the man. If your heart is right, the situation may be difficult, but the difficulty is to be overcome; yes, and out of that difficulty shall arise an excellence which you would not have otherwise known.

Say not in your heart, "I am a soldier, and the barrack-room cannot minister to devotion; therefore I may live as I do because I cannot live as I should." Say not, "I am a working man in the midst of those who blaspheme, and therefore it would be vain for me to talk of holiness and devotion." No, rather remember that in such a case it is your special duty not to talk of these precious things, but to wear them upon you as your daily ornament. Where should the lamp be placed but in the room which otherwise would be dark? Rest assured your calling and your position shall be no excuse for your sin if you continue therein; nor shall your condition be any apology for the absence of integrity and virtue if these are not found in you.

Concerning the centurion, we may remark that perhaps we had never heard of him, though he loved his servant; perhaps we had never read his name, though he tenderly nursed his slave; perhaps he had found no place in the record of inspiration, though he loved the Jewish nation and built them a synagogue; nor perhaps had we read the story of his life, though he had become a proselyte to the Jewish faith. But the one thing that gives him a place in these sacred pages is this, that he was a believer in the Messiah, that he was such a believer in the Son of God that Jesus said concerning him, *I have not found so great faith, no, not in Israel.* There is the vital point. There, my hearer, is the notable matter which shall enroll you among the blessed. If you believe in Jesus Christ, the Son of God, your name is in the Lamb's Book of Life, but if you believe not in him, your outward excellencies, however admirable, shall avail you little.

The faith of the centurion is described both in the eighth chapter of Matthew and in the chapter before us, as being of the highest kind, and the remarkable point in it is that it was coupled with the very deepest humility. The same man who said, *Say in a word, and my servant shall be healed,* also said, *I am not worthy that thou shouldest enter under my roof.* In bringing before you this noble soldier's example, these are two pivots upon which the discourse shall turn. I shall direct you to this double star, shining with so mild a radiance in the sky of Scripture: *this man's deep humility was not injurious to the strength of his faith, and his gigantic faith was by no means hostile to his deep humiliation.*

To begin, then, *the humility of the centurion was not at all injurious to the strength of his faith.* Observe his humble expressions: he insisted that he was not worthy to come to Jesus. *Neither,* said he, *thought I myself worthy to come unto thee*; and then he further felt that he was not worthy that Jesus should come to him. *I am not worthy that thou shouldest enter under my roof.* Was this self-abasement occasioned by the remembrance that he was a Gentile? That may have contributed to it. Was it because he was penitent on account of various rough and boisterous deeds which had stained his soldier life? It may be so. Was it not much more because he had had a deep insight into his own heart, and had learned to see sin in its true colors, and therefore, he who was worthy according to the statement of the Jews, was most unworthy in his own apprehension?

You may have noticed in the biography of some eminent men how badly they speak of themselves. Southey, in his book *The Pilgrim's Progress: With a Life of John Bunyan*, seems to find it difficult to understand how Bunyan could have used such depreciating language concerning his own character. For it is true, according to all we know of his biography, that he was not, except in the case of profane swearing, at all so bad as most of the villagers. Indeed, there were some virtues in the man which were worthy of all commendation. Southey attributes it to a morbid state of mind, but we rather ascribe it to a return of spiritual health. Had the excellent poet seen himself in the same heavenly light as that in which Bunyan saw himself, he would have discovered that Bunyan did not exaggerate, but was simply stating as far as he could a truth which utterly surpassed his powers of utterance.

The great light which shone around Saul of Tarsus was the outward type of that inner light above the brightness of the sun which flashes into a regenerate soul, and reveals the horrible character of the sin which dwells within. Believe me, when you hear Christians making humble confessions, it is not that they are worse than others, but that they see themselves in a clearer light than others; and this centurion's unworthiness was not because he had been more vicious than other men. On the contrary, he had evidently been much more virtuous than the common run of mankind, but only because he saw what others did not see, and felt what others had not felt.

Deep as this man's contrition was, overwhelming as his sense of utter worthlessness was, he did not doubt for a moment either the power or the willingness of Christ. As for the question of willingness, there is no remark made about it at all. The leper had said earlier, *If thou wilt*, but the centurion was so clear about Christ's willingness to relieve suffering humanity that it does not occur to him to mention it. He has long ago settled that matter, and now takes it for granted as a very self-evident truth in the knowledge of Jesus, for such a one as he must be willing to do all the good which is asked of him.

Nor is he at all doubtful about our Lord's power. The palsy which afflicted the servant was a remarkably grievous one, but it did not at all stagger the centurion. He felt not only that Jesus could heal it, could heal it at once, and could heal it completely, but that he could also heal it without moving a step from the place whereon he stood. Let but the word be uttered, and in an instant his servant shall be healed. O glorious humiliation, how low you stoop! O noble faith, how high you soar! Brethren, if we can imitate this noble character in both respects – in the depth of his foundation, in the height of his pinnacle – how near to the model of the temple of God shall we be built up! Empty indeed he was, having nothing of his own; not worthy to receive, much less indulging a thought of giving anything to Christ, and yet confident that all things are possible with the Master, and that he both can and will do according to our faith, and that in a manner gloriously unveiling his kingly power.

My dear friends, especially you who are under concern of soul, you feel unworthy – that is not a mistaken feeling, you are so. You are much distressed by reason of this unworthiness, but if you knew more of it, you might be more distressed still, for the dread which you already have of your sinfulness, although it be very painful, does not at all reach to the full extent of it. You are much more sinful than you think you are, and much more unworthy than you yet know yourself to be. Instead of attempting a foolish and wicked soothing of your dark thoughts, and saying, "You have morbid ideas of yourself, you ought not to speak so," I rather pray you to believe that yours is an utterly hopeless case apart from Christ, and that in your spiritual nature the whole head is sick and the whole heart is faint. I want you not to film the horrible ulcer of your depravity with deceptive hopes and professions. I desire you not to look upon this disease as though it were but skin-deep; it lies in the source and fountain of your life, and poisons your heart. The flames of hell must wrap themselves around you assuredly unless Christ intercedes to save you. You have no merit of any kind or sort, nor will you ever have any; and what's more, you have no power to escape from your lost condition unaided by the Savior's hand. Without Christ you can do nothing, for you are humbly poor, hopelessly bankrupt, and you cannot by the utmost diligence make yourself anything other than you are.

No words that I can utter can exaggerate your deplorable condition, and no feelings which you can ever experience can represent your real state in colors too alarming. You are not worthy that Christ should come to you; you are not worthy to draw near to Christ. But, and here is a glorious contrast, never let this for a single moment interfere with your full belief that he who is God, but who took our nature, that he who suffered in our stead upon the cross, that he who now rules in the highest heavens, is able to do for you, and willing to do for you, exceedingly abundantly above what you ask or even think.

Your inability does not prevent the working of his power; your unworthiness cannot put restrictions on his generosity or limits to his grace. You may be an ill-deserving sinner, but that is no reason for him not to pardon you. You may be in your own dread, and truthfully so, the most unworthy that he ever stooped to bless, yet this is no reason why he should not stoop to press you to his bosom, to accept and to save you. I wish that as the first truth has impressed itself deeply upon you, the second truth may with equal force take up the possession of your heart, that Jesus Christ *is able also to save them to the uttermost that come unto God by him,* and is as willing as he is able, and that your emptiness does not affect his fullness, your weakness does not alter his power, your inability does not diminish his omnipotence, and your undeservedness does not restrain the bowels of his love, which freely move towards the very vilest of the vile.

By some means Satan almost always manages it this way, that when we get a little hope, it is generally a self-grounded hope, a vain idea that we are getting better in ourselves. It is a mischievous conceit: proud flesh, which hinders the cure, and which the Surgeon must cut out; it is no sign of healing, it prevents healing. On the other hand, if we obtain a deep sense of sin, the Evil One manages to put his hoof in there, and to insinuate that Jesus is not able to save such as we are. A great falsehood, for who shall say what the limit of Christ's power is? But if these two things could but meet together, a thorough sense of sin and an immovable belief in the power of Christ to grapple with sin and to overcome it, surely the kingdom of heaven would then have come near unto us in power and in truth, and again it would be said, *I have not found so great faith, no, not in Israel.*

Now, you troubled hearts, I have this word for you, and then I shall pass on to another point. Your sense of your unworthiness, if it be properly used, should drive you to Christ. You are unworthy, but Jesus died for the unworthy. Jesus did not die for those who profess to be by nature good and deserving, for those who are whole have no need of a physician. But it is written, *In due time Christ died for the ungodly.* Christ gave himself for our what? Excellencies and virtues? No, he gave himself for our *sins*, according to the Scriptures. We read that he *suffered for sins* – as the just for the just? By no means, but as *the just for the unjust, that he might bring us to God.* Gospel pharmacy is for the sick; gospel bread is for the hungry; gospel fountains are open to the unclean; gospel water is given to the thirsty. You who do not need shall not have; but you who want it may freely come. Let your huge and painful deficiencies impel you to fly to Jesus. Let the vast cravings of your insatiable spirit compel you to come to him in whom all fullness dwells.

Your unworthiness should act as a wing to bear you to Christ, the sinner's Savior. It should also have this effect upon you: it should prevent your raising those doubts and making those demands which are such a hindrance to some people finding peace. The proud spirit says,

"I must have signs and wonders, or I will not believe. I must feel deep convictions, and horrible tremors, or I must quake because of dreams or threatening texts applied to me with awful power." Ah! but unworthy one, if you are truly humbled, you will not dare to ask for these; you will be done with demands and stipulations, and you will cry, "Lord, give me but a word, speak but a word of promise, and it shall be enough for me. Just say to me, 'Your sins are forgiven you'; give me just half a text; give me one kind, assuring word to sink my fears again, and I will believe it and rest upon it." Thus your sense of unworthiness should lead you to a simple faith in Jesus, and prevent your demanding those manifestations which the foolish so eagerly and contemptuously require.

Beloved, it has come to this: you are so unworthy that you are shut out of every hope but Christ; all other doors are swiftly nailed against you. If there is anything to be done for salvation, you cannot do it. If there is any fitness needed, you do not have it. Christ comes to you and tells you that there is no fitness necessary for coming to him, but that if you will but trust him he will save you. I think I hear you say, "Then, my Lord, since it has come to this,

> I can but perish if I go;
> I am resolved to try;
> For if I stay away, I know
> I must forever die.

And so, sink or swim, upon your precious atonement I cast my guilty soul, persuaded that you are able to save even such a one as I am; and I am so thoroughly persuaded of the goodness of your heart, that I know you will not cast away a poor trembler who comes to you and takes you to be his only ground of trust."

I want you for a moment to wait while we shift the text to the other quarter. The centurion's great faith was not at all hostile to his humility.

His faith was extraordinary. It ought not to be extraordinary. We ought all of us to believe as well in Christ as this soldier did. Observe the form it took: he said to himself, "I am a subordinate officer, under authority. I am not the commander in chief, I am merely the commander of a troop of a hundred men, and yet over those hundred men I exert unlimited control. I say to this one, 'Go,' and he goes. I say to the other, 'Come,' and he comes, and my servant, my poor sick servant (his tender heart comes back to him, and he puts him into the illustration), I say to him, 'Do this,' and he does it at once. I am simply a petty officer, under authority myself; but yet such is the influence of discipline that there are no questions raised, no deliberations tolerated. No soldier turns around and tells me that I have given him too difficult a task; no one out of all the troop ever dares to say to me, 'I shall not do it.'"

The power of discipline among the legions of Rome was exceedingly great. The commander had but to say, "Do it," and it was done, though thousands bled and died. "Now," argued the centurion, "this glorious man is the Son of God. He is not a subordinate, he is the commander in chief. If he gives the word, his will most surely must be done. Fevers and paralysis, good influences and bad, they must be all under his control, and he can therefore heal my servant in a moment. Who can resist the great Caesar of heaven and earth?" That was, I believe, the centurion's idea. Jesus has therefore but to will it, and to the utmost bounds of the earth those influences which are under his control will at once set to work to perform his will. The centurion pictured himself as sitting down in the house and accomplishing his desires without rising, by merely issuing an order; and his faith placed the Lord Jesus in the same position. "You don't need to come to my dwelling; you can stand here, and if you will but say it, the cure will be worked at once." He did in his heart enthrone the Lord Jesus as a captain over all the forces of the world, as the chief commander of the armies of heaven and earth, as, in fact, the Caesar, the imperial governor of all the forces of the universe.

'Twas graciously thought, 'twas poetically embodied, 'twas nobly spoken, 'twas gloriously believed; but it was the truth and nothing more than the truth, for universal dominion is really in the power of Jesus today. If he were a true Caesar before he died, while he was despised and rejected of men, he is much more now that he has trodden through the winepress and stained his clothes with the blood of his vanquished enemies; he is much more now that he has led captivity captive, and sits enthroned by filial right at the right hand of God, even the Father; he is much more now that God has sworn that he will put all things under his feet, and that at the name of Jesus every knee shall bow – of things in heaven, and things on earth, and things that are under the earth; and much more I say can he now work according to his good pleasure. Today he has but to speak and it is done, to command and it shall stand fast.

Beloved, see whether this truth bears us as on eagles' wings. Caesar has but to say, "*Absolvo te*," and his guilty subject is acquitted; Caesar has but to speak, and a province is conquered, an army routed. Stormy seas are navigated at Caesar's bidding, mountains are tunneled, the whole world shall be girded with military roads; Caesar is absolute, and his will is law. So it is on earth, but so much more it is in heaven. Let the imperial Caesar of heaven only say, "I forgive," and the devils of hell cannot accuse you. Let him say, "I will help you," and who shall oppose? If Immanuel be for you, who shall be against you? Let him speak, and the bonds of sinful habits must fall off, and the darkness in which your soul has long been imprisoned must give place to instantaneous light. He reigns as King, Lord over all; let his name be blessed forever. Let each one of us, by our faith, give him the honor that is due unto his name. All hail! great Emperor, once slain, but now forever Lord of heaven and earth!

Here is one point which I want you to hearken back to: this man's faith did not for a moment interfere with his thorough personal humiliation. Interfere with it! My brethren, it was the source of it; it was the very foundation on which it rested. Do you not see that the higher his thoughts of Christ, the more unworthy he felt himself to be of the kind attentions of so good and great a person? If he had thought less of Jesus, he would not have said, *I am not worthy that thou shouldest come under my roof.* There was, of course, a sight of himself to humble him, but the far more wondrous vision of the glory of the Lord Jesus was the true root and parent of his self-abasement. Because Christ was so great, he felt himself to be unworthy either to meet him or entertain him.

Observe, my brethren, that his faith acted upon his humility by making him content with a word from Christ. His faith said, "A word is enough; it will work the cure." Then his humility said, "Ah, how unworthy I am even of so little a thing as a word. If a word will work a miracle, it is so great and powerful a thing that it is more than I deserve; therefore, I will not ask for more. I will not ask for footsteps when a sound will suffice; I will not clamor for his presence when his wish can restore my servant to health." His believing that a word was enough made him humbly decline to pray for more, so that his confidence in Christ – instead of interfering with his sense of unworthiness – aided its manifestation.

Brethren and sisters, never think for a moment, as many foolish persons do, that strong faith in the Lord is necessarily pride; it is the reverse. It is one of the worst forms of pride to question the promise of God. When a man says, "Christ has promised to save those who trust him: I have trusted him, therefore I am saved," then he knows that he is saved. "I am sure of it," he says, "because God says so, and I do not want any better evidence that assurance is humility in action." But if a man says, "God has said that those who trust him shall be saved; I do trust him, but still I do not know that I am saved," why, you do as much as say you do not know whether God is a liar or not, and what is more impertinent, what is more proudly insulting than that? I know it is a most common thing to say, "It seems so presumptuous to say I know I am saved." I think it far more presumptuous to doubt when God speaks positively, and to mistrust where the promise is plain.

> It is one of the worst forms of pride to question the promise of God.

God says, *He that believeth and is baptized shall be saved.* If you believe and are baptized, if God be true, you shall be saved – you are saved. There is no hoping about it; it must be so. Let God be true and every man a liar; and far off from these lips be the insinuation of a doubt that perhaps God can be false to his promise and may break his word. If you question anything, question whether you trust Christ; but that settled, the question is ended. If you believe that Jesus is the Christ, you are born of God; if you rest alone on him, your sins, which are many, are all forgiven you.

Take God at his word as your child takes you at your word. It is not too much for God to ask, for you ask it of your child. Though you be a poor fallible creature, you would not have your child mistrust you. Shall you be believed, and not your God? Shall your little one be expected to confide in you, though you are evil, and will not you believe the voice of your heavenly parent to be the very truth, and rest upon it? Ah! do so, I beg you, and the more you do it, the more you will feel your unworthiness to do so. For it astounds me to think that I shall be saved; it amazes me to think I shall be washed from my every sin in the precious blood of Christ, that I shall be set upon a rock, and a new song shall be put into my mouth. It astounds me, and as I think of it, I say, "How unworthy I am of such favors! I am less than the least of all the benefits which you have bestowed upon me." Your faith will not murder your humility, your humility will not stab at your faith; but the two will go hand in hand to heaven like a brave brother and a fair sister, the one bold as a lion, and the other meek as a dove; the one rejoicing in Jesus, and the other blushing at self. Blessed pair, I would rather entertain you in my heart all the days of my pilgrimage on earth.

I have thus, as best I could, brought before you the example of the centurion with a few incidental lessons. Now for the *application*, with as much earnestness and brevity as we can summon.

The application shall be to three sorts of people. First, we speak to *distressed minds* deeply conscious of their unworthiness. Jesus Christ is able and willing to save you this very morning. What is the form of your distress? Is it that your sins are great? Believe, I charge you, and may God the Holy Spirit help you to believe that all your sins Christ can pardon now. Do you see him upon yonder cross? He is divine, but how he bleeds! He is divine, but how he groans! He hurts! He dies! Do you believe that any sin is too great for those sufferings to put away? Do you think the Son of God offered an inadequate atonement? An atonement of which you can say there is a limit to its efficacy beyond which it cannot operate for the salvation of believers, so that, after all, sin is greater than the sacrifice, and the filth is more full of defilement than the blood is of purification? O crucify not Christ afresh by doubting the power of the eternal God!

My brethren, when in the stillness of the starry night we look up to the orbs of heaven and remember the marvelous truths which astronomy has revealed to us, of the magnificence, the inconceivable majesty of creation, if we then reflect that the infinite God who made all these became man for us, and that as man he was fastened to the wood placed crosswise, and bled to death for us, it will appear to us that if all the stars were crowded with inhabitants, and all those inhabitants had been rebellious against God, and had steeped themselves up to the very throat in scarlet crimes, there must be efficacy enough in the blood of such a one as God himself incarnate to take all their sins away. For this great miracle of miracles, God himself paying honor to his own justice by suffering a substitutionary death, is an exhibition of infinite severity and love, which far down in eternity must appear so glorious as to utterly swallow up the remembrance of creature sin, and to put it altogether out of sight. Yes, sinner, believe that this moment the sins of fifty years can drop from off you, yes, of seventy or eighty years, and that in an instant, you who are as black as hell can be as pure as heaven if Jesus says the word. If you believe in him it is done, for to trust him is to be clean.

Perhaps, however, your difficulty is in getting rid of a hardness of heart. You feel that you cannot repent, but cannot Jesus make you repent by his Spirit? Do you hesitate about that question? See the world during winter hardbound with frost, but how the daffodil, and the crocus, and the snowdrop come up above that once-frozen soil, how snow and ice disappear, and the sweet sun shines out! God does it readily, with the soft breath of the south wind and the kind sunbeams, and he can do the same in the spiritual world for you. Believe he can, and ask him now to do it, and you shall find that the rock of ice shall thaw, that huge, horrible, devilish iceberg of a heart of yours shall begin to drip with showers of crystal repentance, which God shall accept through his dear Son.

But perhaps it is some bad habit which gives you trouble. You have been long in it, and can the Ethiopian change his skin, or the leopard his spots? You cannot get rid of it. I know you cannot. It is a desperate evil, it drags you downward like the hands of demons pulling you from the surface of life's stream down into its black and horrid depths of death and defilement. Ah! I know your dreads and despairs, but man, I ask you, cannot Jesus deliver? He has the key of your heart, and he can turn it so that all its wheels shall revolve differently than now. He who shakes the earth with an earthquake and sweeps the sea with a tornado, can send a heartquake and a storm of strong repentance, and tear up your old habits by the roots. He whose every act is wonderful, can surely do what he will within the little world of your soul, since in the great world outside he rules as he pleases. Believe in his power, and ask him to prove it. He has but to say a word, and this matter of present distress shall be taken away.

Still I hear you say, "I cannot"; a horrible inability hangs over you. But it is not what you can do or cannot do; these have nothing to do with it, it is what Jesus can do. Can there be anything too hard for the Lord? Can the eternal Spirit ever be defeated when he wills to conquer in a man? Can he who bears the earth's huge pillars up, and spreads the heavens abroad, who once was crucified but who now ever lives, can he fail? Put your care into his hand, poor unabled wretch, and ask him to do for you what you cannot do for yourself, and according to your faith so shall it be unto you.

A second application of our subject shall be made to the *patient workers* who are ready to faint. I know that in this house there are many who incessantly plead with God for their unconverted relatives and neighbors that they may be saved. You have pleaded long for your husband, or your son, or your daughter, but they have gone still further into sin. Instead of answers to prayer, it seems as though heaven has laughed at your urgent requests. Take heed of one thing: do not permit unbelief to make you think that the object of your care cannot be saved. While there is life there is hope. Yes, though they add drunkenness to lust, and blasphemy to drunkenness, and hardness of heart and unrepentance to blasphemy, Jesus has but to say the word and they shall be turned every one from his evil way. Under the use of the means of grace, or, church attendance, it may be done, or even without the means it may be done.

There have been men at work, or at their amusements, all in their wickedness, who have had impressions which have made them new men when it was least expected such a thing would occur; and those who have been the ringleaders in Satan's rebellious crew have frequently become the boldest captains in the army of Christ. There is no room for doubt as to the possibility of the salvation of anybody when Jesus gives the word of command. You are unchristian when you shut out the harlot from hope, when you exclude the thief from repentance, when you even despair of the murderer; for the big heart of God is greater than all your hearts put together, and the great thoughts of the loving Father are not as your thoughts when they climb the highest, neither are his ways your ways when they are at their utmost liberality.

Oh, if your friend, your child, your wife, your husband be a very devil incarnate, or if there be seven devils, or a legion of devils within them, while Christ lives, never mutter the word "despair"; for he can cast out the legion of evil spirits and impart his Holy Spirit instead. Therefore have faith. You are unworthy to receive the blessing, but have faith in him who is so able to bestow it. Perhaps you are getting very fainthearted because you do not see the success that you so much desire. Well, perhaps it is good for you to feel how little you can do apart from the divine ministrations. May this humiliation of soul continue, but do not let it degenerate into a distrust of him. If Christ were dead and buried, and had never risen, it would be a horrible case for us poor preachers; but while Christ lives, endowed with the residue of the eternal Spirit which he freely gives, we ought not so much as fear, much less despair. May the church of God pluck up heart, and feel that with a living Christ in the midst of her armies, victory shall before long wait upon her banners.

The last application I shall make is the same as the second, only on a wider scale. There are many who are like *watchers* who have grown weary. We have heard that Christ comes – the great coming man – and the Lord knows right well that there is pressing need for someone to come, for this poor old machine of a world creaks dreadfully, and seems as though it is so laden with the sheaves of human sin that its axles should snap. God's infinite longsuffering has kept a crazy world from utter disintegration by a thousand helps and support, but it is poor work, and seems to get worse and worse.

Our state is rotten at the very core, both in business and politics. No man seems to succeed so well as he who has dispensed with his conscience and laughs at principles; all things are come to that point that there is need for some deliverer to come, or else I do not know where we shall all go to. But he will come, so the promise stands, and to these who wait for him, his coming shall be as the beams of the daystar proclaiming the dawn. He is coming, and at his coming there shall be a glorious time, a millennium, a period of light, and truth, and joy, and holiness, and peace. We are watching and waiting for it. But we say, "Ah, it is hopeless to think of converting the world! How is the truth to be preached? Where are the tongues to speak it? How many proclaim it boldly? Where are the men to carry Christ's cross to the utmost bounds of the globe, and conquer nations for him?" Ah, do not say in your heart, "the former days were better than now." Do not write a book of lamentation and say, "The prophets, where are they? and the apostles have gone and all the mighty confessors who lived and died for Christ have disappeared." At the lifting of his finger the Lord can raise up a thousand Jonahs for every city throughout the land, a thousand bold Isaiahs to declare his glory. He has only to order it and companies of apostles and armies of martyrs shall start up from the quiet nooks of old England's villages, or shall pour forth from the workshops of her cities. He can do wonders when he wills it. The worst plight of the church is but the time when her flood has ebbed in order that it may return in the fullness of its strength.

Have confidence, for even should the instruments fail and the ministry become a dead and decayed thing, yet his coming shall accomplish his purposes, and when he appears, the kingdoms of this world shall become the kingdoms of our Lord and of his Christ. Jesus is not under authority, but he has soldiers under him, and he has but to say to this spirit or to that, "Go," or "Come," and his will shall be done. He has but to stimulate his church by his Holy Spirit, and say, "Do this," and the impossible task shall be accomplished; what seemed beyond all human skill or mortal hope shall be worked, and worked at once. When he says, "Do," it shall be done, and his name shall be praised. O for more faith and more self-abasement. Twin angels abide in this assembly evermore. Go forth with us to battle and return with us from the victory. O Lord, the lover of humility, and the author of faith, grant us to be steeped in both for Jesus' sake. Amen.

Chapter 9

An Astounding Miracle

And they went into Capernaum; and straightway on the sabbath day he entered into the synagogue, and taught. And they were astonished at his doctrine: for he taught them as one that had authority, and not as the scribes. And there was in their synagogue a man with an unclean spirit; and he cried out, saying, Let us alone; what have we to do with thee, thou Jesus of Nazareth? art thou come to destroy us? I know thee who thou art, the Holy One of God. And Jesus rebuked him, saying, Hold thy peace, and come out of him. And when the unclean spirit had torn him, and cried with a loud voice, he came out of him. And they were all amazed, insomuch that they questioned among themselves, saying, What thing is this? what new doctrine is this? for with authority commandeth he even the unclean spirits, and they do obey him. And immediately his fame spread abroad throughout all the region round about Galilee. (Mark 1:21-28)

You will find the same narrative in Luke, in the fourth chapter, from the thirty-first to the thirty-seventh verse. It will be handy for you to be able to refer to the second passage, from which I shall quote one or two matters.

These two evangelists commence the narrative by telling us of the singular authority and power which there was in the Savior's teaching: authority, so that no man dare question his doctrine; and power, so that every man felt the force of the truth which he delivered. *They were astonished at his doctrine: for his word was with power.* Why was it that the Savior's teaching had such a remarkable power about it? Was it not, first, because he preached the truth? There is no power in falsehood except so far as men choose to yield to it because it flatters them; but there is great force in truth, it makes its own way into the soul.

As long as men have consciences, they cannot help feeling when the truth is brought to bear upon them. Even though they grow angry, their very resistance proves that they recognize the force of what is spoken. Moreover, the Savior spoke the truth in a very natural, unaffected manner: the truth was in him, and it flowed freely from him. His manner was truthful as well as his matter. There is a way of speaking truth so as to make it sound like a lie. Perhaps there is no greater injury done to truth than when it is spoken in a doubtful manner, with none of the accent and emphasis of conviction. Our Savior spoke as the oracles of God: he spoke truth as truth should be spoken, honestly and naturally, as one who did not preach professionally, but out of the fullness of his heart. You all know how sermons from the heart go to the heart.

Moreover, our great Example delivered his teaching as one who most heartily believed what he was speaking, who spoke what he knew, yes, spoke of things which were his own. Jesus had no doubts, no hesitancy, and no questions, and his style was as calmly forcible as his faith. Truth seemed to be reflected from his face just as it shone forth from God in all its native purity and splendor. He could not speak otherwise than he did, for he spoke as he was, as he felt, and as he knew. Our Lord spoke as one whose life supported all that he taught. Those who knew him could not say, "He speaks after a right kind, but he acts otherwise." There was about his whole conduct and demeanor that which made him the suitable person to utter the truth, because the truth was incarnate, and embodied, and exemplified in his own person. Well might he speak with great assurance when he could say, *Which of you convinceth me of sin?* He was himself as pure as the truth which he proclaimed. He was not a speaking-machine, sounding out something with which it has no vital connection; but out of the midst of his own heart there flowed rivers of living waters. Truth overflowed at his lips from the deep well of his soul; it was in him and therefore came from him. What he poured forth was his own life, with which he was endeavoring to saturate the lives of others. Consequently, for all these reasons, and many besides, Jesus spoke as one who had authority: his tone was commanding, his teaching was convincing.

Meanwhile, the Holy Spirit, who had descended upon him in his baptism, rested upon him and bore witness by his divine operations in the consciences and hearts of men. If Jesus spoke of sin, the Spirit was there to convince the world of sin; if he set forth a glorious righteousness, the Holy Spirit was there to convince the world of righteousness; and when he told men of the coming judgment, the Holy Spirit was present to make them know that a judgment would surely come at which each of them must appear. Because of his unlimited anointing by the Spirit, our Lord spoke with power and authority of the most astonishing kind, so that all who heard him were compelled to feel that no ordinary rabbi stood before them.

That power and authority was seen all the more in contrast with the scribes, for the scribes spoke hesitatingly; they quoted authority; they begged for permission to offer an opinion; they supported their ideas by the opinion of Rabbi this, although it was questioned by Rabbi the other; they spent their time in tying and untying knots before the people, quibbling about matters which had no practical importance whatever. They were wonderfully clear upon the tithing of mint and dill; they enlarged most copiously upon the washing of cups and basins; they were profound upon phylacteries and borders of garments. They were at home upon such rubbish, which would neither save a soul, nor slay a sin, nor suggest a virtue. While handling the Scriptures they were mere word-triflers and letter-men, whose chief object was to show their own wisdom.

Such attempts at oratory and word-spinning were as far as the poles apart from each other from the discourses of our Lord. Self-display never entered into the mind of Jesus. He himself was so absorbed in what he had to teach that his hearers did not exclaim, "What a preacher is this!" but rather, "What a word is this!" and "What new teaching is this!" – the word and the teaching with their admirable authority and amazing power subduing men's minds and hearts by the energy of truth. Men acknowledged that the great teacher had taught them something worth knowing, and had so impressed it upon them that there was no shaking themselves free of it.

Now, when they were beginning to perceive this authority in his word, our Lord determined to prove to them that there was real power at the back of his teaching, that he had a right to use such authority, for he was Jesus Christ the Son of God, clothed with divine authority and power. It occurred to him to display before their eyes the fact that as there was power in his speech, there was also power in himself, that he was mighty in deed as well as in word, and therefore he worked the miracle now before us. This most astounding deed of authority and power has been passed over by certain expositors as having too little importance about it to be of much interest, whereas, to my mind, it rises in some respects above all other miracles, and is certainly excelled by none in its forcible demonstration of our Lord's authority and power. It is the first miracle which Mark gives us; it is the first which Luke gives us; and it is in some respects the first of the miracles, as I hope I may show before I am done.

> The object of the miracle is to reveal more fully the power and authority of our Lord's word.

Remember, however, that the object of the miracle is to reveal more fully the power and authority of our Lord's word, and to let us see by signs following it that his teaching has an omnipotent force about it. This truth is much needed at the present moment; for if the gospel does not still save men, if it is not still *the power of God unto salvation to every one that believeth*, then the attacks of skepticism are not easily repelled. But if it be still a thing of power over the minds of men, a power conquering sin and Satan, then they may say what they like, and our only answer shall be to lament their doubts and to scorn their scorning. O for an hour of the Son of Man! O where is he that trod the sea, and commanded the rage of hell to subside with a word?

First, then, to show forth this power and authority, *our Lord selects a most unhappy person on whom to prove his power.*

This person was, first, one possessed. A devil dwelt within him. We cannot explain this fact any more than we can explain madness. Many things which happen in the world of the mind are quite inexplicable, and for the matter of that so are many facts in the world of matter. We accept the recorded fact; an evil spirit entered into this man, and continued in him. Satan, you know, is God's ape; he is always trying to imitate him, to caricature him. So, when God became incarnate, it occurred to Satan to become incarnate too; and this man I may call, without any misuse of words, an incarnate devil; or, at any rate, the devil was incarnated in him. He had become like a devil in human form, and so was in a certain manner the opposite of our Lord Jesus. In Jesus dwelt the fullness of the Godhead bodily by an eternal union; in this man the devil dwelt for a while. Is not this an awful picture? But note the fact that the man whom Jesus selects on whom to prove his power and authority was so far gone that the foul fiend controlled his mind and made a kennel of his body.

I wondered, when thinking this over, whether a person of whom this man is the emblem would come into the congregation today, for I have seen such people. I have not dared personally to apply such an epithet to any man, but I have heard it applied. I have heard disgusted friends and indignant neighbors, worn out with the drunken profanity or horrible filthiness of some man, say, "He does not seem to be a man; he acts like the Evil One." Or when it has been a woman, they have said, "All that is womanly is gone; she seems to be a female fiend." Well, if such a one should be reading these words, let them take note that there is help, hope, and health even for them. The power of Jesus knows no limit. Upon one who was the devil's own did our gracious Lord display his authority and power in connection with his gospel teaching; and he is not less able to do so now than then.

This man, further, was one whose personality was to a great extent merged in the Evil One. Read the twenty-third verse: *There was in their synagogue a man with an unclean spirit.* The rendering might be equally accurate if we read it, "A man in an unclean spirit." Do you see that? Not only a man *with* an unclean spirit in him, but also a man *in* an unclean spirit. The phrase is simple enough; we speak of a man being *in drink*. For liquor to be in a man does not mean half so much as for a man to be in liquor. To give a more pleasant illustration, we speak of a person's being *in love*; he is absorbed in his affection, and we could not express a tenth as much if we said that love is in the man. A man can be in a rage or in a passion, and even so was this man in an evil spirit. He was completely ruled by the Evil One. The poor creature had no power over himself whatever, and was not himself actually responsible; in all that I say of him I am not condemning him, but only using him as a type of human sin. Please do not forget this. As far as the narrative is concerned, the man himself scarcely appears; it is the unclean spirit that cries out, *Let us alone; . . . I know thee who thou art.* These are words spoken by the man, but they are the sentiments of the demon who used the man's organs of speech according to his own will. The man was scarcely a man with a will or wish of his own; in fact, you do not notice him till you see him flung down into the midst of the synagogue; you only see the proper man when the Savior raises him up before them all unharmed and rational. Until the miracle is worked, the man is lost in the unclean spirit that dominates him. Have you never seen such men?

You say sometimes, and you say truly, "Alas, poor wretch! The drink has the mastery over him; he would never do such things as he does if he was not in drink." We do not mean to excuse him by such an expression, far from it. Or it may be the man is a gambler, and you say, "He is quite infatuated with gambling; though he impoverishes his wife and children, yet he is possessed by that spirit so completely that he has not the mind nor the will to resist the temptation." Or it may be that such another person is carried away with impure affections, and we say, "How sad! There was something about that man which we used to like; in many points he was admirable, but now he is so deluded by his bad passions that he does not seem to be himself." We almost forget the man, and think mainly of the dreadful spirit which has degraded him below the beasts. The type and emblem of such a person as that, our Lord selected as the platform wherein to show his power. I wonder whether this voice of mine will reach one of that sort. I sincerely hope that none of you are in such a condition; but if you are, still there is hope for you in Christ Jesus. He is able to deliver such as are led captive at the will of Satan.

Though you seem wholly given up and utterly abandoned to the dominion of a terrible sin to which you yield a willing obedience, yet Jesus can break off the iron yoke from your neck and bring you into the liberty of holiness. It will be an awful thing for you to die in your sins, and you surely will unless you believe in the Lord Jesus; but if you look to him, he can make you pure and holy, and create you anew.

Note further, for we must show you how our Lord selects the worst of cases, that it was a man in whom the evil spirit was at his worst. Kindly look at the fourth chapter of Luke, verse 33, and you will see that in this man there was *a spirit of an unclean devil*. Think of that. The devil is never particularly clean at any time; what must an unclean devil be? The ruling spirit in the man was not only a devil, but also an *unclean* devil. Satan sometimes cleans himself up and comes out quite bright and shining, like an angel of light, but do not mistake him; he is still a devil, for all his pretended purity.

> Jesus can break off the iron yoke from your neck and bring you into the liberty of holiness.

There are glittering sins, and respectable sins, and these will ruin souls; but this poor man had a disreputable demon in him, a spirit of the foulest, coarsest, and most abominable order. I suppose this foul spirit would incite its victim to filthy talk and obscene acts. The Evil One delights in sins against the seventh commandment. If he can lead men and women to defile their bodies, he takes special delight in such crimes. I doubt not that this poor creature was reduced to the most brutal form of beastliness; I can well believe that in his body he was filthy, and that in his talk, in all the thoughts that hurried through his poor brain, and in all his actions, he went to a zenith of uncleanness upon which we need not permit a conjecture. If we were to say of such a character as this man pictures, "Let us turn out of the way," who could blame us? If we separated from such sinners, who could censure us?

We do not desire to go near to Satan in any shape, but most of all we would shun him when he is openly and avowedly unclean. You say, "We could not bear to hear the man speak; the very look of him is offensive"; nor is it strange that you should. There are women so fallen that modesty trembles to be seen in their company, and the feeling that makes you shudder at them is not to be condemned, so long as it does not spring from self-righteousness or lead to contempt. Yet now, see it and wonder, our blessed Lord and Master fixed his eye of old on the man with the unclean devil in him, and today he fixes his eye of mercy on the basest and vilest of mankind, that in their conversion he may show the power and authority of his Word. Lord, do so at this moment. Let us see today the miracles of your grace. Bring the chief of sinners to repentance! Raise those who are fallen to the lowest degree!

In this man there did not seem to be anything for the Lord to begin upon. When you are trying to bring a man to the Savior, you look over him to see where you can touch him, what there is in him that you can work upon. Perhaps he is a good husband though he is a drunkard, and you wisely attempt to work upon his domestic affections. If a man has some point of character upon which you can rest your lever, your work is comparatively easy. But with some people you look over them from top to bottom, and you cannot find a spot for hope to rest upon; they seem so utterly gone that there is neither reason, nor conscience, nor will, nor power of thought left in them. Of all this the possessed man in the synagogue is a striking emblem, for when the Lord comes into the synagogue the poor wretch does not begin to pray, "Lord, heal me." No, his first cry is, *Let us alone.* He does not seem to resist this cry of the evil spirit in him, though it was so much to his own injury, but he goes on to say, *What have we to do with thee, thou Jesus of Nazareth? art thou come to destroy us? I know thee who thou art.* The possessed man seems wholly lost in the dominating spirit of evil which permeates his entire being.

Now I look upon this, though it be negative, as a very glaring part of the difficulty; for I do not care how far a man has gone in outward sin, if he has some point left in him of common honesty, or love for his family, or generous heartedness, you know where to commence operations, and your work is hopeful. Even leviathan has some crevice between his scales though they be shut up together as with a close seal. There is some joint in the harness of most men, even though armor plates may cover them from head to foot; but in those outcasts of whom I am now speaking there is neither lodging for hope, nor foothold for faith, nor more than a bare ledge for love. As the man in the synagogue was shut up within the demon's influence, so are some men encompassed by their iniquity, blocked up by their depravity. Yet the great Raiser of the fallen can rescue even these; he is able to save unto the uttermost.

One other matter makes the case still more terrible: he was a man upon whom religious observances were lost. He was in the synagogue on the Sabbath, and I do not suppose that this was anything unusual. The worst man of all is one who can attend church, and yet remain under the full power of evil. Those poor outside sinners who know nothing of the gospel at all, and never go to the house of God at all, for them there remains at least the hope that the very novelty of the Holy Word may strike them; but as for those who are continually in our synagogues, what shall now be done for them if they remain in sin? It is singular, but true, that Satan will come to a place of worship. "Oh," say you, "surely he will never do that?" He did it as far back as the days of Job, when the sons of God came to present themselves before the Lord, and Satan came also among them. The evil spirit led this unhappy man to the synagogue that morning, and it may be that he did so with the idea of disturbing the teaching of the Lord Jesus Christ. I am glad he was there. I wish that more of the slaves of sin and Satan would attend Sabbath worship. They are then within range of the gospel gun, and who can tell how many may be reached?

Yet how sad it was that the influences of religious worship had altogether failed to rescue this man from his enslavement! They sang in the synagogue, but they could not sing the evil spirit out of him; they read the lessons of the day in the synagogue, but they could not read the foul spirit out of him; they gave addresses from passages of Scripture, but they could not address the unclean spirit out of him; no doubt some of the godly prayed for him, but they could not pray the devil out of him. Nothing can cast out Satan but the word of Jesus himself. His own word, from his own lips, has power and authority in it, but everything short of that falls to the ground. O Divine Redeemer, let your omnipotence be displayed in turning great sinners into sincere repentant souls!

You see, then, what a terrible case the Master selected. I have not exaggerated, I am sure. O the comfort which lies in the thought that he still chooses to save people, of whom this wretched being is the suitable emblem and representative! O you vilest of the vile, here is hope for you!

Let us now look a little further and observe that *our Lord encounters a firmly entrenched enemy.*

The evil spirit in this man had shielded himself against the assault of Christ, for as I have said, he had the man fully at his command; he could make him say and do whatever he pleased. He had that man so at his command that he brought him to the synagogue that day, and he compelled him to become a disturber of the worship. Quietness and order should be in the assemblies of God's people, but this poor soul was egged on to cry out and make horrible noises, so as to raise great tumult in the congregation. The Jews allowed all the liberty they could to persons possessed, and so long as their behavior was bearable they were tolerated in the synagogues; but this poor mortal broke through the bounds of propriety, and his cries were a terror to all. But see, the Lord Jesus deals with this disturber; this is the very man in whom he will be glorified. So have I seen my Lord convert his most furious enemy, and enlist unto his service the most violent of opposers.

The Evil One compelled his victim to beg to be left alone: as we have it here, *Let us alone.* In the Revised Version of Luke the same rendering is put in the margin, but in the text we have "Ah!" While the Lord Jesus was teaching, there was suddenly heard a terrible "Ah!" A horrible, hideous outcry startled everyone, and these words were heard: "Ah! *what have we to do with thee?*" It was not the voice of begging, it was distinctly the reverse. It was a prayer not *for* mercy, but *against* mercy. The translation is, however, quite good if we read, *Let us alone.*

Is it not a horrible thing that Satan leads men to say, "Do not trouble us with your gospel! Do not bother us with religion! Do not come here with your tracts! Let us alone!" They claim the wretched right to perish in their sins, the liberty to destroy their own souls. We know who rules when men speak thus: it is the Prince of Darkness who makes them hate the light. Oh, my hearers, do not some of you say, "We do not want to be worried with thoughts of death, and judgment, and eternity; we do not desire to hear about repentance and faith in a Savior. All we want of religious people is that they will let us alone." This cruel kindness we cannot grant them. How can we stand by and see them perish? Yet how sad the moral condition of one who does not wish to be made pure! You would think it impossible for Jesus to do anything with a man while he is crying out, *Let us alone*; yet it was the evil spirit in this man that our Lord met and overcame. Is there not encouragement for us to deal with those who give us no welcome, but shut the door in our faces?

The foul spirit made the man renounce all interest in Christ; he coupled him with himself, and made him say, *What have we to do with thee, thou Jesus of Nazareth?* This was a disclaimer of all connection with the Savior. He almost resented the Savior's presence as an intrusion. The voice seems to cry to Jesus, "I have nothing to do with you; go your way and leave me alone. I do not want you; whatever you can do to save or bless me is hereby refused. Only let me alone." Now, when a man deliberately says, "I will have nothing to do with your Jesus. I want no pardon, no salvation, no heaven," I think most of you would say, "That is a hopeless case; we had better go elsewhere." Yet even when Satan has led a man this length, the Lord can drive him out. He is mighty to save. He can change even the hardest heart.

> You would think it impossible for Jesus to do anything with a man while he is crying out, Let us alone; yet it was the evil spirit that our Lord met and overcame.

The unclean spirit did more than that: he caused this man to dread the Savior, and made him cry out, "Ah! *art thou come to destroy us?*" Many people are afraid of the gospel; to them religion wears a gloomy aspect. They do not care to hear of it for fear it should make them melancholy and rob them of their pleasures. "Oh," say they, "religion would get me into Bedlam; it would drive me mad." Thus Satan, by his detestable falsehoods, makes men dread their best friend, and tremble at that which would make them happy forever.

A further entrenchment Satan had cast up is this: he made his victim yield an outward assent to the gospel. *I know thee who thou art,* said the spirit, speaking with the man's lips, *the Holy One of God*. Of all forms of Satan's devices, this is one of the worst for workers, when men say, "Yes, yes, what you say is very correct!" You call upon them and talk about Jesus, and they answer, "Yes, sir. It is quite true. I am much obliged to you, sir." You preach the gospel, and they say, "He made an interesting conversation, and he is a very clever man!" You buttonhole them and speak about the Savior, and they reply, "It is very kind of you to talk to me so earnestly; I always admire this sort of thing. Zeal is much to be commended in these days." This is one of the strongest of earthworks, for the cannonballs sink into it, and their force is gone. This makes Satan secure in his hold on the heart. Yet the Savior dislodged this demon, and therein displayed his power and authority.

Have I not proved my point? Jesus selected a most unhappy individual to become an instance of his supremacy over the powers of darkness. He selected a most firmly entrenched spirit to be chased out of the nature which had become his stronghold.

We have something more pleasant to think upon as we notice that *our Lord conquered in a most notable manner.*

The conquest began as soon as the Savior entered the synagogue, and was thus under the same roof with the devil. Then the Evil One began to fear. That first cry of "Ah!" or *Let us alone*, shows that the evil spirit knew his Conqueror. Jesus had not said anything to the man. No, but the presence of Christ and his teaching are the terror of fiends. Wherever Jesus Christ comes in, Satan knows that he must go out. Jesus has come to destroy the works of the devil, and the Evil One is aware of his fate. Now, as soon as ever one of you shall go into a house with the desire to bring the inmates to Christ, it will be telegraphed to the bottomless pit directly. Insignificant person as you may think yourself, you are a very dangerous person to Satan's kingdom if you go in the name of Jesus and speak out his gospel. The Lord Jesus Christ opened the book and read in the synagogue, and soon his explanation and his teaching with authority and power made all the evil spirits feel that their kingdom was shaken. *I beheld*, said our Lord at another time, *Satan as lightning fall from heaven*, and that fall was commencing in this *beginning of the gospel of Jesus Christ, the Son of God*. The first token of our Lord's triumph was the evident alarm which caused the evil spirit to cry out.

The next sign was that the devil began to offer terms to Christ, for I take it that is the reason why he said, *I know thee who thou art, the Holy One of God*. He did not confront our Lord with the hostile doubt, *If thou be the Son of God*, but with the complaisant compliment, *I know thee who thou art*. "Yes," the false spirit said, "I will allow this man to say his creed, and declare himself as one of the orthodox ones, and then perhaps I shall be let alone. The man is sound in his views, and so my living in him cannot be a bad thing after all. I am quite willing to admit all the claims of Jesus, so long as he will not interfere with my rule over the man."

The Evil One had read his Bible, and knew how Daniel had called Jesus *the most Holy*, and so he calls him *the Holy One of God*. "I am quite willing to admit it all," says the devil, "only let me stop in the man; do not meddle with me, and this man's lips shall confess the truth." And so, when Jesus comes in his power, and men hear his word, this deceitful compromise is often proposed and attempted. The sinner says, "I believe it all. I deny nothing. I am no infidel, but I mean to keep my sin, and I do not intend to feel the power of the gospel so as to repent and have my sin chased out of me. I will agree to the gospel, but I will not allow it to control my life." However, this coming to terms shows that the fallen spirit knows his Destroyer. He would prefer to be let down easily. He is willing to crouch, to cringe, to fawn, and even to bear testimony to the truth, if he may but be allowed to keep in his den a human soul. Liar as he is, it must go sadly against the grain for him to say, *I know thee who thou art*; yet he will do this if he may be allowed to keep dominion. So when Jesus draws near to men's minds, they say, "We will be orthodox, we will believe the Bible, and we will do anything else you prescribe, only do not disturb our consciences, interfere with our habits, or dislodge our selfishness." Men will accept anything rather than renounce their sin, their pride, or their ease.

Then came our Lord's real work on this man. He gave the evil spirit short and sharp orders. "Silence! Come out!" *Jesus rebuked him.* The word implies that he spoke sharply to him. How else could he speak to one who was maliciously tormenting a man who had done him no harm? The Greek word might be read, "Be muzzled." It is a harsh word, such as an unclean, tormenting spirit deserves. "Silence! Come out!" That is exactly what Jesus means that the devil shall do when he delivers men from him. He says to him, "Come out of the man. I do not want pious talk and orthodox professing; hold your peace and come out of him."

It is not for evil spirits, nor yet for ungodly men, to try to honor Christ by their words. Traitors bring no honor to those they praise. Liars cannot bear witness to the truth, or if they do, they damage its cause. "Be still," says Jesus, and then, "Come out." He speaks as a man might call a dog out of a kennel. "Come out." "Oh," says the unclean spirit, "let me stay, and the man shall go to church; he shall even go to the sacrament." "No," says the Lord, "*Come out of him.* You have no right within him; he is mine, and not yours. *Come out of him!*" I pray that the Master may give one of his mighty calls at this moment, speak to some poor impaired creature, and say to the devil in him, *Come out of him!* O sinners, sin must leave you or it will ruin you forever; are you not eager to be rid of it?

Now see the conquest of Christ over the unclean spirit. The fiend did not dare to utter another word, though he went as near it as he could. He *cried with a loud voice.* He made an inarticulate howling as he left the man. As he came out he tried to do his victim some further injury, but in that also he failed. He tore at him, and threw him down in the midst of the synagogue, but Luke adds, *He came out of him, and hurt him not.* From the moment when Jesus commanded him to come out, his power to harm was gone; he came out like a whipped mongrel. See how Jesus triumphs. As he did this literally in the man in the synagogue, so he does it spiritually in thousands of cases. The last act of the fiend was malicious but fruitless. I have seen a poor creature rolled in the dust of despair by the departing Enemy, but he has soon risen to joy and peace. Have you not seen him in the inquiry room, weeping in the dismay of his spirit? But that has caused him no real harm; it has even been a benefit to him, by causing him to feel a deeper sense of sin, and by driving him quite out of himself to the Savior.

> If the Lord will speak with power today to any soul, however depraved, or impaired, his reigning sins shall come out of him.

Oh, what a splendid triumph this is for our Lord when out of a great sinner the reigning power of sin is expelled by a word! How our Master tramples on the lion and the viper! How he treads under his feet the young lion and the dragon! If the Lord will speak with power today to any soul, however vicious, or depraved, or impaired, his reigning sins shall come out of him, and the poor sinner shall become a trophy of his sovereign grace.

Lastly, *the Savior raises a great wonderment by what he did.* The people that saw this were more astonished than they generally were at the Savior's miracles, for they said, *What thing is this? what new doctrine is this? for with authority commandeth he even the unclean spirits, and they do obey him.* The wonder lay in this: here was man at his very lowest, he could not be worse. I have shown you the impossibility of anybody being worse than this poor creature was. I do not mean that he was evil morally, for, as I have hinted before, the moral element does not actually enter into the man's case; but he is the instructive picture of the worst man morally – utterly and entirely possessed of Satan, and carried away to an extreme degree by the force of evil.

Now, under the preaching of the gospel the worst man that lives may be saved. While he is listening to the gospel, a power goes with it which can touch the hardest heart, subdue the proudest will, change the most perverted affections, and bring the most unwilling spirit to the feet of Jesus. I speak now what I do know, because I have seen it in scores and hundreds of cases, that the least likely persons, about whom there seemed to be nothing whatever helpful to the work of grace or preparatory for it, have nevertheless been turned from the power of Satan unto God. Such have been struck down by the preaching of the gospel, and the devil has been made to come out of them, there and then, and they have become new creatures in Christ Jesus. This creates a great wonderment, and causes great staggering among the ungodly. They cannot understand it, but they ask, *What thing is this? what new doctrine is this?* This is a convincing sign which makes the most callous unbeliever question his unbelief.

Notice, in this case, that Jesus worked entirely and altogether alone. In most of his other miracles he required faith. In order to obtain salvation there must be faith; but this miracle before us is not a parable of man's experience so much as of Christ's working, and that working is not dependent upon anything in man. When a man is commanded to stretch out his withered hand, or told to go to the Pool of Siloam and wash, he does something; but in this case the man is ignored. If he does anything it is rather to resist than to assist. The devil makes him cry, *Let us alone; what have we to do with thee?* The Lord Jesus Christ displays here his sovereignty, his power, and his authority, utterly ignoring the man, consulting neither his will nor his faith, but sovereignly bidding the fiend, "Be silent and come out." The thing is done, and the man is delivered from his enslavement before he has had time to seek or pray.

The miracle seems to me to teach just this, that the power of Christ to save from sin does not lie in the person saved, it lies wholly in Jesus himself. And further, I learn that though the person to be saved may seem to be so far gone that you could scarcely expect faith within him, yet the gospel coming to him can bring faith with itself, and do its own work, *ab initio*, from the very beginning. What if I say that the gospel is a seed that makes its own soil! It is a spark that carries its own fuel with it; a life which can implant itself within the ribs of death, yes, between the jaws of destruction. The eternal Spirit comes with his own light and life and creates men in Christ Jesus to the praise of the glory of his grace. Oh, the marvel of this miracle! I was never led more greatly to admire the splendor of the power of Christ to rescue men from sin than at this hour.

And, to conclude, I notice that our Lord did nothing but speak. In other cases he laid his hand upon the diseased, or led them out of the city, or touched them, or applied clay, or used spittle; but in this case he does not use any instrumentality, his word is all. He says, *Hold thy peace, and come out of him*, and the unclean spirit is evicted. The word of the Lord has shaken the kingdom of darkness, and loosened the bonds of the oppressed. As when the Lord scattered the primeval darkness by the decree, *Let there be light*, so did Jesus give the word, and its own intrinsic power banished the messenger of darkness.

> The eternal Spirit comes with his own light and life and creates men in Christ Jesus to the praise of the glory of his grace.

Oh, you that preach Christ, preach him boldly! No coward lips must proclaim his invincible gospel! Oh, you that preach Christ, never choose your place of labor, never turn your back on the worst of mankind! If the Lord should send you to the borders of hell, go there and preach him with full assurance that it shall not be in vain.

Oh, you that would win souls, have no preference as to which ones they shall be, or, if you have a choice, select the very worst! Remember, my Master's gospel is not merely for the moralist in his respectable dwelling, but it is also for the abandoned and fallen in the filthy dens of the outcast. The all-conquering light of the Sun of Righteousness is not for the dim dawn alone, to brighten it into the full blaze of day, but it is meant for the blackest midnight that ever made a soul to shiver as in the shadow of death. The name of Jesus is high over all, in heaven, and earth, and sky; therefore, let us preach it with authority and confidence, not as though it were an invention of men. He has said he will be with us, and therefore nothing is impossible. The Word of the Lord Jesus cannot fall to the ground, and the gates of hell cannot prevail against it. The pleasure of the Lord shall prosper in his hand. The Lord shall bruise Satan under our feet shortly.

I have gone to great lengths because I desire to reach sinners who have gone to great lengths. Oh, that they would accept this message of amazing mercy! He who has come to save sinners is God, and this is the surest ground of hope for the very worst. Hear this, I pray you: it is the Lord your God who speaks to you, *Look unto me, and be ye saved, all the ends of the earth: for I am God, and there is none else.*

Chapter 10

How to Meet the Doctrine of Election

But he answered and said, I am not sent but unto the lost sheep of the house of Israel. Then came she and worshipped him, saying, Lord, help me. (Matthew 15:24-25)

You who know the loving heart of our Lord Jesus are quite sure that he would never needlessly discourage a soul in coming to him. Yet in this case *he answered her not a word*. Is Jesus dumb when misery begs a word from him? The Friend of Man is usually all attraction, encouragement, drawing, and welcoming, and yet the eager woman cries in vain to him for her tormented daughter! We are not disturbed about this. We know our Lord too well to suspect him of a lack of love. He is not sporting with a wounded bird. He is in no fit of bitterness. He would not even seem to discourage any heart that beats within a human bosom, unless there had been some great necessity for it, some gracious end to be served thereby.

Nobody will have the contempt to accuse our divine Lord of undue harshness toward a soul that sought his help. The world might suspect some of his ministers of being hard and cold, like your pulpits of marble which have in these chill times been exalted among the people. They might think some of us more touchy than tender; for are not some of us great stone creatures, almost without feeling, and not easy to be approached? People may suspect that we are scant in affection, or that we lack earnestness; they may even hint that we are too great sticklers for orthodoxy, or that we are so distrustful of our fellow men that we naturally love to try them with things harsh and forbidding, in order to keep them a good mile off at the least. I know they think us sorry fathers, more ready with the rod than with our cheering sympathies; but for this they have far too much justification. I wish it were not so. You may suppose hard things of us who are his servants: the supposition may be true, it may be slanderous; but you cannot suppose anything of the kind concerning the Lord Jesus Christ. He is so evidently loving, gracious, and cordial that you could not have the heart to suspect him.

If Jesus has ever received you, you have had in that fact unquestionable proof of his tenderness, and you are, and will be hereafter, confident in his compassion. You are sure that the *bruised reed shall he not break, and the smoking flax shall he not quench*, for he neither broke nor quenched you. Yet he did discourage this woman. Not only the disciples did so, but the Master did so too. Therefore, I say that there must have been a secret need for so doing; there must have been a motive for her good which moved the tender Lord to answer her with words so hard, and with language so dispiriting.

I believe that we, dear friends, the humble imitators of the Lord Jesus Christ, are bound to encourage all in whom there is any hopefulness. Whenever we see a wandering soul turning its face homewards, we should be ready to lend a hand to direct its tottering footsteps. Still, if we imitate our Lord, we may be led to say sore things which, like the faithful wounds of a friend, are as sharp as they are beneficial. Love's lips do not always drop honey. Flattery charms with her delightful sentences, but a wise affection often uses tones most harsh and cutting. There is a tendency among certain goody-goody people to comfort too much, and to keep back important truths for fear they should be misunderstood.

Glorious doctrines which made our fathers strong are left in the shade, for fear they should become stumbling blocks to unsettled minds. We are coming to be rather overdone with infants' prepared gospel; they are putting the flour through so many sieves that there will not be an ounce of bone-making material left in it. If it were always wise to comfort and encourage, the Master would have kept to that line of things, but, since he did not do so, I assume – and I think that none will dare to contradict me – that men require something else besides encouragement. Do we not read that *all Scripture is given by inspiration of God, and is profitable for doctrine, for reproof, for correction, for instruction in righteousness: that the man of God may be perfect, thoroughly furnished unto all good works*? There are truths which ought not to be kept back because they may not encourage, for their use is to reprove and correct. There are truths which at certain seasons ought to be told, even though the temporary effect thereof may be to dampen the fervency or to dull the hope of the sinner who is coming to Christ.

Like our Master, we must always long for the salvation of sinners, but, like him, we must go about it wisely. We must exhibit great fatherly tenderness toward sinners, and be very gentle, even as a shepherd is with the lambs; but yet that very love, that very tenderness, will lead the well-instructed teacher to utter many things which the disciple would rather not hear. Our shepherding deals not only with the green pastures, but also with the place of the sheep-washing and the shearing. We have not only to console, but also to correct. Ours is the edification which deals frequently with pulling down dilapidated bits of wall in order to secure the whole fabric, and therefore, we occasionally seem to be destroyers where we are really builders together with God. Our Lord knew that plain speech upon a certain truth would weed out his disciples. Did he therefore preserve a discreet silence? No. In due time he delivered his soul, and we read that *from that time many of his disciples went back, and walked no more with him*.

We come now to consider why the Savior spoke to this woman in this way. Why did he announce to her a fact which could not possibly assist or strengthen her faith? We may learn the answer as we proceed.

Our Lord Jesus more or less discouraged the Syrophenician woman with the doctrine of election. I grant you that there is a difference between the election of the nation of Israel and the election of individuals, but into that we are not going now. The point is this: it was the doctrine of election which the Savior threw in this poor woman's way. He said to her, *I am not sent but unto the lost sheep of the house of Israel.* This was enough to dampen her spirit, surely, and yet the Savior put it before her there and then.

Why? I think he did so, first, at that time, that it might come from him rather than from the disciples. If you feel it needful that a person should be somewhat sharply rebuked, you conclude to do it yourself. You say to yourself, "If I send that message by the best friend I have, he will blunder over it; he will make it more cutting than I meant it to be, and yet he will miss the point. He will inflict more pain than I intended; therefore, I will communicate the unacceptable statement myself." And have you not often felt it to be a matter of real urgency to get before all others? Yes, you who have the care of hearts and minds know that there are times when you want to do all the speaking, and would like to block every other telephone in the world. You know the person, and the effect which statements are likely to have upon him, and therefore you would rather monopolize his ears for a season.

The Savior knew that by and by this woman would hear that the mission of the Christ was only to Israel, and she might hear it in such a way as would much more depress her spirit than if he personally told it to her himself. So he himself said to her, "I am not sent to Tyre and Sidon. *I am not sent but unto the lost sheep of the house of Israel.*" That is to say, Christ's mission as a prophet while he was here in the flesh was to Israel, and to Israel he usually restricted his labors throughout his life. He told her that himself, I think, lest she should hear it secondhand.

It will be wise for us, when we find poor souls hopefully coming to Christ, to manifest thought and prudence, and introduce them to the deeper truths of our theology, because they will hear of them one way or another, and they had better hear of them first from loving, tenderhearted Christians, than from hard, careless, loveless spirits, whose delight is found in mere terms and phrases. You cannot keep these young people in a conservatory; why would you wish to do so? It is poor policy to try and conceal truth. It has a little of a Jesuitical look about it. Why should this particular truth be concealed? Are we ashamed of it? If so, let us revise our creed, but in the name of common honesty let us hide nothing which we believe. The more light the better. The more fully truth is made known, the more surely will good come of it. For one, I bless God that I knew the doctrines of grace from my youth; they have been the staff of my manhood, and I believe they will be the glory of my old age. So far from being ashamed of the election of grace, it commands the enthusiasm of my whole being.

Again, I think that he brought that truth before her mind just then because she might have heard of it otherwise, when she was in a worse condition for the receiving of it. Now, this woman was desperately set on getting a blessing from Christ. Her whole heart was awake; her spirit was on fire; her whole nature was eager for the blessing. If she could stand repression at any time in her life, it was just then. "How do you know?" say you. I know it by a kind of instinct. The story opens for me a window into the woman's soul. I am persuaded that the Master would not have applied anything that looked like a discouraging truth to her unless he had perceived that she was quite able to bear it, and perhaps better able to bear it *then* than upon some future day.

I think there is great wisdom in communicating truth to people at a suitable time. Did not the Lord himself say, *I have yet many things to say unto you, but ye cannot bear them now*? Just at that time his disciples were unfit to hear those many truths, and therefore the oracle of love was silent for a while. At another time the Savior abounded toward them, as he does toward us, in all wisdom and care, and then he made known to them the mystery of his will after a fuller measure. The Lord does not teach us all truth at once, but by degrees he admits us into the chambers of his hidden treasure. You know how a surgeon, when he has operated upon a blinded eye, says to his patient, "Your sight is completely restored, but during the next few days I must ask you to sit in a darkened room. I shall ask you to receive light slowly, that you may retain it surely."

> Infinite is the wisdom of the Holy Spirit in gradually enlightening souls.

Infinite is the wisdom of the Holy Spirit in gradually enlightening souls. The Lord does not all at once let the sinner know the full extent of his sin, nor does he give him a full idea of the punishment due to it; nor, I think, does he give him at the beginning all the knowledge he will have of the complete pardon of his sin, and of the innumerable joys which come to pardoned sinners through Jesus Christ their Savior. It is done little by little, as we must feed needy-born children, not with meat, but with milk; little by little, as you teach the younger scholars in the school. Precept must be upon precept, line upon line, here a little and there a little. His mission to the house of Israel was one of the truths which the Savior saw this poor Canaanite woman would have to learn, and therefore he communicated it to her when she had faith enough to move beyond all discouragement and obtain the blessing upon which her heart was set.

These two things should prove instructive. Now I go on to deal with souls who are somewhat in this woman's case. I shall notice *the discouraging word which has come to them of late,* which is somewhat similar to that which came to her; and then I shall ask them to imitate *the commendable act of this woman* in connection with her discouragement, for though she seemed to be repulsed, she nevertheless came to Christ and worshipped him.

Before concluding, I wish to mention a few helpful considerations to any who may be troubled by that great doctrine which I mentioned just now. Come, Holy Comforter, and fill our hearts with heavenly cheer from this glad hour!

First, then, *is the discouraging word that came to this woman.* It was, as I have said, a certain form of the doctrine of election: the unquestioned truth that God designed to bless the seed of Israel by the personal labors and testimonies of his Son Jesus, and that these blessings were not at that time sent to the people of Tyre and Sidon.

The doctrine of election has been made into a great bugaboo by its unscrupulous opponents and its graceless friends. I have read some very "wonderful" sermons against this doctrine, in which the first thing that was evident was that the person speaking was totally ignorant of his subject. A little knowledge would have made him hesitate and deliberate, and therefore it was like Saul's armor to him; he had rather proceed in his naked folly. The usual way of composing a sermon against the doctrine of grace is this: first exaggerate and misrepresent the doctrine, and then argue against it. If you state the sublime truth as it is found in the Bible, why, you cannot say much against it; but if you collect a number of silly expressions from hotheaded partisans, and denounce these, your task will be easier. Dress up the doctrine like a guy, and then burn it! What a wonderful deal has been done by men in burning figures of their own stuffing!

Nobody ever believed the doctrine of election as I have heard it stated by Arminian controversialists. I venture to say that nobody out of Bedlam ever did believe that which has been imputed to us. Is it remarkable that we are as eager to denounce the dogmas imputed to us as ever our opponents can lie? Why do they earnestly set themselves to debunk what no one defends? They might as well spare themselves the trouble. Our friends abhor the doctrine as it is stated by themselves, and we are much of their mind, though the doctrine itself – as we would state it – is as dear to us as life itself. They suppose that we never preach the gospel freely to sinners, which thing we never fail to do with a freeness which none can excel. Can they tell us how we can improve in gospel preaching, for we should rejoice to learn? They say that if we preach the gospel freely we are inconsistent, to which charge we are at no pains whatever to reply. So long as we believe that we are consistent with Scripture, it never enters into our heads to want to be consistent with ourselves.

To hold all revealed truth is our desire, but to compress it all into a symmetrical creed is beyond our expectation. We are such poor fallible creatures that if we were once to fabricate a system which should be entirely logical, we should feel sure that we must have admitted portions of theory and masses of mere guesswork into the singular fabric. In theology we live by faith, not by logic. We believe and are safe; but the moment we begin to speculate, we are like Peter sinking in the waves. If we will keep simply to what the Word of God says, we shall find in it truths apparently in conflict, but in reality always in agreement.

On every subject there is a truth which is set over against another truth. The one is as true as the other; the one does not take away from the other, nor raise a question upon the other; but the one ought to be stated as well as the other, and the two set side by side. The two relative truths make up the great road of practical truth, along which our Lord travels to bless the souls of men. Some like to run on one rail. I confess a partiality to the two, and I would not like to make an excursion tomorrow on a railway from which one of the rails had been taken.

It must be sorrowfully admitted that the doctrine of election may have discouraged some who were seeking the Savior, but the truth is that *it ought not to do so.* Viewed rightly, it is a royal herald arrayed in silk and gold, freely announcing to the unworthy that the King receives sinners, according to the good pleasure of his will. How it has encouraged some of us! What marrow and fatness it is to us now that we have found the Lord! We feed upon it as upon a divine portion which sustains, satisfies, and satiates the soul. When I first came to Christ I was perfectly satisfied to be as one of the dogs under the table, but I would not be satisfied to be so now, since the Lord has called me to a higher place. Now that I have become one of his children, I am as Lazarus was, of whom we read, *but Lazarus was one of them that sat at the table with him.* The blessed doctrine of election is to my soul as wines on the lees well refined. It is a better, deeper, and more glorious fact of divine love than I ever hoped to realize. *He asked water, and she gave him milk; she brought forth butter in a lordly dish.* We asked for pardon, but he gave us justification; we asked for a little mercy, but the Lord gave us boundless grace, yes, grace upon grace, saying, *I have loved thee with an everlasting love: therefore with lovingkindness have I drawn thee.* If a sinner really knew the doctrine of the choice of grace, he would not run away from it, but he would be inclined to run into its arms.

Yet to many it does seem to be as that black side of the cloud which the Lord turned upon the Egyptians; and therefore I am going to notice the discouragement as Christ put it before this woman. He said to her first, *I am not sent but unto the lost sheep of the house of Israel.* "I am sent," he seemed to say, "to the Jews. I am sent to the house of Israel, but I am not sent to you." That great truth she would have been sure to find out sooner or later, and if she had found it out later, she might have feared that the cure of her daughter would be taken away from her because it had been received contrary to the mission of the Messiah. Jesus lets her know this hard truth at once, so that it may not worry her afterwards. When she did obtain the cure of her daughter, he would have her know that it was given openly and aboveboard, and not by a blunder of pity, or an oversight of charity. She was to be once for all assured that the Lord Jesus had not forgotten himself, that he knew all about the limitation of his commission during his mortal life, and that in overstepping it he knew what he was doing, and had not been wafted beyond himself by the vehemence of his spirit.

Now, there is such a thing as *the choice of God.* The Lord has a people who are redeemed from among men. The Lord Jesus has a people of whom he has said, *Thine they were, and thou gavest them me.* Some are ordained unto eternal life and therefore believe in the Lord Jesus Christ. Does this fact discourage you? I do not see why it should. Why should you not be among that number? "But suppose that I am not?" says one. Why do you not suppose that you are? You do not know anything about it; therefore, why suppose at all? To give up supposing would be a far more sensible thing than to brew for yourself a deadly potion of despair out of the worthless husks of mere supposition. I have enough to do to bear up under facts without overloading myself with conjectures. What God has not revealed we are not bound to know. Indeed, it would seem better for us to be in ignorance where the Lord grants no information.

The Lord has chosen a people to be saved, and I feel glad to think that he has done so, for none can prove that I am not of the number. If there are some whom God will save, then I know also who they are, for he tells me that they are those who repent of sin, confess it, forsake it, and believe in the Lord Jesus Christ unto eternal life. These same things would my soul desire to do, and when I do so, I know that I am of the chosen number, and shall be saved. What is there in this to discourage a soul? Yet it does discourage some. When people are in the dark they are afraid of anything, everything, and nothing! *There were they in great fear, where no fear was.* Once a person gets into a low and nervous state, and the fall of a leaf suggests an avalanche, the least shadow of a cloud foretells the total extinction of the orb of day, while a drop of rain is the commencement of the final conflagration! "Odd expression," say you. Yet it is not so singular and outrageous as many of the inferences drawn by a resolute despondency. Alas, for these troubled ones, they feel that they cannot be saved because there is an Israel whom God has chosen to be saved!

Our Lord put before this woman something worse than the positive fact of the choice of Israel: he declared *the negative side of the sacred choice.* He said, *I am not sent but unto the lost sheep of the house of Israel.* It is very little that you and I who are ministers of the gospel have to do with preaching about what Christ is not sent to do. Here I fear that unrenewed minds, armed with a pitiless logic, have sinned grievously

> **What God has not revealed we are not bound to know.**

against the love of God. Truth treated scripturally is a holy medicine, but treated after the manner of the schools it may sour into a deadly poison. Poor repentant hearts, there is nothing in the divine decree to shut out one of you from hope. The Lord said, *I have not spoken in secret, in a dark place of the earth: I said not unto the seed of Jacob, Seek ye me in vain.* Nevertheless, the Savior did distinctly turn the blackest side of the doctrine to the woman, and say, *I am not sent but unto the lost sheep of the house of Israel.*

What was worse in her case was that she knew that this election, as far as Christ had stated it, must exclude her; for he told her that he was sent to save only the house of Israel, and she well knew that she did not belong to that house. She was a Canaanite woman, a native of Tyre and Sidon, and therefore distinctly shut out, and Jesus himself had told her so. That must have made the sentence fall like a death knell on her ears. If the servants tell us such a thing as that, we can forget it; but if the Master says, *I am not sent but unto the lost sheep of the house of Israel,* then the matter ends in blank despair. The poor Canaanite woman might very logically have ended her pleadings, saying, "What more can be done? I cannot go against the word from Christ's own lips." Yet she did not say so; but like a true heroine she pressed her suit even to the joyful end. You see her cause for discouragement as much worse than yours can ever be, for you do not know that you are shut out: there is nothing in your race or city which excludes you.

> If you have never gathered from any ministry that there is no hope for you, you have no right to come to such a conclusion.

Moreover, Christ has never told you that you are shut out. I do not think that any minister has ever told you so; and if you have never gathered from any ministry under heaven that there is no hope for you, you have no right to come to such a conclusion. In my soul's intent I have never desired the discouragement of a single soul among you all. Far rather would I die that you might live. But if you have spoken out bitter words, and have come to wretched conclusions, then I would urge you to be as sensible and as brave as this woman was, who, when she had not gathered it from ministers but had received it from Christ himself that he was not sent to such as she was, nevertheless she persevered, and pressed forward, and came to him and worshipped him, saying, *Lord, help me.*

Some may say to me this evening, "Why talk about this difficulty at all?" I talk about it because it exists. It frets and worries many minds. Many are troubled, and the servants of God must deal with their trouble. Gladly enough would I leave these fears alone if they would leave my people alone. The stern fact of predestination meets most men somewhere or other, and even in the paths of philosophy it has not escaped; and when it comes darkly over truly gracious souls, much of its power for mischief will lie in the ignorance of the person attacked. If we were better instructed we would probably find no mystery where all is a mystery now.

Men forget that the ordination of God deals with everything: not only with the spiritual, but quite as certainly also with the natural world. Yet they never allow it to interfere with their labor for bread, their struggle for wealth, or their race for fame. Why should they dissociate the matter of salvation from the ten thousand affairs which are enclosed in the same ring? Why will men act in other matters according to common sense, and upon this matter make molehills into mountains? They fancy that the will of God settles one or two matters, and leaves all the rest loose; they dream that it takes away free agency and responsibility, and makes men into machines. They cannot understand that divine plan which interferes with no will of man, and yet secures the will of God; nor can they see how everything proceeds by the free agency of the creature, as much as if there were no God, and yet God rules over all. I wish that this subject did not vex men, but it is vain to wish that. It has vexed them from the beginning, and it will vex them even to the end. Since we cannot alter facts, we must deal with them.

Dear troubled souls, Jesus would have you come to him without fear. He invites you to trust in him; yes, more, he commands you to believe on his name. Nothing he has thought, or ordained, or purposed, or predestinated has any tendency to drive you from him. Whatever predestination may or may not be, this one thing is sure: *Christ Jesus came into the world to save sinners.* Everything beckons towards his cross and himself. Come, and let nothing hinder you even for a single hour.

Now, observe *the commendable act of this woman.* In considering what she did, we shall come to the practical part of the subject. And I notice that she did not attempt for a single moment to deny what Jesus had said. He said, *I am not sent but unto the lost sheep of the house of Israel*, and she did not reply, "Lord, that is not true." She did not question anything which Jesus asserted; that would have been gross presumption on her part. She did not quibble, or object, or raise opposition. She accepted what Jesus said without any argument whatever. She did not attempt to say that it was unjust that the Christ of God should come only to the house of Israel. She did not assert, as some have shamelessly done, that God should deal with one as with another, or else he would be a respecter of persons. All that kind of thing, which we have heard so often, was far from her mind. She was silent and submissive as to the Savior's speech. She did not even argue that surely, in her solitary instance, she might be permitted to break through the regulation. She did not argue at all. She left the truth, which to her was dark, in the keeping of him whose name is light. She sees the black cloud, but she passes through it, feeling that it cannot be anything more than a cloud, and so she comes to the Savior's feet and cries, "Lord, help me. I do not understand this. I am all in a fog, and all in a muddle. Lord, help me. Lord, I do not ask to understand, but I do cry for help. Enable me to believe and to receive the blessing. Let the dark truth say what it may."

Many persons are so weak in judgment that if they have to do battle with a difficulty before they can be saved, they will perish in the attempt. Oh, poor heart, do not battle with a difficulty at all! Learn it alone. If it be a great truth for *men*, and you are nothing but a *babe*, and hardly that, do not choke yourself with man's meat. If a great mystery meddles with you, then fly to Jesus Christ for relief from it, with this prayer in your mouth: "Lord, help me. I am in a difficulty, help my understanding; I am in despondency, help my heart; but especially, I am full of iniquity, help my poor and sorrowful case, and do for me what I cannot do for myself. Save my soul and deliver me." Now then, we have seen what she did not do, and in this she is admirable, but let us see what the woman actually did. She came to Jesus.

Read the words: *Then came she and worshipped him.*

First, she came to Jesus, and did not go round about. She came not to Peter, or James, or John, but she came to Jesus. She did not stand still and cry, as she had done before from a distance, crying unto him; but she came to Jesus, drew near to him, grasped him, and I do not doubt, fell at his feet as though she would have held him. She came to Jesus. Now, from everything beneath the heavens, poor soul, fly you to the living, personal Christ.

There is such a One now living as Jesus Christ, the Savior of sinners, whose delight it is to deal with the sicknesses, infirmities, and diseases of men. Do not, I pray you, stop in doctrines, or in precepts, or in ministers, or in services; but come straightaway to Christ – the living, personal Savior, anointed of the Lord. In him your hope lies. "Which way shall I go?" say you. If it were a matter of physical coming, I know that if the road were long and dreary, you would start upon it now without delay. But it is a mental coming. You are to come to Jesus not with feet and legs, but with mind and heart. Remember that there is such a Person. Consider him. Think of him. Believe him. Reverence him, for he is the Son of the Highest. Trust him, for he is *mighty to save.*

> Sooner shall heaven and earth pass away than Jesus fail to save the soul that trusts in him.

This is coming to him. Since he is a Savior, let him fulfill his office upon you. You greatly need saving, so give him the opportunity of showing what he is able to do. Say within your own soul, "I, the chief of sinners, am lost, ruined, and undone. Behold, I come to him. If I perish, I will perish trusting in him." It cannot be that a soul can die relying upon Jesus; sooner shall heaven and earth pass away than Jesus fail to save the soul that trusts in him.

The woman came to Jesus immediately after he uttered this word of discouragement. We read in the text, "*Then* she came." *Then came she and worshipped him.* What, *then*? When he seemed to drive her away? Then? Why, he had just told her that he was not sent to her. *Then came she.* He had just uttered a most mysterious and discouraging truth, but *then came she.* That kind of faith which comes to Christ only on a summer's day among the lilies of the field is not of much account. Flowers and butterflies and all things which come of the calm and the bright are soon gone; we need a hope which can survive the frost. That is the sort of faith which comes to Jesus in the middle of winter, when the cold kicks, and the fierce blast prowls among the snowdrifts. That is the faith which saves the soul – the faith which ventures to the Savior in all types of weather. Saving faith learns to credit contradictions, to laugh at impossibilities, and to say, "It cannot be, but yet it will be."

Our poor friend who was buffeted by our Lord's word was secretly upheld by the sight of his person. What can a word be compared with a person – compared with such a person as that of Jesus, the Sinner's Friend? She believes *him* rather than his way of speaking. He says that he is not sent, but there he is. He says that he is not sent but to the lost sheep of the house of Israel, and yet *there he is.* He has come here where there are none of the house of Israel. She seems to say to herself, "Whether he was sent or not, here he is. He has come among Tyrians and Sidonians, and I have come to him; therefore, he is not kept from me by his commission. I do not understand his language, but I do understand the look of his face, I do understand his manner. I do understand the winsomeness of his blessed person. I can see that compassion dwells in the Son of David. I am sure that he has all power given to him to heal my daughter, and here he is. I do not know about his commission, but I do know him, and I shall still plead with him." So she came to Jesus there and *then*, and why should you not also?

Now, soul, is this the darkest night that ever was over you? Come to Jesus now. Are you quite sure that your case is hopeless? Quite certain that your doom is sealed? Have you written out your own death warrant? Have you made a covenant with death and are in league with hell? Do you feel sure that you will be damned before the morning light breaks on you? Then come to Jesus Christ *now. Then came she.* That is the thing: to come to Christ when he has a drawn sword in his hand, as Bunyan puts it; to come to Christ when he frowns; to come to Christ when everything says, "Keep back." *Then came she.* Brave woman! I will even do the same.

But now notice how she came. *Then came she* **and worshipped him** (emphasis added). My heart greatly rejoices. I wish I could picture the scene. She did not stop to work out the difficult question which he posed to her, but she looked at him, and she came to him, and when she got near to him she did the best thing she could: she worshipped him. Down she went on her face before him, and when she did look up it was with a look of reverent awe and childlike confidence. Blessed be his name, if we cannot understand him, we can worship him.

Now, you have been thinking about yourself, and the more you do this the more you will become despondent and despairing. No possible comfort can come to you by that road. If I were you, I would give up that task and now begin to think about Jesus, the Son of God, the Savior of men. "Oh, but I am such a sinner!" Yes, and he is such a Savior. "Sir, I am so black!" But he is able to make us whiter than snow. "Alas, I greatly deserve his curse!" Yes, but he was *made a curse for us: for it is written, Cursed is every one that hangeth on a tree.* By death the Lord has put that curse away. Behold him, then, upon the cross removing human sin, and see if you cannot copy the woman's example: *Then came she and worshipped him.* Now try, poor fainthearted spirit, try and worship. This is a homage which a humble heart can render in acceptable style.

A self-conceited heart will do anything sooner than worship. Pride, and self, and rebellion cannot worship, but humble hearts are happy in the deed. Oh, that you would now bow with me before the Lamb of God! Worship him now! "Blessed Son of God! Blessed Son of God! that ever you should become man for men, and die in the sinner's stead! Oh, your love! Your wondrous love! And you are gone up into glory now. You sit at the right hand of God, and there I worship you as my Lord and my God. If I may not call you my Savior, yet you shall be my God. If I may not rejoice in you, at least I will worship you." This is holy talk. It has a perfume about it which the Lord loves. That way faith will come to you. That way life and peace and rest will come to you. This trembling Canaanite came to him and worshipped him. Follow her and share her blessedness.

> Pride, and self, and rebellion cannot worship, but humble hearts are happy in the deed.

Then, notice *her prayer.* One has well observed that if you were on a rotten piece of ice, and you could not get to the shore, or feared that you could not, one of the very best ways would be to go down on all fours and try to crawl along as gingerly as you could, and long to leave the ice and get on to the shore somehow. This woman proceeds this way. She seems to fall flat upon that awful truth which she cannot understand. She adores and worships and reverences him who spoke it, and thus she outspreads her weakness upon every possible resting place, and comes safely to shore. "Lord," she says, "help me. Oh, do not put me back, but help me. Lord, do not leave me, but help me. Whatever you have to say to me, say it, and I will worship you while you say it.

> Though you slay me, I will trust,
> Praise you even from the dust;

but Lord, help me." My dear hearer, do that, and do it *now*. No doctrine will trouble you for long. I am sure it will not. On the contrary, you will ask why you did ever let it trouble you. Do you ever let predestination trample you in the matter of your daily business? Tomorrow you hope to make a few shillings at your daily calling, but it may be that you will not, you may lose it. Why do you not say to yourself, "It may be that the providence of God has arranged that I shall not earn anything tomorrow; therefore, I shall stop at home and do nothing"? Why, you are not such a fool. You will take down your shop shutters, display your goods, and do your best, or you will go out to your calling and look for your usual wage. Let the providence of God do what it may, your business is to do what you can. So it is with a poor seeking soul; that soul's business is to let the Lord do what he wills, but meanwhile to cry, "Lord, help me." Wholly submissive, but heartily adoring, lie at Jesus' feet and believe that this divine Savior must and will save every soul that hangs upon him. This is the way of wisdom, follow it. God help you to do so, and to do so at once.

> There never was yet a soul that came to Christ and Christ did cast it away.

I do not think that I need to say anything more by way of comforting you, for that may well suffice, if the Lord shall incline your heart to seek his face at once. Remember this, however, that there never was yet a soul that came to Christ and Christ did cast it away. Remember, again, that there never can be such a soul, for he has said, *Him that cometh to me I will in no wise cast out*. Remember, again, that every soul that ever did come to Christ came because the Father drew him, and that every soul that came found out afterwards that there was an election of grace that encompassed him, and that he was in it. Even this poor woman turned out to be one whom Christ was sent to bless. Although, as a general matter of fact, in his lifetime he came to the seed of Israel, just as the prophets came to Israel, yet there always appeared to be an exception with the prophets, and therefore it was no marvel that there should be exceptions in the case of their Lord.

Many widows were in Israel in the days of Elijah, but unto none of them was the prophet sent except to a woman of Zarephath, who belonged to the very city out of which this woman came. Many lepers were in Israel in the days of Elisha, yet none of them was healed except Naaman the Syrian. Naaman did not belong to the favored race at all, but was a far-off stranger, and yet he received the blessing of healing from the Lord God of Israel. The election of God as to these temporal things did seem to exclude all but the seed of Israel, but it only seemed that way; there were always some strangers in the chosen line, and so that particular form of election which consisted of our Lord's personal ministry being only to the Jews did not cause the exclusion of this poor believing woman. To her Jesus Christ had manifestly come in the chosen line, for *there he was!* He was outside his own boundary! He had come to her!

Now, at this moment, whatever you may think about this doctrine or that, *Jesus Christ has come to you*. I have preached to you his truth, and you have heard it. Yes, and you have felt something of its power. Yield to it, I beg you. If you yield to it, and come to him and trust him, then rejoice that the lines of electing love have encompassed you. You are his. You could not and would not have come to him in prayer and simple faith if it had not been so. Your coming to him proves that his eternal love of old went after you. Go home, O woman of a sorrowful spirit, and be sad no more. The Lord bless you, for Christ's sake. Amen.

Chapter 11

The Little Dogs

But he answered and said, It is not meet to take the children's bread, and to cast it to dogs. And she said, Truth, Lord: yet the dogs eat of the crumbs which fall from their masters' table. (Matthew 15:26-27)

But Jesus said unto her, Let the children first be filled: for it is not meet to take the children's bread, and to cast it unto the dogs. And she answered and said unto him, Yes, Lord: yet the dogs under the table eat of the children's crumbs. (Mark 7:27-28)

I quote the two records of Matthew and Mark so that we may have the whole matter before us. May the Holy Spirit bless our meditations thereon.

The brightest jewels are often found in the darkest places. Christ had not found such faith, no, not even in Israel, as he discovered in this poor Canaanite woman. The borders and fringes of the land were more fruitful than the center, where the agriculture had been more abundant. In the headlands of the field, where the farmer does not expect to grow much beyond weeds, the Lord Jesus found the richest ear of corn that as yet had filled his sheaf. Let those of us who reap after him be encouraged to expect the same experience. Never let us speak of any district as too depraved to yield us converts, nor of any class of persons as too fallen to become believers. Let us go even to the borders of Tyre and Sidon, though the land be under a curse, for even there we shall discover some elect one, ordained to be a jewel for the Redeemer's crown. Our heavenly Father has children everywhere.

In spiritual things it is found that the best plants often grow in the most barren soil. Solomon spoke of trees, and discussed the hyssop on the wall and the cedar in Lebanon. So it is in the natural world, where the great trees are found on great mountains, and the minor plants in places adapted for their tiny roots. But it is not so among the plants of the Lord's right-hand planting, for there we have seen the cedar grow upon the wall – great saints in places where it was apparently impossible for them to exist; and we have seen hyssops growing upon Lebanon – a questionable, insignificant devotion, where there have been innumerable advantages. The Lord is able to make strong faith exist with little knowledge, little present enjoyment, and little encouragement; and strong faith in such conditions triumphs and conquers, and doubly glorifies the grace of God. Such was this Canaanite woman, a cedar growing where soil was scant enough. She was a woman of amazing faith, though she could have heard but little of him in whom she believed, and perhaps had never seen his person at all until the day when she fell at his feet and said, *Lord, help me.*

Faith has a strong attraction for the Lord Jesus.

Our Lord had a very quick eye for spying faith. If the jewel was lying in the mire, his eye caught its glitter; if there was a choice ear of wheat among the thorns, he failed not to perceive it. Faith has a strong attraction for the Lord Jesus; at the sight of it *the king is held in the galleries* and cries, *Thou hast ravished my heart with one of thine eyes, with one chain of thy neck.* The Lord Jesus was charmed with the fair jewel of this woman's faith, and watching it and delighting in it he resolved to turn it around and set it in other lights, so that the various facets of this priceless diamond might each one flash its brilliance and delight his soul. Therefore he tried her faith by his silence and by his discouraging replies so that he might see its strength; but he was all the while delighting in it and secretly sustaining it, and when he had sufficiently tried it, he brought it forth as gold, and set his own royal mark upon it in these memorable words: *O woman, great is thy faith: be it unto thee even as thou wilt.*

I am hopeful that perhaps some poor soul that is under very discouraging circumstances may nevertheless be led to believe in the Lord Jesus Christ with a strong and persevering faith; and though as yet it enjoys no peace and has seen no gracious answer to prayer, I trust that its struggling faith may be strengthened by the example of the Canaanite woman.

I gather from the story of her appeal to the Lord Jesus and her success therein, four facts. The first is: *faith's mouth cannot be closed*; the second is: *faith never disputes with God*; the third is: I perceive that *faith argues mightily*; and the fourth is: *faith wins her suit.*

The mouth of faith can never be closed, for if ever the faith of a woman was tried so as to make her cease from prayer, it was that of this daughter of Tyre. She had difficulty after difficulty to encounter, and yet she could not be put off from pleading for her little daughter, because she believed in Jesus as the great Messiah, able to heal all manner of diseases, and she meant to pray to him until he yielded to her urgency, for she was confident that he could chase the demon from her child.

Observe that *the mouth of faith cannot be closed even on account of the closed ear and the closed mouth of Christ.* He answered her not a word. She spoke very pitifully, she came and threw herself at his feet, her child's case was very urgent, her motherly heart was very tender, and her cries were very piercing, and yet he answered her not a word. As if he were deaf and dumb, he passed her by; yet she was not staggered. She believed in him, and even he himself could not make her doubt him, let him try silence even if he would.

It is hard to believe when prayer seems to be a failure. I wish to God that some poor seeker here might believe that Jesus Christ is able and willing to save, and so fully believe it that his unanswered prayers shall not be able to make him doubt. Even if you should pray in vain by the month together, do not allow a doubt about the Lord Jesus and his power to save to cross your mind. What if you cannot yet grasp the peace which faith must ultimately bring you? What if you have no certainty of forgiveness of your sin? What if no gleams of joy should visit your spirit? Yet you believe him who cannot lie. *Though he slay* me, said Job, *yet will I trust in him.* That was splendid faith. It would be a big deal for some if they could say, "Though he strikes me, yet will I trust him"; but Job said, *Though he slay me.* If he puts on the garb of an executioner, and comes out against me as though he would destroy me, yet will I believe him to be full of love. He is good and gracious still, I cannot doubt it, and therefore at his feet I will lie down and look up, expecting grace at his hands. Oh, for such faith as this! O soul, if you have it, you are a saved man, as sure as you are alive. If even the Lord's apparent refusal to bless you cannot close your mouth, your faith is of a noble sort, and salvation is yours.

In the next place, *her faith could not be silenced by the conduct of the disciples.* They did not treat her well, but yet perhaps not altogether ill. They were not like their Master, but frequently repulsed those who would come to him. Her noise annoyed them, she kept to them with boundless perseverance, and therefore they said, *Send her away, for she crieth **after us*** (emphasis added). Poor soul, she never cried after *them*, but after their Master.

Sometimes disciples become very important in their own eyes, and think that the pushing and crowding to hear the gospel is caused by the people's eagerness to hear *them*, whereas nobody would care for their poor talk if it were not for the gospel message which they are charged to deliver. Give us any other theme, and the multitude would soon melt away. Though weary of the woman's urgent cries, they acted somewhat kindly towards her, for they were evidently desirous that she should obtain the blessing she sought, or else our Lord's reply would not have been appropriate: *I am not sent but unto the lost sheep of the house of Israel.* It was not her daughter's healing that they cared for, but they considered their own comfort, for they were anxious to be rid of her. *Send her away,* said they, *for she crieth after us.* Still, though they did not treat her as men should treat a woman, as disciples should treat a seeker, and as Christians should treat everybody, yet for all that, her mouth was not stopped.

Peter, I have no doubt, looked in a very scowling manner, and perhaps even John became a little impatient, for he had a quick temper by nature. Andrew and Philip and the rest of them considered her very impertinent and presumptuous. But she thought of her little daughter at home, and of the horrible miseries to which the demon subjected her, and so she pressed up to the Savior's feet and said, *Lord, help me.* Cold, hard words, and unkind, unsympathetic behavior could not prevent her pleading with him in whom she believed. Ah, poor sinner, perhaps you are saying, "I am longing to be saved, but such and such a good Christian man has dealt very bitterly with me. He has doubted my sincerity and questioned the reality of my repentance, and caused me the deepest sorrow; it seems as if he did not wish me to be saved." Ah, dear friend, this is very trying, but if you have true faith in the Master, you will not mind us disciples, neither the gentlest of us nor the most crooked of us, but just press on with your appeal to your Lord till he condescends to give you an answer of peace.

Her mouth, again, was not closed by exclusive doctrine, which appeared to confine the blessing to a favored few. The Lord Jesus Christ said, *I am not sent but unto the lost sheep of the house of Israel*, and though properly understood, there is nothing very severe in it, yet the sentence must have fallen on the woman's heart like a weight of lead. "Alas," she might have thought, "then he is not sent to me; vainly do I seek for that which he reserves for the Jews." Now, the doctrine of election, which is assuredly taught in Scripture, ought not to hinder any soul from coming to Christ, for, if properly understood, it would rather encourage than discourage; and yet often to the uninstructed ear the doctrine of the divine choice of a people from before the foundation of the world acts with very depressing effect.

We have known poor seekers mournfully say, "Perhaps there is no mercy for me. I may be among those for whom no purpose of mercy has been formed." They have been tempted to cease from prayer for fear they should not have been predestinated unto eternal life. Ah, dear soul, if you have the faith of God's elect in you, you will not be kept back by any self-condemning inferences drawn from the secret things of God, but you will believe in that which has been clearly revealed, and you will be assured that this cannot contradict the secret decrees of heaven. What if our Lord was only sent to the house of Israel? Yet there is a house of Israel not after the flesh but after the spirit, and therefore the Syrophenician woman was included even where she thought she was shut out, and you may also be included within those lines of gracious destiny which now distress you. At any rate, say to yourself, "In the election of grace others are included who were as sinful as I have been, so why should I not be? Others have been included who were as full of distress as I have been on account of sin, and why should I not be also?" Reasoning thus you will press forward, in hope believing against hope, suffering no plausible deduction from the doctrine of Scripture to prevent your believing in the appointed Redeemer.

The mouth of faith in this case was not even closed by a sense of admitted unworthiness. Christ spoke of dogs: he meant that the Gentiles were to Israel as the dogs. She did not at all dispute it, but yielded the point by saying, *Truth, Lord.* She felt she was only worthy to be compared to a dog. I have no doubt her sense of unworthiness was very deep. She did not expect to win the blessing she sought for on account of any merit of her own; she depended upon the goodness of Christ's heart, not on the goodness of her cause, and upon the excellence of his power rather than upon the prevalence of her plea. Yet conscious as she was that she was only a poor Gentile dog, her prayers were not hindered. She cried, notwithstanding all, *Lord, help me.*

> O sinner, if you feel yourself to be the worst sinner out of hell, still pray for mercy.

O sinner, if you feel yourself to be the worst sinner out of hell, still pray – believingly pray – for mercy. If your sense of unworthiness is enough to drive you to self-destruction, I implore you, out of the depths, out of the dungeon of self-loathing, still cry unto God, for your salvation rests in no measure or degree upon yourself, or upon anything that you are or have been or can be. You need to be saved *from* yourself, not *by* yourself. It is yours to be empty that Jesus may fill you; yours to confess your filthiness that he may wash you; yours to be less than nothing that Jesus may be everything to you. Permit not the number, blackness, frequency, or heinousness of your transgressions to silence your prayers, but though you be a dog, yes, not worthy to be set with the dogs of the Lord's flock, yet open your mouth in believing prayer.

There was besides this a general tone and spirit in what the Lord Jesus said which tended to depress the woman's hope and restrain her prayer, yet *she was not kept back by the darkest and most depressing influences. It is not meet,* said the Lord Jesus, "it is not becoming, it is not proper, it is hardly lawful, to take children's bread and throw it to dogs." Perhaps she did not quite see all that he might have meant, but what she did see was enough to pour cold water upon the flame of her hope, and yet her faith was not quenched. It was a faith of that immortal kind which nothing can kill; for her mind was made up that whatever Jesus meant, or did not mean, she would not cease to trust him, and urge her appeal to him.

There are a great many things in and around the gospel which men see as in a haze, and being misunderstood they rather repel than attract seeking souls; but be they what they may, we must resolve to come to Jesus at all risks. *If I perish, I perish.* Besides the great stumbling stone of election, there are truths and facts which seekers magnify and misconstrue till they see a thousand difficulties. They are troubled about Christian experience, about being born again, about inbred sin, and all sorts of things. In fact, a thousand lions are in the way when the soul attempts to come to Jesus, but he who gives Christ the faith which he deserves, says, "I fear none of these things. Lord, help me, and I will still confide in you. I will approach you, I will press through obstacles to you, and throw myself at your dear feet, knowing that him who comes to you, you will in no wise cast out."

Faith never disputes with the Lord. Faith worships. You notice how Matthew says, *Then came she and worshipped him.* Faith also begs and prays. You observe how Mark says, *She besought him.* She cried, *Lord, help me*, after having said, *Have mercy on me, O Lord, thou Son of David.* Faith pleads, but never disputes, not even against the hardest thing that Jesus says. If faith disputed (I am uttering a *faux pas*), it would not be faith, for that which disputes is unbelief. Faith in God implies agreement with what God says, and consequently it excludes the idea of doubt. Genuine faith believes anything and everything the Lord says, whether discouraging or encouraging. It never has a *but* or an *if* or even a *yet* to put in, but it stands to it: "You have said it, Lord, and therefore it is true. You have ordained it, Lord, and therefore it is right." She never goes beyond that.

Observe in our text that *faith assents to all the Lord says.* She said, *Truth, Lord.* What had he said? "You are comparable to a dog!" "Truth, Lord; truth, Lord, so I am." "It would not be proper that the children should be robbed of bread in order to feed dogs." "Truth, Lord, it would not be fitting, and I would not have one of your children deprived of grace for me." "It is not your time yet," said Jesus. "The children must *first* be fed; children at the mealtimes and dogs after dinner; this is Israel's time, and the Gentiles may follow after. But not yet." She virtually replies, "I know it, Lord, and agree thereto."

She does not raise a question or dispute the justice of the Lord's dispensing his own grace according to his sovereign good pleasure. She fails not, as some do who fuss at divine sovereignty. It would have proved that she had little or no faith if she had done that. She disputes not as to the Lord's set time and order. Jesus said, "Let the children first be filled," and she does not dispute the time, as many do, who will not believe it that now is the accepted time, but are as much for postponing – as this woman was for anticipating – the day of grace. She entered into no argument against its being improper to take the covenant bread from the children and give it to the uncircumcised heathen: she never wished Israel to be robbed for her. Dog as she was, she would not have any purpose of God nor any propriety of the divine household shifted and changed for her. She assented to all the Lord's appointments. That is the faith which saves the soul, which agrees with the mind of God, even if it seems adverse to itself, which believes the revealed declarations of God whether they appear to be pleasant or terrible, and which assents to God's Word whether it be like a balm to its wound or like a sword to cut and slay.

> **If the Word of God be true, O man, do not fight against it, but bow before it.**

If the Word of God be true, O man, do not fight against it, but bow before it. It is not the way to a living faith in Jesus Christ, nor to obtain peace with God, to take up arms against anything which God declares. In yielding lies safety. Say, *Truth, Lord*, and you shall find salvation.

Note that she not only assented to all that the Lord said, but also *she worshipped him in it. Truth,* she said, "but yet you are my Lord." You call me 'dog,' but you are my Lord for all that. You account me unworthy to receive your bounties, but you are my Lord, and I still own you as such." She is of the mind of Job: *Shall we receive good at the hand of the Lord, and shall we not receive evil?* She is willing to take the evil and say, "Whether the Lord gives, or whether he refuses, blessed be his name; he is my Lord still." Oh, this is grand faith, which has thrown aside the contentious spirit, and not only assents to the Lord's will, but also worships him in it. "Let it be what it may, O Lord; even if the truth condemns me, yet still you are Lord, and I confess your deity, confess your excellence, own your crown rights, and submit myself to you: do with me what you will."

And, you observe, when she said, *Truth, Lord,* she did not go on to suggest that any alteration should be made for her. "Lord," she said, "you have classed me among the dogs." She does not say, "Put me among the children," but she only asks to be treated as a dog is. *The dogs eat of the crumbs,* she says. She does not want a purpose altered nor an ordinance changed, nor a decree removed. "Let it be as it is; if it be your will, Lord, it is my will"; only she spies a gleam of hope, where, if she had not possessed faith, she would have seen only the blackness of despair. May we have such a faith as hers, and never enter into controversy with God.

Now I come to an interesting part of our subject, namely, that faith argues, though it does not dispute. *Truth, Lord,* she said, *yet the dogs eat of the crumbs.* This woman's argument was correct and strictly logical throughout. It was an argument based upon the Lord's own premises, and you know if you are reasoning with a man you cannot do better than take his own statements and argue upon them. She does not proceed to lay down new premises, or dispute the old ones by saying, "I am no dog"; but she says, "Yes, I am a dog." She accepts that statement of the Lord, and uses it as a blessed *argumentum ad hominem,* such as was never excelled in this world. She took the words out of his own mouth and vanquished him with them, even as Jacob overcame the angel. There is so much force in the woman's argument that I quite despair of being able to set it all forth to you.

I would, however, remark that the translators have greatly injured the text by putting in the word *yet,* for there is no *yet* in the Greek; it is quite another word. Jesus said, *It is not meet to take the children's bread, and to cast it to dogs.* "No," said she, "it would not be meet (proper) to do this, because the dogs are provided for, for the dogs eat the crumbs that fall from their masters' table. It would be very improper to give them the children's bread, because they have bread of their own. Truth, Lord, I admit it would be improper to give the dogs the children's bread, because they already have their share when they eat the crumbs which fall from the children's table. That is all they want and all I desire. I do not ask you to give me the children's bread, I only ask for the dogs' crumbs."

Let us see the force of her reasoning, which will appear in many ways. The first is this: *She argued with Christ from her hopeful position.* "I am a dog," said she, "but Lord, you have come all the way to Sidon. Here you are close on the borders of my country, and therefore I am not like a dog out in the street; I am a dog under the table." Mark tells us that she said, *The dogs under the table eat of the children's crumbs.* She as good as says, "Lord, you see my position: I was a dog in the street, afar off from you, but now you have come and preached in our borders, and I have been privileged to listen to you. Others have been healed, and you are in this very house doing deeds of grace while I look on, and therefore, though I am a dog, I am a dog under the table; therefore, Lord, let me have the crumbs." Do you see, dear hearer? You admit that you are a sinner, and a great sinner, but you say, "Lord, I am a sinner that is permitted to hear the gospel; therefore, bless it to me. I am a dog, but I am under the table, deal with me as such. When there is a sermon preached for the comfort of your people, I am there to hear it. Whenever the saints gather together, and the precious promises are discussed, and they rejoice therein, I am there, looking up, and wishing that I were among them; but still, Lord, since you have had the grace to let me be a hearer of the gospel, will you reject me now that I desire to be a receiver of it? To what end and purpose have you brought me so near, or rather come so near to me, if after all you will reject me? Dog I am, but still I am a dog under the table. It is a favor to be privileged to be among the children, even if I may only lie at their feet. I pray you then, good Lord, since now I am permitted to look up to you and ask this blessing, do not reject me." To me it seems that this was a strong point with the woman, and that she used it well.

Her next plea was *her encouraging relationship. Truth, Lord,* she says, "I am a dog, but the dogs eat the crumbs *which fall from their masters' table.*" See the stress laid there by Matthew: *from their masters' table.* "I cannot say that you are my Father, I cannot look up and claim the privilege of a child, but you are my Master, and masters feed their dogs; they give at least the crumbs to those dogs which own them as their lord." The plea is very like that suggested to the mind of the poor returning prodigal. He thought to say to his father, *Make me as one of thy hired servants*, only his faith was far weaker than hers. "Lord, if I do not stand in relation to you as a child, still I am your creature. You have made me, and I look up to you and entreat you not to let me perish. If I have no other hold upon you I have at least this, that I ought to have served you, and therefore I am your servant though I am a runaway. I do belong to you at least under the covenant of works if I do not under the covenant of grace, and oh, since I am your servant, do not utterly reject me. You have some property in me by creation, at any rate; oh, look upon me, and bless me. The dogs eat what falls from their masters' table, let me do the same." She spies out a dog's relation to its master, and makes the most of it with blessed ingenuity, which we shall do well to imitate.

Notice next, she pleads *her association with the children*. Here I must tell you that it is a pity that it was not, I suppose, possible for our translators to bring clearly out what is after all the crux of the passage. She was pleading for her *little* daughter; and our Lord said to her, "It is not meet to take the children's bread and cast it to the *little* dogs." The word is petty, but the woman pitched upon it. The word *dogs* could not have served her turn one-half as well as that of *little dogs*, but she said, "Truth, Lord, yet the little dogs eat of the crumbs." In the East, as a rule, a dog is not allowed indoors; in fact, dogs are there looked upon as foul creatures, and they roam about uncared for and half wild. Christianity has raised the dog and made him man's companion, as it will raise all the brute creation, till the outrages of vivisection and the cruelties of the vulgar will be things unheard of except as horrors of a past barbarous age. In the East, a dog is far down in the scale of life, a street wanderer, prowling for scanty food, and in temper little better than a reformed wolf. So the adult Easterners do not associate with dogs, having a prejudice against them; but children are not so foolish, and consequently the Eastern children associate with the little dogs. The father will not have the dog near him, but his child knows no such folly, and seeks out a little dog to join him in his sports; thus the little dog comes to be under the table, tolerated in the house for the child's sake. The woman appears to me to argue thus: "You have called me and my daughter whelps, little dogs, but then the little dogs are under the children's table; they associate with the children, even as I have been with your disciples today. If I am not one of them, I have been associating with them, and would be glad to be among them."

How heartily do I wish that some poor soul would take hold of this and say, "Lord, I cannot claim to be one of your children, but I love to sit among them, for I am never happier than when I am with them. Sometimes they trouble and distress me, as little children pinch and hurt their little dogs, but oftentimes they caress me, and speak kindly and comfortably to me, and pray for me, and desire my salvation. So Lord, if I am not a child, yet you call me a little dog, then so I am, but give me a little dog's treatment, give me the crumb of mercy which I seek."

His argument goes further, for *the little dog eats the crumbs of the children's bread with the child's full consent.* When a child has its little dog to play with while he is eating, what does the child do? Why, of course, it gives a little bit to the dog every now and again, and the doggie himself takes great liberties and helps himself as much as he dares. When a little dog is with the children at mealtime, it is sure to get a crumb from one or other of its playmates, and none will object to its eating what it can get.

So the woman seems to say, "Lord, there are the children, your disciples. They do not treat me very well. Little children do not treat little dogs always so kindly as they might, but still, Lord, they are quite willing that I should have the blessing I am seeking. They have a full portion in you; they have your presence, they have your word, they sit at your feet, they have obtained all sorts of spiritual blessings. I am sure they cannot grudge me so much less a blessing. They are willing that I should have the devil cast out of my daughter, for that blessing compared with what they have is but a crumb, and they are content that I should have it; so Lord, I answer your argument. You say it is not proper until the children are filled to give bread to dogs, but Lord, the children are filled and are quite willing to let me have my portion, they consent to allow me the crumbs; will you not give them to me?"

I think there was another point of force in her plea, and it was this:

the abundance of the provision. She had a great faith in Christ, and believed big things of him, and therefore she said, "Lord, there is no great strength in your argument if you intend to prove that I ought not to have the bread for fear there should not be enough for the children, for you have so much that even while the children are being fed, the dogs may get the crumbs, and there will be enough for the children still."

Where it is a poor man's table, and he cannot afford to lose a crumb, dogs should not be allowed; but when it is a king's table where bread is of small account, and the children are sitting and feeding to the full, the little dogs may be permitted to feed under the table for the mere droppings – not the bread the master *casts* down, but the crumbs which fall by accident are so many that there is enough for the dogs without the children being deprived of a mouthful. "No, Lord," said she, "I would not have you take away the bread from your own children; God forbid that such a deed should be done for me. But there is enough for your children in your overflowing love and mercy, and still enough for me, for all I ask is but a crumb compared with what you are daily bestowing upon others."

Now, here is the last point in which her argument had force: *she looked at things from Christ's point of view.* "If, great Lord," she said, "you look at me as a dog, then behold, I humbly take you at your word, and plead that if I be a dog to you, then the cure I ask for my daughter is but a crumb of your great power and goodness to bestow on me." She used a petty word too, and said, "A little crumb."

The little dogs eat of the little crumbs which fall from the children's table. What bold faith this was! She valued the mercy she sought beyond all price, she thought it worth ten thousand worlds to her, but yet to the Son of God she knew it to be a mere crumb, so rich is he in power to heal and so full of goodness and blessing. If a man gives a crumb to a dog, he then has a little less, but if Jesus gives mercy to the greatest of sinners, he does not have less, for he is just as rich in condescension and mercy and power to forgive as he was before. The woman's argument was most potent. She was as wise as she was earnest, and, best of all, she believed most marvelously.

I shall close this outline of the argument by saying that at bottom the woman was, in reality, arguing according to the eternal purpose of

God; for what was the Lord's grand design in giving the bread to the children, or, in other words, sending a divine revelation to Israel? Why, it always was his purpose that through the children the dogs should get the bread; that through Israel the gospel should be handed to the Gentiles. It had always been his plan to bless his own heritage so that his way might be known upon earth, his salvation among all nations; and this woman somehow or other, by a divine instinct, fell into the divine method. Though she had not spied out the secret, or at least it is not told us that she did so in so many words, yet there was the innate force of her argument. In other words, it ran thus: "It is through the children that the dogs have to be fed. Lord, I do not ask you to cease giving the children their bread, nor do I even ask you to hurry on the children's meal; let them be fed first, but even while they are eating, let me have the crumbs which drop from their well-filled hands, and I will be content." There is a brave argument for you, poor coming sinner. I leave it in your hands, and pray the Spirit of God to help you to use it, and if you can turn it to good account you shall prevail with the Lord this day.

Our last and closing head is this: *faith wins her suit.* This woman's faith first *won a commendation for itself.* Jesus said, *O woman, great is thy faith.* She had not heard of the prophecies concerning Jesus; she was not bred and born and educated in a way in which she was likely to become a believer, and yet she did become a believer of the first class. It was marvelous that it should be so, but grace delights in doing wonders. She had not seen the Lord before in her life, she was not like those who had associated with him for many months; and yet, with but one view of him, she gained this great faith. It was astonishing, but the grace of God is always astonishing. Perhaps she had never seen a miracle. All that her faith had to rest upon was that she had heard in her own country that the Messiah of the Jews had come, and she believed that the Man of Nazareth was him, and on this she relied.

O brethren, with all our advantages, with the opportunities that we have of knowing the whole life of Christ, and understanding the doctrines of the gospel as they are revealed to us in the New Testament, with many years of observation and experience, our faith ought to be much stronger than it is. Does not this poor woman shame us when we see her with her slender opportunities nevertheless so strong in faith, so that Jesus himself, commending her, says, *O woman, great is thy faith*?

But her faith prevailed further, in that it *won a commendation for the mode of its action,* for, according to Mark, Jesus said, *For this saying go thy way; the devil is gone out of thy daughter,* as if he rewarded the saying as well as the faith which suggested it. He was so delighted with the wise, and prudent, and humble yet courageous manner in which she turned his words against him, that he said, *For this saying . . . the devil is gone out of thy daughter.* The Lord who commends faith afterwards commends the fruits and acts of faith. The tree consecrates the fruit. No man's actions can be acceptable to God till he himself is accepted, but for the woman having been accepted on her faith, the results of her faith were agreeable to the heart of Jesus.

The woman also *gained her desire: The devil is gone out of thy daughter,* and he was gone at once. She had only to go home and find her daughter on the bed taking a quiet rest, which she had not done since the demon had possessed her. Our Lord, when he gave her the desire of her heart, gave it in a grand manner. He gave her a sort of *carte blanche,* and said, *Be it unto thee even as thou wilt.* I do not know that any other person ever had such a word said to him as this woman: *Be it unto thee even as thou wilt.* It was as if the Lord of glory surrendered at his discretion to the conquering arms of a woman's faith. The Lord grant to you and me in all times of our struggling to be able thus by faith still to conquer, and we cannot imagine how great will be the spoil which we shall divide when the Lord shall say, *Be it unto thee even as thou wilt.*

The close of all is this: this woman is a lesson to all outsiders, to you who think yourselves beyond the pale of hope, to you who were not brought up to attend the house of God, who perhaps have been negligent of all religion for almost all your lifetime. This poor woman is a Sidonian; she comes from a race that had been condemned to die many centuries before, one of the accursed seed of Canaan, and yet for all that she became great in the kingdom of heaven because she believed, and there is no reason why those who are reckoned to be quite outside the church of God should not be in the very center of it, and be the most burning and shining lights of the whole. O you poor outcasts and far-off ones, take heart and comfort, and come to Jesus Christ and trust yourselves in his hands.

This woman is next of all an example to those who think they have been repulsed in their endeavors for salvation. Have you been praying, and have you not succeeded? Have you sought the Lord, and do you seem to be more unhappy than ever? Have you made attempts at reformation and alteration, and believed that you made them in the divine strength, and have they failed? Yet trust in him whose blood has not lost its efficacy, whose promise has not lost its truth, and whose arm has not lost its power to save. Cling to the cross, sinner. If the earth sinks beneath you, hold on; if storms should rage, and all the floods be out, and even God himself seems to be against you, cling to the cross. There is your hope. You cannot perish there.

This is a lesson, next, to every intercessor. This woman was not pleading for herself, she was asking for another. Oh, when you plead for a fellow sinner do not do it in a coldhearted manner; plead as for your own soul and your own life. That man will prevail with God as an intercessor who solemnly bears the matter upon his own heart and makes it his own, and with tears begs for an answer of peace.

Lastly, recollect that this mighty woman, this glorious woman, is a lesson to every mother, for she was pleading for her little daughter. Maternal instinct makes the weakest strong, and the most timid brave. Even among poor beasts and birds, how powerful is a mother's love. Why, the poor little robin that would be frightened at the approach of a footstep will sit upon its nest when the intruder comes near when her little ones are in danger. A mother's love makes her heroic for her child; and so when you are pleading with God, plead as a mother's love suggests to you, till the Lord shall say to you also, "O woman, great is your faith; the devil is gone out of your daughter, be it unto you even as you will." I leave that last thought with parents as an encouragement to pray. The Lord stir you up to it, for Jesus' sake. Amen.

Chapter 12

Children's Bread Given to Dogs

And she said, Truth, Lord: yet the dogs eat of the crumbs which fall from their masters' table. (Matthew 15:27)

In this narrative we have the portrait of a soul for whom a sure blessing is reserved. If the story closed without its final verse, one might be quite sure as to what the result of the woman's pleading would be. Christ must change his nature if a person coming as she is said to have come could be sent away empty. I shall with a few touches sketch the woman's picture, and shall beg you to see if you are like her; for if so, it will be evidence to you that the time to favor you, yes, the set time, has come. This woman had *a great and pressing need*. Her daughter was vexed with a devil, and she could not endure to see the misery which that evil spirit caused her child; the pain and anguish, the delirium and horror into which the child was thrown were too much for her to bear. Her need was conscious, troublesome, and burdensome; she had grown desperate under it, and she *must* be rid of it. Is it so with you, dear hearer? Does your sin plague you? Does your transgression come up before you like a continual offense? Does it vex you both day and night till it has come to this pass – that you cannot live without pardon, that you must be forgiven or driven into madness? Do you feel that things are at such a point with you that you cannot live any longer under the sentence of divine wrath? This is a very blessed and hopeful sign. If there be many such here, there is music in store for angels.

When her case had come to such a point, *she heard of the Lord Jesus; and what she heard she acted upon.* They told her that he was a great healer of the sick, and was able to cast out devils. She was not content with that information, but she set to work at once to test its value. She went to Jesus with all speed. Finding that it was a convenient season, for he had come near to her land, she hastened to cry unto him. Ah! dear hearer, you too have heard of Jesus. I shall not ask you whether you know the doctrine of his Godhead and of his manhood and of his atonement for sin; you know it well, but have you put it to the test? You understand that he saves souls; have you taken your own soul to him to be saved? You know that he can forgive sin; are you looking to him now to forgive your sin? If it be so, though as yet you sit in the shadow of death, your hour of deliverance hastens on swiftly; for a soul that under a sense of need honestly seeks the Savior's face is not far from the kingdom of heaven.

This woman was *most desperately resolved.* She had made up her mind, I believe, that she would never go back to the place from where she came till she had received the blessing. She would dog the Savior's footsteps, she would waylay him; if the disciples pushed her back, she would wait for another opportunity, and if not then successful, she would try the next occasion, and if that would not suffice, she would venture yet again. She was sorely tested by the Savior, for he sometimes tests those whom he knows to be strong enough to bear the trial; and when she obtained no answer from him, but rather met with a rebuff, she was not at all daunted but pressed her appeal, for she had drunk deep into the spirit of the hymn:

> Resolved, for that's my last defense,
>   If I must perish there to die.

If there is here a soul who has come to this, that he will never give up praying until he receives a comfortable answer, that he will never cease to weep for sin until the blood has washed it out, then rejoice, you heavens, and be glad, O earth, for there are souls here who have come to the birth, and they shall be brought forth this day. There are souls here who are *now* upon the edge of liberty, upon the verge of peace; they shall even this day obtain a complete liberation from all their bondage. I said at the start that this woman was a correct portrait of the most hopeful case in the world; can you spy your own face in her story, even as men see their countenances in a glass? Then I am happy, for your position is full of hopefulness.

I may not leave this picture, however, without observing that this woman *triumphantly endured a trial very common among seeking souls.* Brethren, those evangelists who are not pastors will perhaps differ from me in what I am about to say, but if they knew more about souls, they would not. It is customary in the pulpit to exhort people to believe in Jesus Christ; it is not only customary but it is also most proper and right, and the more of it the better. But there are some who are content with giving the exhortation generally, and do not with affectionate discrimination deal with the individual cases of men. There are cases in which the bare exhortation to believe is not enough. I wonder what mere exhorters would do with certain peculiar instances which I now have under my own hand. I have explained the gospel to them to the best of my ability many times, and have prayed with them and for them. I have given them books which God has blessed in other cases. I have directed them to passages of Scripture which have been the means of giving light to thousands, yet these persons month after month remain in as much doubt and distress of mind as at first; no, they are even worse. This was my own case for years as a child.

The gospel was taught me by my parents, but I was in such darkness and despondency of spirit that I could not do what I was bidden to do, and felt as if when bidden to look to Christ I had no eyes to look with. Even the gospel did not then appear to suit my case; it was my sinful blindness, my guilty folly which made me think so; but alas! how many are there equally blinded who need to have their cases handled gently and wisely. Albeit that we say to them, "Believe," they are far from being comforted by the advice. There is needed some further explanation, some simpler opening up of the saving truth, and perhaps a laborious answering of their difficulties before they can find peace. Genuine seekers who as yet have not obtained the blessing may take comfort from the story before us. The Savior did not at once give the blessing, even though this woman had faith. Do not be startled, it is the truth. She had real and genuine faith in Christ when she came to Jesus, else she would never have put up with the rebuffs of the disciples. Yet, believer as she was, she did not at first obtain the blessing which she sought. The Savior always intended to give it, but he waited awhile. *He answered her not a word.* Were not her prayers good? Never better in the world. Was not her case needy? Sorrowfully needy. Did she not *feel* her need sufficiently? She did feel it overwhelmingly. Was she not earnest enough? She was as earnest as ever a woman could be. Had she no faith? She had such a high degree of it that even Jesus wondered, and said, *O woman, great is thy faith.* Yet for a while she could not obtain an answer to her prayers.

See then, dear friends, although it is true that faith brings peace, yet it does not always bring it instantaneously. There may be certain reasons calling for the trial of faith rather than the reward of faith. Genuine faith may be in the soul like a hidden seed, but as yet it may not have budded and blossomed into joy and peace. Comfort is the child of faith, but it is not always as old as its mother. I say this to cheer some of you. Do not, I beg you, give up seeking; do not give up trusting my Master, because you have not yet obtained the conscious joy which you long for. I doubt not but that you certainly will be saved, even though as yet no kindly promise has gladdened your heart. "Slow breaks the light" on many a heart, but surely will it break before long.

A painful silence from the Savior is the grievous trial of many a seeking soul, but heavier still is the affliction of a harsh, cutting reply such as this: *It is not meet to take the children's bread and to cast it to dogs.* Many in waiting upon the Lord find immediate delight, but this is not the case with all. Some, like the jailer, are in a moment turned from darkness to light, but others are plants of slower growth. A deeper sense of sin may be given to you instead of a sense of pardon, and in such a case you will have need of patience to bear the heavy blow. Ah! poor heart, though Christ beats and bruises you or even slays you, trust him; though he should give you an angry word, believe in the love of his heart; and even if for the next few months you should not be able to say, "I know comfortably that he is mine," yet cast yourself on him, and perseveringly depend even where you cannot rejoicingly hope.

We come to the text itself. The woman's case is an instance of prevailing faith, and if we would conquer, we must imitate her tactics. If I were called to be a commander in an army, I should observe how other commanders who have been successful have managed the matter. Here is a woman who conquered Christ, so let us go by her rule, and we will conquer Christ too by his own grace.

In the first place, observe that *she admits the accusation brought against her.* Jesus called her a dog, and she meekly said, *Truth, Lord*. Here is no controversy with Christ; no setting up of oppositions, excuses, or mitigations. She is frank, prompt, humble, and open. *Truth, Lord* – that is her only answer to him. When a man wrestles, much depends upon his foothold. If he does not stand firmly he cannot win the day; and if we would wrestle with the angel of mercy, we must find a foothold where this woman did, in a deep sense of unworthiness. She knew herself to be an outcast from Israel, and at once confessed it. Most men, if they had been called dogs, would either have turned on their heel and gone away in sullen despair, or else would have blazed into a bad temper and replied to the master, "I am no more a dog than you, and if I come to ask for mercy, can you not at least give me a civil refusal?"

The natural heart rebels against what the Scripture says about it. Until a man is truly humbled, he scorns to admit the depravity of his nature. Though he may be quite willing to use the common terms of humility, he does not mean them, for if they were applied to him in another shape he would grow very angry, like the monk who said he had broken all the commandments and was as bad as Judas Iscariot, and when a bystander remarked, "I always thought so," the monk grew dreadfully angry, and vowed vengeance on the man who so insulted him.

Call me a horse if you will, but it is quite another thing to put a saddle on my back. I have heard of a woman who told her minister who visited her that she was a shocking sinner. "Well," said the minister, "I have no doubt you are; let us go over your sins." So beginning with the first commandment, she declared that she had never broken that; she had never worshipped any other god but God. As to the second commandment, she had never set up any graven images that she knew of, nor had she broken the Sabbath day; she had honored her father and mother; she had never coveted, never borne false witness, never killed anybody, and in fact she pleaded that she had not broken one of the Ten Commandments, notwithstanding she had confessed herself so sad a sinner.

We plead guilty to stealing a forest, but deny that we ever stole so much as a couple of sticks. The woman before us believed in her heart in the degradation of her state, so that when the Savior addressed her in apparently the coarsest manner as a dog, she was so thoroughly familiar with her own fallen condition that it did not startle her to be called what she knew herself to be. She had heard sin balk within her so often and so loudly that when the Savior called her a dog, she only felt that he was calling things by their right names. If I were to go over the whole statement of the fall and the mischief of sin, everybody in this place would say, "That is true"; but oh! how few there are who really feel it to be true and are deeply grieved over it! We are all sinners, *so we say;* but we all have our excellencies, *so we feel.*

> **We are all sinners, so we say; but we all have our excellencies, so we feel.**

The Word of God does not give us a very complimentary picture of humanity. It informs us that our first father sinned, and that through him, as he stood for all of us, we all fell and lost the favor of God. The Herald's College of Scripture draws up for us a miserable pedigree.

Those aristocrats who are so proud of their Norman ancestors would do well to trace the family tree to its still earlier date, and they will find the one of blue blood ending in the gardener who stole his Master's fruit, and was sent adrift without a rag to cover his nakedness. A beggarly pedigree this, you nobles of the earth; this is a *bar sinister* on your ornamental plate which nothing can wipe out. The inspired Word goes on to tell us that, in consequence of this, we are all born in sin and shaped in iniquity, that in sin do our mothers conceive us. It testifies that we are not only sinners with the hand, but also with the heart; that sin is not merely a scab upon the skin, but also a leprosy in the soul; that *the whole head is sick, and the whole heart faint*; that the heart itself is *deceitful above all things, and desperately wicked*. No, it goes further, and certifies that we are not simply sick and depraved, but are utterly perverted; that through our sin our wills have become perverse, so that we will not come to Christ that we might have life, habitually putting the bitter for sweet and the sweet for bitter, choosing the evil and shunning the good. It tells us that this inability of ours to do good is so great as to be tantamount to spiritual death. It describes us as being by nature *dead in trespasses and sins*, in such a state that we can no more restore ourselves to salvation than the dead in their graves can raise themselves of their own power, and put themselves into a state of life and health.

The Book of God says all against man that can be said, and more than man is willing to confess except when the Spirit of God comes, and then our heart answers, *Truth, Lord*. Moreover, God's Word goes on to say that our sin is so great that it must be always hateful to God, that it deserves that we who have committed it should be banished from his presence into unutterable woe. But human nature kicks at this and says, "No, sin is a weakness, a foible, a mistake, and nothing more"; but when the Holy Spirit enters the heart we cry, "*Truth, Lord*; it *is* a black thing, a devilish thing, an infernal thing, and if you cast us into hell, you only do with sin what ought to be done with it."

Beloved friends, whenever you meet with a sinner bowed down with the burden of sin, never try to make his sin appear to be lighter. On the contrary, say to the soul that is most despairing, "You feel that you are a great sinner, but you are a much greater sinner than you feel yourself to be." When the soul cries, "My sin is very heavy," do not attempt to comfort it by making excuses for it; but on the contrary, say, "Heavy as you think your sin to be, it is much heavier than you know of."

Never play into the devil's hands by excusing sinners in their sins. If you give comfort to your friend by saying to him, "Well, you have not been such a sinner as you think you are," you are giving him ruinous comfort; you are presenting to him a poisonous drug which may lull him to sleep, but which will therefore lull him to destruction. Tell him that sin is in itself so horrible, that if a man could see a naked sin it would drive him mad; that the very least offense against God is so intolerable, that if hellfire were put out, one sin could kindle it again. The woman in this case, if it had been a sound way of getting comfort, would have argued, "No, Lord, I am not a dog. I may not be all I ought to be, but I am not a dog at any rate; I am a human being. You speak too sharply. Good Master, do not be unjust." Instead of that, she admits the whole. This showed that she was in a right state of mind, since she admitted in its blackest, heaviest meaning whatever the Savior might choose to say against her. By night the glowworm is bright like a star, and rotten tinder glistens like molten gold. By the light of day the glowworm is a miserable insect, and the rotten wood is decayed and nothing more. So with us; until the light comes into us we count ourselves good, but when heaven's light shines, our heart is discovered to be rottenness, corruption, and decay.

Do not whisper in the mourner's ear that it is not so, and do not delude yourself into the belief that it is not so. You *are* a lost sinner; you do deserve damnation; *you* deserve it especially, if no one else deserves it; you have sinned against light and against knowledge; you are ruined, and ruined utterly. Bad as you think yourself to be, your case is infinitely worse than you conceive it to be, and I am not here to give you any comfort by saying peace, peace, where there is no peace. Your state, O sinner, is horribly bad, and will soon be worse, hopelessly worse; and before God may you be made to feel this and to say, Truth, Lord.

But notice, in the second place, *she adheres to Christ nevertheless.* Did you notice the force of what she said? *Truth, Lord: yet the dogs eat of the crumbs which fall from*—where? *From their masters' table.* Dogs in the East very seldom have any master. There are big dogs in every Eastern city that live on the garbage thrown from the houses, and these big dogs are such a nuisance that I am not aware that there is one word in the whole of Scripture in favor of them. The dog, as we know him, is a most affectionate, faithful servant of man, and deserves great honor; but the dog as he is in the East deserves nothing but contempt; he is simply a big howling brute who will bark at or bite anybody who is passing by. In the Savior's days the Easterners had learned Roman manners, and had introduced little household dogs; and it is remarkable that our Lord did not call this woman one of the big dogs without a master, but one of the little lapdogs. It was a name of contempt certainly, but still not the severest form of it. "It is not proper to give the children's bread to these little dogs."

There is a word here which I want you to notice. The woman does not say, "the dogs eat the crumbs that fall from the table," but *from their masters' table.* Notice her adherence to Jesus. She says in effect to him, "You are my master." She seems to say, "Lord, I am asking for a great blessing, and say what you will to me, I mean to have it; but if I cannot obtain the blessing, at any rate I will always follow *you;* you shall be my master. If you shall never say, 'Go in peace, your faith has given you the blessing,' yet I take you to be my master." As a stray dog picks up with a stranger and follows him home, and seems to say, "You may kick me or shut the door, but I have taken you to be my master. If you shut me out of one door, I will go in through the other; if you shut me out of both doors, I will lie on the doormat; and if you kick me into the street, I will stand there until you come out, and then I will follow you. I have taken you to be my master, and my master you shall be." Now, poor soul, is this your case? If not, I urge you to take that stand.

You have admitted that all Jesus has said is true, but you say, "For all that, whether I am a dog or a devil, I will never leave off coming to Christ as my Savior. If I be a dog, I will follow at the heels of mercy; morning, noon, and night I will crouch at my Master's feet, and I will never give up trusting Jesus, even if I have no comfort from him. I have argued out the case with my own heart, and I have concluded that if God becomes a Savior, there can be no case beyond his infinite power; if the Son of God dies and sheds his blood, there can be no scarlet sin which his blood cannot wash out; and if he rose again and is gone up on high, then he is able to save unto the uttermost them that come unto God by him. I am resolved therefore to wait and wrestle until he condescends to give me an answer."

> Fear frequently intensifies faith. The more afraid I am of my sins, the more firmly do I grasp my Savior.

No man clings more closely to Christ than he who is most sensible of his lost estate. Who holds the plank the tightest? Why, the man who is the most afraid of being drowned. Fear frequently intensifies faith. The more afraid I am of my sins, the more firmly do I grasp my Savior.

Fear is sometimes the mother of faith. One who was walking in the fields was surprised to find a trembling lark fly into his bosom. A strange thing for a timid bird to do, was it not? But there was a hawk after it, and therefore fear of the hawk made the bird bold enough to fly to man for shelter. And oh! when the fierce vultures of sin and hell are pursuing a poor sinner, he is driven by the courage of despair to fly into the heart of the blessed Jesus. John Bunyan has somewhere words to this effect: "I was brought into such a dread and horror under the wrath of God that I could not help trusting in Christ; I felt that if he stood there with a drawn sword in his hand I must even run right upon its point sooner than endure my sins." I hope and pray that the Lord may drive you to Jesus in such a way as this if you will not be drawn by gentler means.

Brethren, a soul set upon Jesus, and clinging to him with a death grip, can by no means perish; the thing is utterly impossible. I have sometimes tried to picture a soul in hell that has sought Jesus, and resolved to die at the foot of his cross. Such a thing cannot be; but suppose it for a moment, and the supposition will destroy itself. "Alas," says that lost soul, "Jesus, I did hang alone upon you, but I am undone; I was worthless, I deserved nothing of your favor; but I did trust in you as the Savior of the vile, I did depend upon your power to deliver me, and here I am in the pit." Can you fancy such a sound as that amid the wailings of hell? How the devils would laugh! "Ha, ha! where are the promises? Where is the great heart of Christ to let a sinner perish who twined his arms around him? Was it because he *could not*?" Then cries Satan, "Ha, ha! he was not able to save to the uttermost them that came to God by him; though he claimed to be a physician, he could not heal." "Or else," says the archfiend, "he *would not* save those who longed and panted to be saved."

You shudder to think what fearful blasphemy all this would be, and how it would tarnish the honor of the glorious Redeemer. It shall not be, sinner, it shall not be. If you are the blackest offender that ever lived, cast yourself at the feet of Jesus, resolved never to leave until he gives you pardon. He will not refuse you. We must not limit God and say what he can or cannot do; but we do read that he cannot lie, and certainly if Jesus were to cast out a soul that came to him he would lie. Therefore be of good cheer. Only stand to it that you will never leave the Savior, that you will die at the foot of the cross, and all shall be well with you.

Furthermore, the woman's great master weapon, the rifle which she used in her battle, was this: *she had learned the art of getting comfort out of her miseries.*

Jesus called her a dog. "Yes," she said, "but then dogs get the crumbs." She could see a silver lining in the black cloud. Christ threw a bone at her; she took it up and cracked it, and got marrow out of it. It looked to be a very hard stone, but it had a lump of gold inside, and she knocked away the quartz and found the clear, bright bullion and was enriched. "Call me a dog!" she says. "Very well, I will be a dog, and I shall get the crumbs." She draws water of comfort from the deep well of her miseries.

Now, poor soul, in the same state try by the Holy Spirit's aid to do the same thing. Satan has been saying to you, "You have broken God's law, you have offended him, you have been a sinner." Soul, if you have any wit left, cut the devil's head off with his own sword. Say to him, "I am a sinner, but it is written, *This is a faithful saying, and worthy of all acceptation, that Christ Jesus came into the world to save sinners.* What do you say to that, Satan? If I am a sinner, he came into the world to save sinners. If I had not been a sinner, Jesus would not have come to save me, for it is nowhere written that he came to save those who are not sinners." The more clearly I prove that I am a sinner, the more clearly I prove that I am an object for the Savior's mercy.

> If I had not been a sinner, Jesus would not have come to save me, for it is nowhere written that he came to save those who are not sinners.

Perhaps conscience whispers, "You are not a sinner of an ordinary kind; you have gone to the greatest lengths until you have made your heart hard; you are *a lost sinner.*" "Ah!" say you, "I will take hold of that, then, for the Son of Man is come to seek and to save that which was lost. He did not come to seek those who did not want seeking; he did not come as the great Shepherd to find the sheep that were in the fold, but those which had gone astray; and I being a lost one, when I see the Shepherd going over the mountains after the lost ones, I will bleat like a lost sheep, for perhaps he has come to look for me."

But conscience says to you again, "You are such an undeserving one; you are not only a lost sinner, but you are also utterly unworthy." Sinner, take hold of that and say, "God is a God of mercy. If I deserved anything, there would be less room for mercy; for something would be due to me as a matter of justice. But as I am a sheer mass of undeservedness, there is room for the Lord to reveal the abundance of his grace." There is no room for a man to be generous among yonder splendid mansions in Belgravia. Suppose a man had thousands of pounds in his pocket and desired to give it away in charity; he would be terribly hampered amid princely palaces. If he were to knock at the doors of those great houses, and say he wanted an opportunity of being charitable, powdered footmen would slam the door in his face and tell him to be gone with his brashness. But come along with me; let us wander down the Mews all among the dunghills, and get away into back alleys where crowds of ragged children are playing amid filth and squalor, where all the people are miserably poor, and where cholera is festering. Now, sir, down with your money bags; here is plenty of room for your charity; now you may put both your hands into your pockets, and not fear that anybody will refuse you. You may spend your money right and left now with ease and satisfaction.

When the God of mercy comes down to distribute mercy, he cannot give it to those who do not want it; but you need forgiveness, for you are full of sin, and you are just the person likely to receive it. "Ah!" says one, "I am so sick at heart; I cannot believe, I cannot pray." If I saw the doctor's carriage driving along at a great rate through the streets, I should be sure that he was not coming to my house, for I do not need him. But if I had to guess where he was going, I should conclude that he was hastening to some sick or dying person. The Lord Jesus Christ is the Physician of souls. The more sick you are, the more room is there for the Physician's art.

When a man sets up a trade, he likes to find a locality where his articles are wanted, and there he opens his shop. What if I say it is my Master's trade to save sinners? What if I say it is the only business and calling that he undertook, to become a Savior of lost and ruined souls? Then he can drive a brisk trade in your heart, and I believe that he will open shop there, and enrich himself with your praise and your love by saving you! Do try now, my hearer, thus to find hope in the very hopelessness of your condition, in whatever aspect that hopelessness may appear to you.

The Bible says that you are *dead in sins;* then conclude that there is space for Jesus to come, since he is the resurrection and the life. If you were alive, you would not want two lives; but since you are dead, there is room for Jesus to give you life. The Bible tells you that you are dead; do not deny it. Say, *Truth, Lord,* but then there is room for Christ's fullness. If you were full, you could not hold two fullnesses; your own fullness would keep Christ's fullness out. But now that you are empty, there is room for him. Dear heart, instead of trying to make your case out to be better, believe in its thorough badness, and yet be of good cheer. You cannot exaggerate your sin, and even if you could, it would be wiser to err in that direction than the other.

A man called at my house some time ago for charity; a regular beggar, I have no doubt. Thinking that the man's rags and poverty were real, I gave him a little money, some of my clothes, and a pair of shoes. After he had put them on and gone out, I thought, "Well, after all, I have done you a bad turn very likely, for you will not get so much money now as before, because you will not look like so wretched an object." Happening to go out a quarter of an hour afterwards, I saw my friend, but he was not wearing the clothes I had given him; why, I should have ruined his business if I could have compelled him to look respectable. He had been wise enough to slip down an archway, take all the good clothes off, and put his rags on again. Did I blame him? Yes, for being a rogue, but not for carrying on his business in a businesslike manner. He only wore his proper garb, for rags are the uniform of a beggar, The more ragged he looked the more he would get. Just so is it with you. If you are to go to Christ, do not put on your good doings and feelings, or you will get nothing; go in your sins, they are your garb. Your ruin is your argument for mercy; your poverty is your plea for heavenly charity; and your need is the motive for heavenly goodness. Go as you are, and let your miseries plead for you.

> Your ruin is your argument for mercy; your poverty is your plea for heavenly charity; and your need is the motive for heavenly goodness.

If I were wounded on the battlefield, and the surgeon was going about to attend to the sick, he would be sure to first visit those whose wounds were the worst; for in the hurry of a battle, of course they do not look after a man who has had his finger shot off, when there are others whose arms and legs are gone. I would take care to state my case as fully as I could, by no means speaking lightly of my hurts, in order to have my bleeding wounds bound up as soon as possible. I should not feel inclined to say, "Oh, it is nothing, I am very little injured, it does not matter." I should be taking hold of time by the hair of my head, and getting what help I needed as soon as possible. Now you, sinner, learn this art. Do not paint yourself in bright colors, but own yourself to be lost and ruined, and then clinging still to Christ, make your very wants, and needs, and death, and ruin to be an argument for why the Lord of mercy should show his mighty power in you.

Let me, in the fourth place, notice the way in which the woman gained comfort: *she thought great thoughts of Christ.*

I must have your attention to this. The Master had talked about the children's bread. "Now," she argued, "since you are the Master of that table, I know that you are a generous housekeeper, and there is sure to be an abundance of bread on your table. You are no miserly provider; there will be such an abundance for the children that there will be crumbs to throw on the floor for the dogs, and the children will fare none the worse because the dogs are fed." She did not think the Lord Jesus to be a workhouse master who must serve out so many ounces of bread for each one, but she thought him to be a generous provider who kept so good a table that all that she needed would only be a crumb in comparison. Yet remember, what she wanted was to have the devil cast out of her daughter. It was a very great thing to her, but she had such a high esteem of Christ that she said, "It is nothing to him; it is but a crumb for Christ to give." This is the royal road to comfort.

> Great thoughts of your sin alone will drive you to despair; but great thoughts of Christ will soon bear you upwards upon eagles' wings.

Great thoughts of your sin alone will drive you to despair; but great thoughts of Christ will soon bear you upwards upon eagles' wings. "My sins are many, but oh! it is nothing to Jesus to take them all away; he can as easily lift the mountain of my sin as I could lift a molehill on a shovel. It is true that the weight of my guilt presses me down as a giant's foot would crush a worm, but it would be no more than a grain of dust to him, because he has already borne its curse in his own body on the tree. It will be but a small thing for *him* to give me full remission, although it will be an infinite blessing for *me* to receive it." She opens her mouth to expect great things of Jesus, and he fills it with his love.

I ask you, dear friends, to do the same. Oh, may the Holy Spirit enable you. But you may say, "Help me." Well, I will help you. You ought to think great thoughts of Jesus when you remember that *he is God*. What limit can you set when you have God to deal with? He with his span measures the heavens, in the hollow of his hand he holds the seas, and he takes up the islands as a very little thing. If Jesus Christ be God, how can you think he cannot save you? O man, when you have to deal with the Eternal and Infinite One, let your doubts fly to the winds. Think again that he being God, *suffered the penalty of sin*, a grief which man alone could not have endured. The weight of his Father's wrath fell upon Jesus at Calvary. Can you see him with his pierced hands and feet, can you read the lines of agony written upon his thorn-crowned brow, and not believe that he is able to save? God over all, the glory of whose countenance fills heaven with splendor, yields his face to be covered with shameful spit, and his brow to be moistened with drops of bloody sweat. Is anything impossible to the merits of the agonizing God?

Think of that, sinner, and you will put no limit on what Jesus can do. But Jesus *rose again*. See him as he rises from the tomb, ascending to his Father's throne amidst the jubilation of ten thousand angels; see how he wears the keys of heaven, and death and hell, swinging from his belt. What can he not do? Not save you? He who is exalted on high to give repentance, who *is able also to save them to the uttermost*, seeing that he ever lives to intercede – can you doubt his power to save? Oh, do not dishonor my Master. Trust him now.

But you are still doubting. Then I will bring you one thing more that shall by God's sweet love drive your doubts away and make you cling to the Savior. There are some country towns in the eastern counties where there is a celebrated doctor, and I have heard of wagons leaving from remote hamlets loaded with people to go twenty or thirty miles to consult the famous man. Whether he did them good or not, I am sure I cannot tell, but the illustration serves my turn. Suppose one of you were to set off to see this doctor. Feeling very sick and ill, you are afraid that he will be of no service to you when you get there, but on the road you meet wagonloads of persons journeying cheerfully home. They say, "Where are you going?" and you reply, "I am going off to Doctor So-and-so, for I am ill." "Oh!" they say, "you are very fortunate to be able to go. We have been there; we were all as bad as you and we have been cured, and are now going home." "But," say you, "did any of you have a bad leg like mine?" "Oh, yes," one replies, "I had two bad legs, my case was even worse than yours." "Well, were you perfectly restored?" "Yes," says the man, "see how I can walk. I am fully restored." Would you not go on with confidence? You were half afraid before, but you say, "Now I shall proceed joyfully, for these cures are so many proofs of the physician's power." There are many who can say, "Yes, Jesus is able to save," and they can give the very best proof of it too by adding, "He saved me!" Dear hearers, I know that Christ can save sinners, for I have seen his salvation in thousands of cases; but the best proof I ever had was when he saved me. When I looked to him and was lightened, and my face was not ashamed, then I knew I wanted no further arguments. O sinner, he has saved drunkards, swearers, harlots, whoremongers, and adulterers.

Paul says that he saved those who defiled themselves with nameless sins, for he says, *Such were some of you: but ye are washed.* Even the murderer can have deeds of blood washed out by the blood of Jesus. All manner of sin and blasphemy shall be forgiven unto men, for *the blood of Jesus Christ his Son cleanseth us from all sin.* He is a great Savior, he is the greatest Savior, he is a Savior greater than the greatest; and as for your sins, they shall sink beneath the sea of his atoning blood, and shall be found against you no more forever. The woman thought great thoughts of Christ, and that brought her comfort.

And so you see, in the last place, *she won the victory.*

She confessed what Christ laid at her door; she laid fast hold upon him, and drew arguments even out of his hard words; she believed great things of him, and she thus overcame him. Now let me say that the reason why she overcame Christ was really here, that she had first of all overcome herself. She had conquered in another fight before she wrestled with the Savior, and that was with her own soul. I think I see her before she started away from home. She was sitting down one day when a talkative neighbor came in and said, "Have you heard about the new prophet?" "No, I have not; what about him?" "Oh! he is a great healer of diseases." "Tell me all about it," said the woman, for that subject interested her. She heard the story; she knew that her friend talked a great deal more than she needed, and she did not quite believe it. The next day she came to the house and said, "Are you certain that what you told me was quite true?" "Well," she said, "I heard it from So-and-so, whose daughter was healed."

The woman then determined to hunt the matter out, and at last found an eyewitness whose word could be taken. "Yes," said the friend, "it is the Messiah, the Son of God, who has come down to earth, and I am sure he is able to cure, for I have seen some wonderful miracles worked by him; there can be no doubt about his power." At first the woman was puzzled. She had been brought up as a heathen; she had tried her heathen gods, and they had failed her; she had tried her priests, and they had only deluded her, and she thought that this perhaps was a delusion too. But she thought it over. There were fifty objections, but then she said, "I have heard that there will be such-and-such signs attending the coming of the Messiah, and this man is just what they said the Messiah would be. I believe he is the Messiah, and if he is God's Son, he must be able to heal my daughter." Then hosts of difficulties came up. "You are a Canaanite." "Yes, but it was said of the Messiah, *A bruised reed shall he not break, and smoking flax shall he not quench*; therefore, I will go and try him. And again it is written, *In his name shall the Gentiles trust*. I am a Gentile, and I will trust in him." I can suppose that she debated all this over in her mind, and having first conquered herself, she easily overcame the willing Savior.

> Sinner, there is nothing between you and salvation but yourself.

Possibly some of you may suppose that there is a degree of difficulty in bringing the Lord Jesus to save a sinner. There is none whatever. The difficulty is in bringing the sinner to trust Jesus. This is the work, this is the labor. In this woman's case the conflict with Jesus was only external but not real. He was already on her side. The true conflict was with her own unbelief, and when her faith had proved itself victorious, within it she became victorious with Christ. Sinner, there is nothing between you and salvation but yourself. Do I speak boldly? Christ has leveled every mountain that stood in your way, he has filled up every valley, and he has made a high road from you to the very throne of God. The difficulty is with you, not with God. How then is it with you? Can you trust Christ, dear hearer? Can you throw yourself wholly upon Jesus crucified? If so, your sins are forgiven you, go your way and rejoice. But if you cannot, here is your difficulty. Oh, may God help you to contend with it. It is a sin to doubt Christ, it is a cruelty; it is an unkind cut to suspect that he is unwilling to forgive. Cast away, I pray you, your wicked unbelief! May God the Holy Spirit help you to do so! Do come just as you are, and rest in Jesus, and you shall find eternal life.

Chapter 13

Pleading, Not Contradicting

She said, Truth, Lord: yet. (Matthew 15:27)

Do you notice, in the reading of this narrative of the Syrophenician woman, the two facts mentioned in the twenty-first and twenty-second verses? *Then Jesus went thence, and departed into the coasts of Tyre and Sidon. And, behold, a woman of Canaan came out of the same coasts.* See, Jesus goes towards the coast of Sidon on the land side, and the woman of Canaan comes from the seashore to meet him, and so they come to the same town. May we find that case repeated today! May our Lord Jesus come into our midst with power to cast out the devil; and may one – no, may many – seek grace at his hands! Jesus and the seeker have a common attraction. He comes, and she comes. It would have been of no use her coming from the seacoast of Tyre and Sidon if the Lord Jesus had not also come down to the Israelite border of Phenicia to meet her. His coming makes her coming a success. What a happy circumstance when Christ meets the sinner, and the sinner meets his Lord!

Our Lord Jesus, as the Good Shepherd, came that way, drawn by the instincts of his heart: he was seeking after lost ones, and he seemed to feel that there was one to be found on the borders of Tyre and Sidon, and therefore, he must go that way to find that one. It does not appear that he preached or did anything special on the road; he left the ninety and nine by the Sea of Galilee to seek that one lost sheep by the Mediterranean shore. When he had dealt with her, he went back again to his old haunts in Galilee.

Our Lord was drawn towards this woman, but she also was driven towards him. What made her seek him? Strange to say, a devil had a hand in it; but not so as to give the devil any of the praise. The truth was, that a gracious God used the devil himself to drive this woman to Jesus, for her daughter was *grievously vexed with a devil*, and she could not bear to stay at home and see her child in such misery. Oh, how often does a great sorrow drive men and women to Christ, even as a fierce wind compels the mariner to hasten to the harbor! I have known a domestic affliction, a daughter sorely vexed, influence the heart of a mother to seek the Savior; and, doubtless, many a father, broken in spirit by the likelihood of losing a darling child, has turned his face towards the Lord Jesus in his distress.

Ah, my Lord! you have many ways of bringing your wandering sheep back; and among the rest you even send the black dog of sorrow and of sickness after them. This dog comes into the house, and his howlings are so dreadful that the poor lost sheep flies to the Shepherd for shelter. God make it so with any of you who have a great trouble at home! May your boy's sickness work your health! Yes, may your girl's death be the means of the father's spiritual life! Oh, that your soul and Jesus may meet this day! Your Savior drawn by love, and your poor heart driven by anguish – may you thus be brought to a gracious meeting place!

Now, you would suppose that as the two were seeking each other, the happy meeting and the gracious blessing would be very easily brought about, but we have an old proverb, that "the course of true love never does run smooth"; and for certain, the course of true faith is seldom without trials. Here was genuine love in the heart of Christ towards this woman, and genuine faith in her heart towards Christ; but difficulties sprang up which we would never have looked for. It is for the good of us all that they occurred, but we could not have anticipated them. Perhaps there were more difficulties in the way of this woman than of anybody else that ever came to Jesus in the days of his flesh.

I never saw the Savior before in such a mood as when he spoke to this woman of great faith. Did you ever read of his speaking such rough words? Did such a hard sentence, at any other time, ever fall from his lips as, *It is not meet to take the children's bread, and to cast it to dogs*? Ah! he knew her well, and he knew that she could stand the trial, and would be greatly benefited by it, and that he would be glorified by her faith throughout all future ages. Therefore, with good reason he put her through the athletic exercises which train a vigorous faith. Doubtless, for our sakes, he drew her through a test to which he would never have exposed her had she been a weakling unable to sustain it. She was trained and developed by his rebuffs. While his wisdom tried her, his grace sustained her.

Now, see how he began. The Savior had come to the town, wherever it was, but he was not there in public; on the contrary, he sought seclusion. Mark tells us, in his seventh chapter, in the twentyfourth and twenty-fifth verses, *From thence he arose, and went into the borders of Tyre and Sidon, and entered into an house, and would have no man know it: but he could not be hid. For a certain woman, whose young daughter had an unclean spirit, heard of him, and came and fell at his feet.*

> While his wisdom tried her, his grace sustained her.

Why is he hiding from her? He does not usually avoid the quest of the seeking soul. "Where is he?" she asks of his disciples. They give her no information; they had their Master's orders to let him remain in hiding. He sought quiet, and needed it, and so they discreetly held their tongues. Yet she found him, and fell at his feet. Half a hint was dropped; she took up the trail, and followed it until she discovered the house, and sought the Lord in his abode. Here was the beginning of her trial: the Savior was in hiding. *But he could not be hid* from her eager search; she was all ear and eye for him, and nothing can be hidden from an anxious mother, eager to bless her child. Disturbed by her, the Blessed One comes into the street, and his disciples surround him. She determines to be heard over their heads, and therefore she begins to cry aloud, *Have mercy on me, O Lord, thou son of David.*

As he walks along, she still cries out with mighty cries and pleadings, till the streets ring with her voice, and he who *would have no man know it* is proclaimed in the marketplace. Peter does not like it; he prefers quiet worship. John feels a great deal disturbed by the noise: he lost a sentence just now, a very precious sentence, which the Lord was uttering. The woman's noise was very distracting to everybody, and so the disciples came to Jesus, and they said, "Send her away, send her away. Do something for her, or tell her to be gone, for she cries after us, and we have no peace for her clamor; we cannot hear you speak because of her pitiful cries." Meanwhile, she, perceiving them speaking to Jesus, comes nearer, breaks into the inner circle, falls down before him, worships him, and utters this plaintive prayer: *Lord, help me.* There is more power in worship than in noise; she has taken a step in advance. Our Lord has not yet answered her a single word. He has heard what she said, no doubt; but he has not answered a word to her as yet. All that he has done is to say to his disciples, *I am not sent but unto the lost sheep of the house of Israel.* That has not prevented her nearer approach, or stopped her prayer; for now she pleads, *Lord, help me.*

Finally, the Blessed One does speak to her. Greatly to our surprise, it is a chill rebuff. What a cold word it is! How cutting! I dare not say, how cruel! yet it seemed so. *It is not meet to take the children's bread, and to cast it to dogs.* Now, what will the woman do? She is near the Savior; she has an audience with him, such as it is; she is on her knees before him, and he appears to repulse her! How will she act now? Here is the point about which I am going to speak. She will not be repulsed, she perseveres, she advances nearer, and she actually turns the rebuff into a plea. She has come for a blessing, and a blessing she believes that she shall have, and she means to plead for it till she wins it. So she deals with the Savior after a very heroic manner, and in the wisest possible style. From this I want every seeker to learn a lesson at this time, that he, like her, may win with Christ, and hear the Master say to him, *Great is thy faith: be it unto thee even as thou wilt.*

Three pieces of advice can be gathered from this woman's example. First, *agree with the Lord about whatever he says.* Say, "Truth, Lord; truth, Lord." Say yes to all his words. Secondly, *plead with the Lord*: "Truth, Lord, yet . . . ." Think of another truth, and mention it to him as a plea. Say, "Lord, I must maintain my hold; I must plead with you, yet . . . ." And thirdly, *in any case have faith in the Lord, whatever he says.* However he tests you, still believe in him with unstaggering faith, and know for sure that he deserves your utmost confidence in his love and power.

My first advice to every heart here seeking the Savior is this: Agree with the Lord. In the Revised Version we read that she said, "Yea, Lord," or "Yes, Lord." Whatever Jesus said, she did not contradict him in the least. I like the old translation, *Truth, Lord*, for it is very expressive. She did not say, "It is hard," or "It is unkind," but "It is true. It is true that it is not proper to take the children's bread and to cast it to dogs. It is true that compared with Israel I am a dog: for me to gain this blessing would be like a dog's feeding on the children's bread. Truth, Lord; truth, Lord." Now, dear friend, if you are dealing with the Lord for life and death, *never contradict his Word*. You will never come unto perfect peace if you are in a contradicting temperament, for that is a proud and unacceptable condition of mind. He that reads his Bible to find fault with it will soon discover that the Bible finds fault with him. It may be said of the Book of God as of its Author: "If you walk contrary to me, I will walk contrary to you." Of this Book I may truly say, *With the [contrary] thou wilt show thyself [contrary]*.

> However he tests you, still believe in him with unstaggering faith, and know that he deserves your utmost confidence in his love and power.

Remember, dear friends, that *if the Lord reminds you of your* unworthiness and your unfitness, he only tells you what is true, and it will be your wisdom to say, *Truth, Lord*. Scripture describes you as having a depraved nature: say, *Truth, Lord*. It describes you as going astray like a lost sheep, and the charge is true. It describes you as having a deceitful heart, and just such a heart you have. Therefore, say, *Truth, Lord*. It represents you as *without strength* and *without hope*. Let your answer be, *Truth, Lord*. The Bible never gives unrenewed human nature a good word, nor does it deserve it. It exposes our corruptions, and lays bare our falseness, pride, and unbelief. Fuss not at the faithfulness of the Word. Take the lowest place, and own yourself a sinner, lost, ruined, and undone. If the Scripture should seem to degrade you, do not take offense at it, but feel that it deals honestly with you. Never let proud nature contradict the Lord, for this will only increase your sin.

This woman took the very lowest possible place. She not only admitted that she was like one of the little dogs, but she also put herself under the table, and under the children's table, rather than under the master's table. She said, *The dogs eat of the crumbs which fall from their masters' table.* Most of you have supposed that she referred to the crumbs that fell from the table of the master of the house himself. If you will kindly look at the passage you will see that it is not so. *Their masters'* refers to several masters: the word is plural, and refers to the children who were the little masters of the little dogs. Thus she humbled herself to be not only as a dog to the Lord, but also as a dog to the house of Israel – to the Jews. This was going very far indeed, for a Tyrian woman, of proud Sidonian blood, to admit that the house of Israel was to her as masters, that these disciples who had said just now, *Send her away,* stood in the same relation to her as the children of the family stand in relation towards the little dogs under the table. Great faith is always sister to great humility. It does not matter how low Christ puts her, she sits *there. Truth, Lord.*

> Great faith is always sister to great humility.

I earnestly recommend every hearer of mine to consent unto the Lord's verdict, and never to raise an argument against the Sinner's Friend. When your heart is heavy, when you have a sense of being the greatest of sinners, I pray you remember that you are a greater sinner than you think yourself to be. Though conscience has rated you very low, you may go lower still, and yet be in your right place; for, truth be told, you are as bad as bad can be; you are worse than your darkest thoughts have ever painted you; you are a wretch most undeserving and hell-deserving; and apart from sovereign grace your case is hopeless. If you were now in hell, you would have no cause to complain against the justice of God, for you deserve to be there. I wish to God that every hearer here who has not yet found mercy would consent to the severest declarations of God's Word; for they are all true, and true for him. Oh, that you would say, "Yes, Lord, I have not a syllable to say in self-defense."

And next, *if it should appear to your humbled heart to be a very strange thing for you to think of being saved, do not fight against that belief.* If a sense of divine justice should suggest to you, "What! You saved? Then you will be the greatest wonder on earth! What! You saved? Surely, God will have gone beyond all former mercy in pardoning such a one as you are. In that case, he would have taken the children's bread and cast it to a dog. You are so unworthy, and so insignificant and useless, that even if you are saved, you will be good for nothing in holy service." How can you expect the blessing? Do not attempt to argue to the contrary. Seek not to magnify yourself, but cry, "Lord, I agree with your valuation of me. I freely admit that if I am forgiven, if I am made a child of God, and if I enter heaven, I shall be the greatest marvel of immeasurable love and boundless grace that ever yet lived in earth or heaven."

We should be all the more ready to give our assent and consent to every syllable of the divine Word, since *Jesus knows us better than we know ourselves.* The Word of God knows more about us than we can ever discover about ourselves. We are partial to ourselves, and therefore we are half blind. Our judgment always fails to hold the balance evenly when our own case is in the weighing. What man is there who is not on good terms with himself? Your faults, of course, are always excusable; and if you do a little good, why, it deserves to be talked of, and to be estimated at the rate of diamonds of the greatest brilliance and transparency.

Each one of us is a very superior person; so our proud heart tells us. Our Lord Jesus does not flatter us, he lets us see our case as it is. His searching eye perceives the naked truth of things, and as *the faithful and true witness,* he deals with us according to the rule of uprightness. O seeking soul, Jesus loves you too well to flatter you. Therefore, I pray you, have such confidence in him that, however much he, by his Word and Spirit, may rebuke, reprove, and even condemn you, you may without hesitation reply, "Truth, Lord! Truth, Lord!"

Nothing can be gained by quibbling with the Savior. A beggar stands at your door and asks for charity; he goes the wrong way to work if he begins a discussion with you and contradicts your statements. If beggars must not be choosers, certainly they must not be argumentative. If a beggar will dispute, let him dispute; but let him give up begging. If he fusses over how he shall receive your gift, or how or what you shall give him, he is likely to be sent about his business. A critical sinner disputing with his Savior is a fool in capitals. As for me, my mind is made up that I will quarrel with anybody sooner than with my Savior; and especially I will contend with myself, and pick a desperate quarrel with my own pride, rather than have a shade of difference with my Lord. To contend with one's Benefactor is folly indeed! For the justly condemned to quibble with the Lawgiver in whom is vested the prerogative of pardon would be folly. Instead of that, with heart and soul I cry, "Lord, whatever I find in your Word, whatever I read in Holy Scripture, which is the revelation of your mind, I do believe it, I will believe it, I must believe it; and I, therefore, say, *Truth, Lord*! It is all true, though it condemns me forever."

Now mark this: if you find your heart agreeing with what Jesus says, even when he answers you roughly, you may depend upon it that *this is a work of grace*; for human nature is very upstart, and stands very much upon its silly dignity, and therefore it contradicts the Lord, when he deals truthfully with it and humbles it. Human nature, if you want to see it in its true condition, is that naked thing over yonder, which so proudly aims at covering itself with a dress of its own invention. See, it sews fig leaves together to make itself an apron! What a destitute object! With its withered leaves around it, it seems worse than naked! Yet this wretched human nature proudly rebels against salvation by Christ. It will not hear of imputed righteousness: its own righteousness is far dearer. Woe be to the crown of pride which rivals the Lord Christ! If, my hearer, you are of another mind, and are willing to own yourself a sinner, lost, ruined, and condemned, it is well with you. If you are of this mind, that whatever humbling truth the Spirit of God may teach you in the Word, or teach by the conviction of your conscience, you will at once agree with that, and confess, "It is even so." Then the Spirit of God has brought you to this humble and truthful and obedient condition, and things are going in a hopeful manner with you.

The Lord Jesus has not come to save you, proud and arrogant ones, who sit on your thrones and look down contemptuously on others. Sit there as long as you can, until your thrones and yourselves dissolve into perdition: there is no hope for you. But you who lie upon the dunghill, you who feel as worthless as the broken potsherds around you, you who mourn that you cannot rise from that dunghill without divine help – you are the men whom he will lift from your contemptible condition and set you among princes, even the princes of his people. See the spokes of yonder wheel! They that are highest shall be lowest; they that are lowest shall be raised on high. This is how the Lord turns things upside down. *He hath put down the mighty from their seats, and exalted them of low degree. He hath filled the hungry with good things; and the rich he hath sent empty away.* If you find it in your heart to say, *Truth, Lord* to all that the Holy Spirit teaches, then surely that same Spirit is at work upon your soul, leading you to look to Jesus, and causing you to give your heart's consent to the way of salvation through the merit of the Redeemer's blood.

And now my second point is this: although you must not quibble with Christ, you may *plead with him. Truth, Lord*, she says, but she adds, *yet*.

Here, then, is my first lesson: *set one truth over against another.* Do not contradict a frowning truth, but bring up a smiling one to meet it. Remember how the Jews were saved out of the hands of their enemies in the days of Haman and Mordecai. The king issued a decree that, on a certain day, the people might rise up against the Jews, and slay them, and take their possessions as spoil. Now, according to the laws of the Medes and Persians, this could not be altered: the decree had to stand. What then? How was it to be got over? Why, by meeting that ordinance by another. Another decree is issued, that although the people might rise against the Jews, yet the Jews might defend themselves; and if anybody dared to hurt them, they might slay them, and take their property as prey. One decree thus counteracted another. How often we may use the holy art of looking from one doctrine to another!

If a truth looks black upon me, I shall not be wise to be always dwelling upon it; but it will be my wisdom to examine the whole range of truth, and see if there be not some other doctrine which will give me hope. David practiced this when he said of himself, *So foolish was I, and ignorant: I was as a beast before thee.* And then he most confidently added, *Nevertheless I am continually with thee: thou hast holden me by my right hand.* He does not contradict himself, and yet the second utterance removes all the bitterness which the first sentence left upon the palate. The two sentences together set forth the supreme grace of God, who enabled a poor beast-like being to commune with himself. I beg you to learn this holy art of setting one truth side by side with another, that thus you may have a fair view of the whole situation, and may not despair.

For instance, I meet with men who say, "O sir, sin is an awful thing, it condemns me. I feel I can never answer the Lord for my iniquities, nor stand in his holy presence." This is assuredly true, but remember another truth: *The Lord hath laid on him the iniquity of us all; He hath made him to be sin for us, who knew no sin; There is therefore now no condemnation to them which are in Christ Jesus.* Set the truth of the sin-bearing of our Lord over against the guilt and curse of sin due to yourself apart from your great Substitute.

"The Lord has an elect people," cries one, "and this discourages me." Why should it? Do not contradict that truth; believe it as you read it in God's Word, but hear how Jesus puts it: *I thank thee, O Father, Lord of heaven and earth, because thou hast hid these things from the wise and prudent, and hast revealed them unto babes.* To you who are weak, simple, and trustful as babes, the doctrine is full of comfort. If the Lord will save a number that no man can number, why should he not save me? It is true that it is written, *All that the Father giveth me shall come to me;* but it is also written, *And him that cometh to me I will in no wise cast out.* Let the second half of the saying be accepted as well as the first half.

Some are tripped up by the sovereignty of God. He will have mercy on whom he will have mercy. He may justly ask, "Shall I not do as I will with my own?" Beloved, do not dispute the rights of the eternal God. It is the Lord: let him do as seems good to him. Do not quarrel with the King, but come humbly to him and plead thus: "O Lord, you alone have the right to pardon; but then your Word declares that if we confess our sins, you are faithful and just to forgive us our sins; and you have said that whosoever believes in the Lord Jesus Christ shall be saved." This pleading will prevail. Kick not at truth, lest you dash your naked foot against iron pricks. Yet dwell not on one truth till it distracts you, but look at others till they cheer you. Submit to all truth, but plead on your own behalf that which seems to you to look favorably upon you.

When you read, *Ye must be born again,* do not be angry. It is true that to be born again is a work beyond your power: it is the work of the Holy Spirit, and this need of a work beyond your reach may well distress you. But that third chapter of John, which says, *Ye must be born again*, also says, *For God so loved the world, that he gave his only begotten Son, that whosoever believeth in him should not perish, but have everlasting life.* Thus it is clear that he that believes in Jesus is born again. I pray you, have an eye to all the land of truth, and when you seem to be persecuted in one city of truth, flee to another; for there is a refuge city even for you. Besides, there is a bright side to every truth, if you have but the wit to spy it out. The same key which locks will also unlock: very much depends on the turn of the key, and still more on the turn of your thoughts.

This brings me to a second remark: *draw comfort even from a hard truth*. Take this advice in preference to that which I have already given. The Authorized translation here is very good, but I must confess that it is not quite so true to the woman's meaning as the Revised Version. She did not say, *Truth, Lord:* **yet** (emphasis added), as if she were raising an objection, as I have already put it to you; but she said, *Truth, Lord,* **for** (emphasis added). I have gone with the old translation because it expresses the way in which our mind too generally looks at things. We fancy that we set one truth over against another, whereas all truths are agreed, and cannot be in conflict. Out of the very truth which looks darkest we may gain consolation.

She said, "Yes, Lord, *for* the dogs eat the crumbs which fall from their masters' table." She did not draw comfort from another truth which seemed to neutralize the first; but, as the bee sucks honey from the nettle, so did she gather encouragement from the severe word of the Lord: *It is not meet to take the children's bread, and to cast it to dogs.* She said, "That is true, Lord, for even the dogs eat the crumbs that fall from their masters' table." She did not turn what Christ said upside down; she took it as it stood, and spied out comfort in it. Earnestly would I urge you to learn the art of deriving comfort from every statement of God's Word; not necessarily bringing up a second doctrine, but believing that even the present truth which bears a threatening aspect is yet your friend.

Do I hear you say, "How can I have hope? for salvation is of the Lord." Why, that is the very reason why you should be filled with hope and seek salvation from the Lord alone. If it were of yourself, you might despair; but since it is of the Lord, you may have hope.

Do you groan out, "Alas! I can do nothing!" What of that? The Lord can do everything. Since salvation is of the Lord alone, ask him to be its Alpha and Omega to you. Do you groan, "I know I must repent, but I am so unfeeling that I cannot reach the right measure of tenderness." This is true, and therefore the Lord Jesus is exalted on high to give repentance. You will no more repent in your own power than you will go to heaven in your own merit; but the Lord will grant you repentance unto life, for this also is a fruit of the Spirit.

Beloved, when I was under a sense of sin I heard the doctrine of divine sovereignty, "He will have mercy on whom he will have mercy"; but that did not frighten me at all, for I felt more hopeful of grace through the sovereign will of God than by any other way. If pardon be not a matter of human deserving, but of divine prerogative, then there is hope for me. Why should I not be forgiven as well as others? If the Lord had only three elect ones, and these were chosen according to his own good pleasure, why should I not be one of them? I laid myself at his feet, and gave up every hope but that which flowed from his mercy. Knowing that he would save a number that no man could number, and that he would save every soul that believed in Jesus, I believed and was saved.

It was well for me that salvation was not based upon merit, for I had no merit whatever. If it remained with sovereign grace, then I also could go through that door, for the Lord might as well save me as any other sinner; and inasmuch as I read, *Him that cometh to me I will in no wise cast out*, I even came, and he did not cast me out. Rightly understood, every truth in God's Word leads to Jesus, and no single word drives the seeking sinner back. If you are a fine fellow, full of your own righteousness, then every gospel truth looks black on you. But if you are a sinner deserving nothing from God but wrath, and if in your heart you confess that you deserve condemnation, then you are the kind of man that Christ came to save, you are the sort of man that God chose from before the foundation of the world, and you may, without any hesitancy, come and put your trust in Jesus, who is the sinner's Savior. Believing in him, you shall receive immediate salvation.

I will not give you further instances and particulars, for time would fail me. I leave you just there with this advice: it is not yours to raise questions, but submissively to say, *Truth, Lord*. Then it is your wisdom to set one truth over against another, till you have learned the better plan of finding light-in-the-dark truth itself. God help you to fetch honey from the rock and oil out of the flinty rock, by a simple and unquestioning faith in the Lord Jesus Christ.

Thirdly, in any case, whatever Christ says or does not say, have faith in him. Look at this woman's faith and try to copy it. It grew in its understanding of Jesus.

First, he is *the Lord of mercy*. She cried, *Have mercy on me*. Have faith enough, dear hearer, to believe that you need mercy.

Mercy is not for the meritorious: the claim of the meritorious is for justice, not for mercy. The guilty need and seek mercy, and only they. Believe that God delights in mercy, delights to give grace where it cannot be deserved, and delights to forgive where there is no reason for forgiveness but his own goodness. Believe also that the Lord Jesus Christ whom we preach to you is the incarnation of mercy: his very existence is mercy to you. His every word means mercy; his life, his death, his intercession in heaven all mean mercy, mercy, mercy, nothing but mercy. You need divine mercy, and Jesus is the embodiment of divine mercy, he is the Savior for you. Believe in him, and the mercy of God is yours.

This woman also called him *son of David*, in which she recognized his manhood and his kingship towards man. Think of Jesus Christ as God over all, blessed forever, he that made the heavens and the earth, and upholds all things by the word of his power. Know that he became man, veiling his Godhead in this poor clay of ours. He hung as a babe upon a woman's breast, he sat as a weary man upon the curb of a well, he died with felons on the cross, and all this out of love for man. Can you not trust this son of David? David was very popular because he went in and out among the people, and proved himself the people's king. Jesus is such. David gathered to him a company of men who were greatly attached to him, because when they came to him they were a broken-down crew; they were in debt, and discontented. All the outcasts from Saul's dominions came around David, and he became a captain to them.

My Lord Jesus Christ is one chosen out of the people, chosen by God on purpose to be a brother to us, a brother born for adversity, a brother who has come to associate with us, despite our meanness and misery. He is the friend of men and women who are ruined by their guilt and sin. *This man receiveth sinners, and eateth with them.* Jesus is the willing leader of a people sinful and defiled, whom he raises to justification and holiness, and makes to dwell with him in glory forever. Oh, will you not trust such a Savior as this? My Lord did not come into the world to save superior people who think themselves born saints. I say again, you may sit upon thrones till you and your thrones go down to perdition. But Jesus came to save the lost, the ruined, the guilty, and the unworthy. Let such come clustering around him like the bees around the queen bee, for he is ordained on purpose to collect the Lord's chosen ones, as it is written, *Unto him shall the gathering of the people be.*

This believing woman might have been cheered by another theme. Our Lord said to his disciples, *I am not sent but unto the lost sheep of the house of Israel.* "Ah!" thinks she, "he is a shepherd for lost sheep. Whatever his flock may be, *he is a shepherd,* and he has bowels of compassion for poor lost sheep. Surely he is one to whom I may look with confidence." Ah, dear hearer! my Lord Jesus Christ is a shepherd by office and by nature, and if you are a lost sheep this is good tidings for you. There is a holy instinct in him which makes him gather the lambs with his arms, and causes him to search out the lost ones who were scattered in the cloudy and dark day. Trust him to seek you; yes, come to him now, and leave yourselves with him.

Further than that, this woman had a faith in Christ that he was like *a great householder.* She seems to say, "Those disciples are children who sit at the table, and he feeds them on the bread of his love. He makes for them so great a feast, and he gives to them so much food, that if my daughter were healed, it would be a great and blessed thing to me, but to him it would be no more than if a crumb fell under the table and a dog fed on it." She does not ask to have a crumb thrown to her, but only to be allowed to pick up a crumb that has fallen from the table. She asks not even for a crumb which the Lord may drop, but for one which the children have let fall: they are generally great crumb-makers. I notice in the Greek that as the word for *dogs* is "little dogs," so the word rendered *crumbs* is "little crumbs" – small, insignificant morsels which fall by accident.

Think of this faith. To have the devil cast out of her daughter was the greatest thing she could imagine, and yet she had such a belief in the greatness of the Lord Christ that she thought it would be no more for him to make her daughter well than for a great housekeeper to let a poor little dog eat a tiny crumb that had been dropped by a child. Is not that splendid faith? And now, can you exercise such a faith? Can you believe it – you, a condemned, lost sinner – that if God saves you it will be the greatest wonder that ever was, and yet that to Jesus, who made himself a sacrifice for sin, it will be no more than if this day your dog or your cat should eat a tiny morsel that one of your children had dropped from the table? Can you think Jesus to be so great that what is heaven to you will be only a crumb to him? Can you believe that he can save you readily?

As for me, I believe my Lord to be such a Savior that I can trust my soul wholly to him, and do it without difficulty. And I will tell you something else: if I had all your souls in my body, I would trust them all to Jesus. Yes, and if I had a million sinful souls of my own, I would freely trust the Lord Christ with the whole of them, and I would say, "I am persuaded that he is able to keep that which I have committed to him against that day." Do not suppose that I speak thus because I am conscious of any goodness of my own. Far from it: my trust is in no degree in myself, or in anything I can do or be. If I were good I could not trust in Jesus. Why should I? I should trust in myself. But because I have nothing of my own, I am obliged to live by trust, and I rejoice that I may do so. My Lord gives me unlimited credit at the Bank of Faith. I am very deeply in debt to him, and I am resolved to be more indebted still. Sinner as I am, if I were a million times as sinful as I am, and then had a million souls with each one a million times more sinful than my own, I would still trust his atoning blood to cleanse me, and himself to save me. By your agony and bloody sweat, by your cross and passion, by your precious death and burial, by your glorious resurrection and ascension, by your intercession for the guilty at the right

> **If I were good I could not trust in Jesus. Why should I? I should trust in myself.**

hand of God, O Christ, I feel that I can rest in you. May you come to this point, all of you, that Jesus is abundantly able to save.

You have been a thief, have you? The last person that was in our Lord's near company on earth was the dying thief. "Oh!" but you say, "I have been foul in life; I have defiled myself with all manner of evil." But those with whom he associates now were all of them once unclean; for they confess that they have washed their robes and made them white in his blood. Their robes were once so foul that nothing but his heart's blood could have made them white. Jesus is a great Savior, greater than my tongue can tell. If we were somehow able to speak his worth, even if we could speak heaven in every word and express infinity in every sentence, not all the tongues of men or of angels could fully set forth the greatness of the grace of our Redeemer. Trust him! Are you afraid to trust him? Then make a dash for it. Venture to do so.

> Venture on him, venture wholly;
> Let no other trust intrude.

Look unto me, says he, *and be ye saved, all the ends of the earth: for I am God, and there is none else.* Look! Look now! Look to him alone; and as you look to him with the look of faith, he will look on you with loving acceptance and say, *Great is thy faith: be it unto thee even as thou wilt.* You shall be saved at this very hour; and though you came into this house of prayer grievously vexed with a devil, you shall go out at peace with God and as restful as an angel. God grant you this blessing, for Christ's sake. Amen.

Chapter 14

Little Faith and Great Faith

O thou of little faith, wherefore didst thou doubt? (Matthew 14:31)

O woman, great is thy faith: be it unto thee even as thou wilt. (Matthew 15:28)

Between the very lowest degree of faith and a state of unbelief there is a great gulf. An abyss immeasurable yawns between the man who has even the smallest faith in Christ and the man who has none. One is a living man, though feeble, the other is *dead in trespasses and sins*; the one is a justified man, the other is *condemned already, because he hath not believed in the name of the only begotten Son of God.* The weakest believer is on the road to heaven; the other, having no faith, is going the downward road, and he will find his portion at last among the unbelievers – a terrible portion indeed.

Although we thus speak of believers as all of one company, yet there is a great distance between weak faith and strong faith. Thank God, it is a distance upon the one safe road: the King's highway. No gulf divides little faith from great faith; on the contrary, little faith has only to travel along the royal road, and he shall overtake his stronger brother, and himself become *strong in the Lord, and in the power of his might.* I want to revive souls of the more tardy travelers along the sacred way.

I would have doubts slain and faith revived. I want Mr. Feeble-Mind, and Mistress Much-Afraid, and Miss Despondency, and the whole tribe of the little ones to take heart of hope, and observe that they have not yet enjoyed all that the Lord has prepared for them. Although a little faith saves, there is more faith to be had: faith which strengthens, gladdens, honors, and makes useful is a most desirable grace. It is written, *He giveth more grace*, and therefore God has more in readiness for us. Little faith may increase exceedingly until it ripens into full assurance with all its mellowness and sweetness.

There are three things I am going to point your attention to. The first is *little faith gently rebuked: O thou of little faith, wherefore didst thou doubt?* In the second place is *little faith tenderly commended*; for it is no small benefit to have any faith at all, even though it has to be called little. Thirdly, I shall conclude by speaking of *great faith as much more to be commended*. In this last matter I shall dwell upon our Master's gracious words: *O woman, great is thy faith: be it unto thee even as thou wilt.*

I have read in your hearing two stories in the fourteenth and fifteenth chapters of this Gospel according to Matthew. It is memorable that the incidents, illustrating little and great faith, come so closely together. I shall take it for granted that you have the stories of Peter and the Canaanite woman clearly before your minds. Keep your Bibles open while I preach, and may the Spirit of God open your hearts to understand them!

First, we have *little faith gently rebuked.*

What shall I say about it, to begin with, but this? That *it is frequently found where we expected greater things.* This man who is chided for little faith is Peter. Peter, to whom the Lord had communicated a very clear knowledge of himself; Peter, the foreman of the twelve; Peter, in afterdays the great preacher of Pentecost; Peter, who has been exalted by some into the role of leader or pope of the apostolic church, though he claimed no such position. This is Peter, who was a true piece of stone from the foundation rock, to whom the Master gave the keys, and to whom he delivered the commission, *Feed my sheep*, and *Feed my lambs.* It is Peter to whom Jesus says, *O thou of little faith.*

And, my dear brother or sister, may it not be true that you have obtained great mercy, enjoyed high privileges, received gracious protection, and been eminently favored with fellowship with Christ, most near and dear? By this time you ought to be strong in faith. But yet you are not so. You will soon be home; your gray hairs are silvered with the light of Immanuel's land; you can almost hear the singing of the saints across the narrow stream. At your time of life, so long taught of God, so deeply experienced in the things of Christ, you ought to be fathers in faith, whereas you are still children; you ought to be mothers in Israel, and yet you are mere babes. Is it not so? Why is this sad fact so undeniable?

Solomon spoke of the cedar in Lebanon and of the hyssop on the wall, but I have too often seen a hyssop on Lebanon, and I have sometimes seen a cedar upon a wall. I mean that I have seen great grace where there seemed to be nothing to assist it, and I have seen little grace where everything was advantageous to its growth. These things ought not to be so. You and I, who are no children now; you and I, who are no longer coasters, but have launched out into the deep, and have had experience in many a storm; you and I, who are no strangers to our Lord now, for the King has often brought us into his banqueting-house, and his banner over us has been love, we ought to be ashamed if we are still lamenting our little faith. It is an infirmity in which we cannot glory, for unbelief is exceedingly sinful. Well might the Master lift his finger to us and say to us one by one, *O thou of little faith, wherefore didst thou doubt?*

Continuing our very gentle rebuke, we note that *little faith is far too eager for a sign.* I do not think that Peter's faith became suddenly little; it was always little, and the sight of the boisterous wind made its littleness apparent. When he said, *Lord, if it be thou, bid me come unto thee on the water,* his faith was weak. Why did he want to walk on the water? Why did he seek such a wonder? It was because his faith was little. Strong faith is content without signs, without tokens, and without marvels. It believes God's bare word, and asks for no confirming miracle; its trust in Christ is such that it asks for no sign in the heavens above, or in the seas beneath. Little faith, with her *If it be thou*, must have signs and wonders, or she yields to doubt.

Joyful meditations, remarkable dreams, singular providences, choice answers to prayer, and special fellowships – little faith must be having something out of the common, or she collapses. The perpetual cry of little faith is, "Show me a token for good." Little faith is not satisfied with the bow which God sets in the cloud, but she would prefer to have the whole heavens painted with celestial colors. She is not satisfied with the usual portion of the saints, but must have more, do more, and feel more than the rest of the disciples. Why could not Peter keep himself in the ship like the rest of his brethren? Because his faith was weak he must leave the deck for the deep; he cannot think that it really is his Master walking on the sea unless he walks with him. How dare he ask to do what his divine Lord was doing! Let him be content to share his Lord's humiliation; he ventures far when he asks to partake in a miracle of omnipotence.

Am I to doubt unless I can do miracles like those of my Lord? But this is one of the failings of weak faith: it is not content to drink of his cup and be baptized with his baptism; it wants to share his power and partake in his throne.

Weak faith is apt to have too high an opinion of its own power. "Oh," says one, "surely you are wrong. Is it not the error of weak faith to have too low an opinion of its own ability?" Brethren, no man can have too low an opinion of his own power, because he has no power whatever. The Lord Jesus Christ said, *Without me ye can do nothing*; and his witness is true. If we have strong faith we shall glory in our powerlessness, because the power of Christ rests upon us. If we have weak faith, we shall diminish our trust in Jesus and put into our hearts instead of it so many measures of confidence in self. Just in proportion as faith in our Lord is weakened, our idea of ourselves will be strengthened. "But I thought," says one, "that a man who had strong self-reliance was a man of great faith." He is the man who has no faith at all, for self-reliance and Christ-reliance will not abide in the same heart. Peter has an idea that he can go upon the water to his Master; he is not so sure of the others, but he is clear about himself. James, and John, and Andrew, and the rest of them are in the ship. It does not occur to Peter that any one of these can tread the waves; but he cries, *Lord, if it be thou, bid **me** come unto thee on the water* (emphasis added).

Self-consciousness is no attribute of faith, but it is a nest for doubt.

Had he known himself, he might have said, "Lord, bid John come to you on the water; I am unworthy of so high a dignity." But no. Being weak in faith, he was strong in his own opinion of himself, and he hurried to the front, as usual; he hastened into a pathway that was quite unfit for his trembling feet to tread, and before long he found out his error. It is weak faith that allows high ideas of self. Great faith hides self under its mighty wings.

Note another point about weak faith: *it is too much affected by its surroundings.* Peter went on pretty well till he noticed that the wind tossed the waves about tremendously, and then he was afraid. Are not many Christians too apt to live by what they feel and see? Do we not often hear a young beginner say, "I know that I am converted, for I feel so happy"? Well, but a new dress will make many a girl happy, or a few coins in the pocket will make a youth rejoice. Is this the best evidence that you can bring? Why, if you are very troubled, it may be a better sign of conversion than feeling happy. It is well to mourn over sin, and struggle against it, and try to overcome it; this is a sure mark of grace, a far surer one than overflowing joy.

> It is weak faith that allows high ideas of self. Great faith hides self under its mighty wings.

Ah, believer! you will be happy in the highest and best sense if you trust in Jesus, but you will soon lose your happiness if your happiness becomes the ground for your confidence. Happiness is a thing that depends upon how things happen. It is too often happiness, and nothing more. It is too much a haphazard thing. But faith rests in Christ whatever "hap" may happen; and so it is happy in the happening of sorrow and grief, because it relies wholly upon God. Faith rests upon the Lord's faithful word and promise, come what may. "Ah!" says another, "I feel very low and dull. I am heavy even when I try to pray; I cannot pray as I would like." And so you doubt your salvation because of that, do you? Does your salvation depend upon the liveliness of your prayers? It is the mark of weak faith, that it is all up, and then all down.

If we live by feelings, brethren, we shall live a very wretched life; we shall not dwell in the Father's house, but we shall lie as a kind of gypsies, whose tents are too frail to shut out the weather. God save us from being like the barometer, which at one time is "set fair"; but "set fair" with the barometer does not last long. It is soon back again to "rain," and then it drops down to "much rain," before we know where we are.

Strong faith knows where its true standing is, and, perceiving this to be unchanging, it concludes that its foundation is as good one day as another day, for its standing is in Christ. Since the promise upon which strong faith leans is not a variable quantity but is always the same, so its rest is the same. Our faithful God will save all those who put their trust in him; and there is the top and the bottom of it: we need not go any further. But poor weak faith is always looking out to see whether the wind is in the east; and if it be so, down she goes. Is the wind quiet? Peter walks on the wave. Does the wind howl? Peter begins to sink. This is weak faith all over. It pins us down to its environment. God help us to rise out of it!

Weak faith, in the next place, *is forgetful of its constant danger,* and has not learned to believe in the teeth of it. When Peter was walking on the waves, he was in as much danger as when he began to sink. Practically, he never was in any danger at all; for Jesus, who enabled him to tread the sea, was equally near all the way. When he was standing, he could not have walked another step if the Master had not upheld him; and when he began to sink, his Master was still able to prevent his drowning. Would his Master withdraw the divine strength and permit his poor servant to perish? Peter's strength is gone, but will his Master take away the divine strength, and leave him to perish?

> **Strong faith takes Jesus only as her basis, but feeble faith tries to add to it.**

Weak faith frequently makes this mistake; she does not know that she is at all times in extreme danger, wherever she may be, when she looks to herself; and that she is never in any danger, wherever she may be, if she looks to her Lord. If you get a cloudy view of your confidence, and begin to trust not in Christ pure and simple, but in Christ Jesus as you enjoy him, in Christ as you are like him, or in Christ and yourself as taught by him; if you allow any amalgamations in your trust, they will turn out to be adulterations; and when a sense of danger falls upon your mind, you will not know where to turn for the re-establishment of your confidence.

Strong faith takes Jesus only as her basis, but feeble faith tries to add to it. Beloved, weak faith tries to make up for lack of confidence in the Lord Jesus Christ with an indistinct confidence in herself, or her works, or prayers, or something else. If Peter had been trusting wholly in Jesus, whether he walked on the billows or sank in the waves, he would have done what his Master told him to do, and the reason for his safety would not have been in the least affected by the wind. If his reliance was on Jesus only, the ground for his confidence was never questionable. I pray that we may climb above that weak faith which rises and falls with the passing incidents of this life's story.

Weak faith, when conscious of her danger, swings as a pendulum to the opposite extreme, and *in an instant exaggerates her peril.* One moment Peter walks upon the sea, the next moment he is going to be drowned. It is a curious thing that he never thought of swimming. When the soul trusts Christ, it is robbed of reliance upon self. When once a man has found out the way to walk upon the top of the water, he forgets his skill in swimming in it.

Self-confidence goes when confidence in Christ comes in. It was the Lord's will that Peter should know his weakness, and should most clearly see that his standing depended upon his faith, and that faith found all its strength in the Lord Jesus. Down goes Peter, and now it is, *Lord, save me.* He is at his wits' end. Peter is going to be drowned – drowned with the Master standing by! He will die while Jesus lives. Will he? He will perish when he is doing what Jesus bid him do! Do you think he will? It is evident he has that fear upon him. I have been foolish enough to feel that I should sink under trouble and need. It is folly.

Having mixed up our confidence in brighter days, when dark days come, a large part of our confidence is gone, and we fear that we shall perish. Have not some of you that believed in the doctrine of the final perseverance of the saints still said, "I shall one day fall by the hand of the Enemy"? You know that Christ has promised to keep you, and yet, because you are not quite keeping yourself as you ought to do, you dream that he will not keep you. You know that he will never give you up, and yet you are almost ready to give it all up yourself and say, "I shall prove an apostate after all." In this way little faith forgets her Lord. She is too bold one day, and too timid another, and all because she mixes up her confidences.

Little faith speaks unreasonably. Notice how our Lord puts it: *O thou of little faith, wherefore didst thou doubt?* Faith is spiritual common sense, unbelief is treasonable. Look: if Christ was worth trusting at all, and Peter had proved that he thought he was by throwing himself into the sea to go to him, then, if he was worth trusting at all, he was worthy to be trusted to the full. You cannot say of a man, "He is a faithful man, for you may at times rely upon his word." That qualifying phrase, "at times," is fatal to his character. Unless he is always to be relied upon, he is not an honest, truth-speaking man. And if you say of God's promises, "I can believe some of them, and therefore I expect him to help me under certain difficulties," you are accusing the Lord of unfaithfulness. O sir, you are cutting away the foundation of what little faith you have. Your Lord might ask you, "Why do you believe as much as you do believe? Having gone so far, why do you not go on to the end? The reason which makes you believe as much as you do believe should make you believe to a still greater degree.

O you of little faith, why did you doubt? If you have any faith, why do you doubt? If any doubt, why any faith?" The two things are inconsistent with each other. You are not occupying a logical position in being a weak believer in a strong Christ. Why wavering faith in an unwavering promise? Why feeble faith in a mighty Savior? Let your faith take its color from him on whom it rests, and from the Word which you believe, and then you will be standing upon good, solid, reasonable ground, which can be justified to conscience and understanding.

> If you have strong faith you will often escape a sea of troubles, which weak faith will be immersed in.

One word more about our trembling misgivings. *Weak faith often gets a wetting.* Although Peter was not drowned, yet you may be sure he was soaked to the skin with the water. If you have strong faith you will often escape a sea of troubles, which weak faith will be immersed in. Weak faith is a great fabricator of terrors. I know friends who have a trouble-factory in their back garden, where they are always making rods for their own backs. They disbelieve God about this and about that, and therefore they are always fretting and worrying and getting wet through with trouble.

I have heard it said that homemade clothes very seldom fit; and, certainly, homemade troubles are very hard to bear. I have also heard that a homemade suit will last longer than other garments, and I believe that homemade troubles stick to us far longer than those which God appoints for us. Shut up that fear factory, and make songs instead! If God sends you a trouble, it comes not wrongly to you. But who wetted Peter through and through, and soaked him in the deep? Who but Peter himself! Peter, afflicted Peter! If he had possessed strong faith, he might have had a dry coat. His Master prevented the waters from destroying him, but he permitted them to make him very uncomfortable. If you have weak faith, you will have broken joys and many discomforts.

Thus have I very gently rebuked weak faith. I did not mean to hurt a hair of its head. It is a blessed thing, this little faith – not its littleness, but its faith. If I could kill the weakness and revive the faith, if the littleness could be removed and the faith could be increased, how glad I should be!

Now, *little faith shall be tenderly commended*. I shall praise it, not because it is little, but because it is faith. Little faith needs to be tenderly handled, and then it will be seen to be a precious thing.

First of all, *it is true faith*. Faith which begins and ends with Jesus is true faith. The least faith in Jesus is the gift of God; and it is *like precious faith*, though it is not like strong faith. If you have faith as a grain of mustard seed, you can do wonders. Though your faith be so little that you have to look for it with all your eyes, yet if it be there, it is of the same nature as the strongest faith. A threepence piece is silver, as surely as the crown piece, and it bears the mint-mark quite as certainly. A drop of water is of the same nature as the sea; a spark is fire as assuredly as the flames of Vesuvius.

Nobody knows what may come of a spark of faith: behold, it sets a thousand souls on fire! Little faith is true faith, for did not our Lord say this to Peter: *Blessed art thou, Simon Bar-jona: for flesh and blood hath not revealed it unto thee, but my Father which is in heaven*? Peter had true faith, and yet it was little faith. O my hearer, if you believe that Jesus is the Christ, you are born of God. If you do feebly cast yourself on Christ's finished work, your weakness in the act of reliance does not alter the fact that you have fallen into strong hands, which will surely save you. Jesus says, *Look unto me, and be ye saved*; and though your look be a very unsteady one, and though tears of sorrow dim your eyes so that you cannot see him as he is, yet your looking to him has saved you. Little faith is born from above, and belongs to the family of the saved. The weakest faith is real faith.

Next, notice that *little faith obeys the precept, and will not go a step without it*. Little faith cries, *If it be thou, bid me come unto thee on the water. And he said, Come. And when Peter was come down out of the ship, he walked on the water, to go to Jesus.* If Jesus says, *Come*, then little faith answers, *Behold, I come*! Though her gait be staggering, and her knees be feeble, yet she will go where Jesus calls her, whether it be through flood or flame. I know some of the Lord's children who very seldom have much enjoyment, and yet I almost envy them for their tenderness of conscience. Their shrinking from the least contact with sin, their carefulness to keep the way of the Lord's commandments, are admirable traits in their character. Gracious walking is, after all, more precious than comfortable feeling. How can I blame you, poor little faith, when I see you afraid to put one foot before the other for fear you should step aside? I would rather see you in all your timidity be carefully obedient than hear you talking loudly about your great faith, and then see you tampering with sin and folly, and feeling as if when you have greatly erred it is a matter of no great consequence. When tenderness of conscience flourishes side by side with little faith, they are as two lilies for delicate beauty.

Peter's little faith did not try to walk upon water until Jesus gave the word of permission. Peter asked, *Bid me come.* Oftentimes I have noticed men and women very despondent and greatly fearful, and yet they would not do anything for the life of them until they heard the voice behind them saying, *This is the way, walk ye in it.* They hesitate till they have consulted the map of the Word; they dare not go at random, but they kneel and cry for guidance, for they are afraid of taking even a single step apart from their Master's will. They have a holy dread of running without warrant from the Lord. Little faith, if this be your mind and temper, we commend you much!

And next, *little faith struggles to come to Jesus.* Peter did not leave the ship for the mere sake of walking on the waters, but he ventured on the waves that he might come to Jesus. He sought not a promenade upon the waves, but the presence and company of his Lord. *When Peter was come down out of the ship, he walked on the water, to go to Jesus.* That was the one point he aimed at – to get to Jesus. Some of you, I know, have but little faith, but you long to get nearer to Jesus. Your daily panting is, "Lord, reveal yourself to me, reveal yourself in me, and make me more like you." He who seeks Jesus has his face turned in the right direction. Though your knees knock together, and your hands hang down, yet what little headway you do make is towards Jesus. You strive to serve him and to honor him; is it not so? Though the winds be contrary, you still pull for the shore. Well, though you be little in faith, yet am I glad you are struggling, despite your feebleness, to reach your Lord. Struggle on, for Jesus comes to meet you; and when you do begin to sink, though you lack confidence, he will catch you up and set you on your feet again. Therefore, be of good cheer!

Little faith deserves commendation again, in that *it does behave grandly for a time.* Though Peter had little faith, yet he walked from one billow to another in rare style. I think I see him after he leaped out of the ship, astonished to find himself standing upon the waters which lay beneath him like solid glass. Then he takes one step, like a child that begins to walk; and, with growing confidence, he takes another. Though the waves roll under his feet, yet he stands firmly upon them, for a time. Little faith can play the man for a while. When Jael took the nail and slew Sisera, the timid woman became a warrior, as she slew the enemy of Israel. Many a time the lame and the feeble, who could not usually lift a hand in the holy war, have felt stimulated, and have developed heroism for the time being. Little faith, like David's sling, has slain the giant; like Ehud's lefthanded dagger, little faith has brought deliverance. So I commend you, little faith, for you have your high days and holidays, and you too can count your victories, brought about in the name of Jesus. If it were always with you as it is at times, you would be glorious indeed! Even now you can move mountains and pluck up trees by the roots.

Little faith I must commend yet further, because *when it finds itself in trouble it commits itself to prayer.* Peter begins to sink. What does Peter do? Peter prays, *Lord, save me.* Little faith knows where her strength lies. When she is in trouble, she does not then turn her face to human confidences, or natural forces; but she turns immediately to prayer. Little faith pours out her heart before the Lord. I love to see a man, in the hour of his distress, begin to pray at once, as naturally as frightened birds take to their wings. Some of you run to your neighbors, or hold a council with your own mind, but the profit of this course has never made you rich. Let us try a surer method. Instead of stopping to turn over all the old stock we have, let us go at once to Jesus for new help. Alas! we do not go to Jesus until we have knocked at every other door, and then the mercy is that he does not turn us away from his gate.

Peter did not try the natural resort of swimming; he took to praying, *Lord, save me.* O little faith, you are great at pleading in prayer. Perhaps your very weakness drives you more often to your knees. You are not so prevalent in prayer as in strong faith, but you are quite as abundant in it. I see you trembling and faint, then you cry unto the Lord for strength, and he helps you. This cry of yours proves you to be of the spiritual stock, even as it was with one of old, of whom it was said, *Behold, he prayeth.*

Weak faith has this commendation again, that *it is always safe, because Jesus is near.* Peter was safe on the water, because Christ was on the water. Though his faith was weak, he was not saved by the strength of his faith; he was saved by the strength of that gracious hand which was stretched out to catch him when he was sinking in the flood. If you believe in Christ with all your heart, if he is the first and last of your confidence, then, though you be full of trembling and alarm, Jesus will never let you perish. If you are depending upon him, and upon him alone, it is not possible that he should make light of your faith and let you die. God forbid we should so insult our Lord as to suppose he would let a believer drown, however weak his faith! Since Christ lives, how can we die? Since Christ stands on the waters, how can we sink beneath them? Are we not one with him?

One thing I may say in commendation of weak faith, and that is, that *Jesus himself acknowledges that it is faith.* He said to Peter, *O thou of little faith.* He rebuked him because it was little, but he smiled on him because it was faith. I love to feel that the Holy Spirit is the Creator, not of the littleness of our faith, but of our faith, be it ever so little. Our

Lord acknowledges that to be faith which we suspect to be little better than unbelief. *Lord, I believe; help thou mine unbelief* is an admirable prayer for many of us. Christ forgives the unbelief, but he very graciously accepts the faith, despite its weakness. He can spy out faith when, like a lone spark, it is all but smothered under a heap of rubbish.

Once more, I commend little faith because, though it may sometimes sink, *it recovers itself, and does its old wonders over again*. Peter is ready to sink, but when his Master catches him, what do you see? There is not one person now walking on the water, there are two. Christ is there, and Peter too. Peter, my man, you walk on the sea as one fitted to that role! Oh yes, his little faith has learned, by a touch from the Lord, to do what it did at first: he walked the waves at first, and now he does it again. See! he comes up with his Lord into the ship. You that used to have good times and at this hour look back upon them with deep regret, may have the same again. You that have grown despondent and sad, be of good courage; you shall have your festival days back again, and much brighter than they were. "Oh, but I have wasted so much time," says one, "through this feeble faith of mine." Well, it is a great pity, but there is a promise which I commend to your faith: *I will restore to you the years that the locust hath eaten*. The locust has eaten up our harvests – this locust of weakness has devoured our pleasant fruits; yet our Lord Jesus Christ can restore to us those wasted years; he can pack ten years of usefulness into one; he can put seven days of joy into one day, and so make up to us the lost past. Our Lord can make you forget the shame of your youth, and not remember the reproach of your widowhood any more.

> Put your trust in the Lord, and quietly wait for him, and then shall your morning surely come in due time.

Be of good courage, little faith! You come to a good family, though you be but a babe as yet. Be of good courage, little faith! You may be sick on board the vessel, but the vessel on which you have embarked is safe for all that, and you will get to shore as surely as strong faith will do. Put your trust in the Lord, and quietly wait for him, and then shall your morning surely come in due time. Thus have I gently rebuked and kindly commended little faith.

But now I want to say a few words to finish with, and this is the motto of them: *great faith is much more commended.*

It is sometimes found where we least expected it. Our Lord beheld it, not in the manly Peter, but in the tender woman who pleaded for her child. She was a woman, but she had faith which put the men to shame. She was a Canaanite woman, of a race concerning which it was said, *Cursed be Canaan,* and yet she had stronger faith than Israelite Peter, who had known the Scriptures from his youth up. She was a woman who had great discomfort at home, for the devil was there, tormenting her daughter. It is a dreadful thing to have the devil in your husband, or the devil in your daughter, when you go home; yet many a Christian has this to bear. Notwithstanding this grave trial, though there was nothing to comfort her at home, she was a woman of great faith. And why should we not be like her?

My brother, although your condition and circumstances are greatly against your growth in grace, why should you not grow to manhood in Christ? The Lord Jesus can cause you to do so. Though it seems to you that you must be stunted by the chill blast and the cruel soil which surround you, yet the great husbandman can so foster you that you shall become a plant of renown. God can turn disadvantageous circumstances into means of growth. By the holy chemistry of his grace he can bring good out of evil. I commend great faith with special emphasis when I see it where all its surroundings are hostile to it.

Next, great faith is to be commended because *it perseveres in seeking the Lord.* This woman came to Jesus to have her daughter healed, and at first he answered her not a word. Oh, the misery of silent suspense! Next, he speaks coolly of her to his disciples, but she seeks on. She has come for a blessing, and she so believes in the Lord, the Son of David, that she will not take no for an answer; she means to be heard, and so she presses her action with urgency even to the end. Oh, for a strong faith, a persevering faith! Brethren, have you got it? You men, are you using it? Here is a woman that had it, and kept it at work till she won her object. May we have it abundantly!

Great faith also *sees light in the thickest darkness.* I do not think Peter was half so tested as the Canaanite was. What was it that frightened Peter? The wind. What might have frightened her? Why, the harsh words of Jesus himself. Who is afraid of the wind? Who would not be afraid of a rejecting Christ speaking hard words? *It is not meet to take the children's bread, and to cast it to dogs.* Why, if our Lord had spoken thus to any one of us, we should never have dared to pray again. We should have said, "No, that hard sentence shuts me out altogether." But not so for strong faith. "No," says she, "he called me a dog. Dogs have a position in society; little dogs are carried by their little masters indoors at dinner time, that they may get a crust or a crumb; and, Lord, I will be a dog, and get my crumb. It is only a crumb for you to give it, though it would be everything to me to get it." So she pleads with him as readily as if he had given her a promise instead of a rebuff.

Great faith can see the sun at midnight: great faith can reap harvests at mid-winter, and find rivers in high places. Great faith is not dependent upon sunlight: she sees that which is invisible by other light. Great faith rests upon the certainty that such a thing is so because God has said it, and she is satisfied with his bare word. If she neither sees, nor hears, nor feels anything to corroborate the divine testimony, she believes God for his own sake, and all is well with her. O brethren, I hope you will be brought to this condition, that you will believe in God though your feelings give God's promise the lie, and though your circumstances give it the lie. Though all your friends and companions give the Lord the lie, may you come to this: let God be true with every man, and every man a liar; but doubt God we dare not, and we will not. His sure promise must stand. Such a faith as this deserves to be commended, and our Lord himself praises it. *O woman, great is thy faith.*

Great faith prays and prevails. How she did prevail! Her daughter was made whole, and she received a broad grant of whatever she willed. *Be it unto thee even as thou wilt.* I wish we had this mighty faith in connection with prayer. One man praying with faith will get more from God than ten men, or, for that matter, ten thousand men, who are unstable and unbelieving. Believe me, there is a way of praying in which you may have what you will of God. You may go up to your closet, and ask and have; yes, and come out of your solitude saying, "I have it." Even though you have it not as a matter of actual enjoyment, yet your faith has grasped it, realized it, and believed in it, and so has taken immediate possession. Did not Luther often, in his worst times, come down from his chamber crying, "*Vici!*" ("I have conquered!") He wrestled with God in prayer, and then he felt that all else that he had to wrestle with was just nothing. If he had overcome heaven by prayer, he could overcome earth and death and hell. Strong faith does all this, and goes on to do more.

She has extraordinary reverence for God, but she has a wonderful familiarity with him. If you were to hear what strong faith has sometimes dared to say to God, you would think it irreverent; and irreverent it would be from any lips but hers. But when God indulges her to know the secret of the Lord, which is with them who fear him, and when he says, "Ask what you will, and it shall be done for you," she has a blessed liberty with God which is to be commended and not forbidden. If the Son makes you free in prayer, you shall be free indeed. Strong faith is ever on the winning side. It wears the keys of heaven on its belt. The Lord can deny nothing to the pleadings of an unstaggering faith.

I commend strong faith because *Jesus, our Lord, was delighted with it*. What music there was in his words, *O woman, great is thy faith*. There was no smile on his face when he said to Peter, *O thou of little faith*. It grieved him that his follower should have such little faith in him. But now it gladdened him that this poor woman had such splendid faith. He looks at her faith as jewelers do at some famous stone worth more than they can tell. "*O woman,*" said he, "*great is thy faith*. I am charmed with your faith. I am amazed at your faith. I am delighted with your faith." Well, brethren, you and I long to do something to please our Redeemer. I know we have often cried, "Oh, what shall I do, my Savior, to praise?" Believe him then. Believe his promise without doubt. Believe him greatly. Believe him unstaggeringly. Believe him to the full, and go on in faith till there seems to be nothing further to believe. Believe evermore in Christ Jesus.

> Strong faith is ever on the winning side. It wears the keys of heaven on its belt.

How enriched that woman became! She had pleased her Lord, and then her Lord pleased her: *Be it unto thee even as thou wilt*. She went away the happiest woman under the skies. God had given her desire to her, and she was over-glad and ever glad.

What benefits we could confer upon others if we had strong faith!

Her daughter was made whole. Mother, if you had more faith, your child would soon be brought to Jesus. Father, if you had more faith, your boy would not be such a plague to you as he is now. Have more faith in your God, and when you treat your Father better, your children shall treat you better. If you will dishonor your God by doubting him, do you wonder that your children dishonor you by disobeying you? O preacher, if you had more faith, you would have more converts! Sunday school teacher, if you had more faith, more children would be brought to the Savior out of your class. *Lord, Increase our faith.* I hope we are all saying that in our hearts at this moment.

I will conclude by asking, is there not great reason why our faith in Christ should be strong? Is there not every reason why we should have the strongest faith in him? I told you the other day of John Hyatt, when he was dying. Someone said to him, "Mr. Hyatt, can you trust your soul with Christ now?" He said, "I would trust him with ten thousand souls, if I had them." We can go even further than that. If all the sins against Christ that men had committed since the world was made, and time began, were laid upon one poor sinner's head, that sinner would be justified in believing that Christ could take that sin away. Whoever you are, and whatever you are, bring your burdens, and lay them at his feet, casting all your care upon him, for he cares for you; and from this point on may he never have to say to you, *O thou of little faith, wherefore didst thou doubt?* Oh, may he often exclaim, with joy, of you, *O woman, great is thy faith: be it unto thee even as thou wilt.* May the Holy Spirit bless these simple words of mine to your edification! Amen.

Chapter 15

The Perseverance of Faith

Then Jesus answered and said unto her, O woman, great is thy faith: be it unto thee even as thou wilt. And her daughter was made whole from that very hour. (Matthew 15:28)

I have frequently spoken to you concerning the faith of this Canaanite woman, of the way in which Christ tested it, and of the manner in which, at length, he honored it, and granted all that the pleading one sought. The story is so full of meaning that one might turn it this way, and that way, and the other way, and always see jewels in it. But now I am going to use it with only one end and aim, namely, to encourage those who have faith enough to seek Jesus, but have not yet, to their joy and peace, been quite able to find him.

This woman had come to her last word. I do not see what more she could have said. When Christ had likened her to a dog, she had consented to it and said, *Truth, Lord: yet the dogs eat of the crumbs which fall from their masters' table.* She had come to her last word, and now Christ gives her his best word. It is his way, sometimes, to make us wait till we are completely exhausted, and can say and do no more; then he comes in with the fullness of his divine power, and gives to us what we have urgently sought at his hands. Our extremity is his opportunity.

The first remark which I shall make, and enlarge upon, is that *faith alone can keep a soul seeking after Christ under discouragement.* Other causes may send us a certain distance along the road, but only faith will bring us to the goal of assured rest.

That which made this woman seek the Savior was, first of all, parental love. She loved her daughter. She longed to have the devil cast out of her so that her daughter might not be so grievously vexed. That started her going, and carried her some way towards the blessing; but she would have stopped short of the blessing she desired if she had relied upon natural love alone.

Her earnestness also to a large extent urged her forward. When she desired healing for her daughter, she meant what she said. When she cried, *Have mercy on me, O Lord, thou Son of David*, it was with a shrill and pitiful voice. She could not bear to be refused. Nobody ever came to Christ who pleaded more from the heart than did this poor Canaanite. She was not an idle repeater of forms of prayer. Her prayer leaped, red-hot, from her soul: *Have mercy on me, O Lord, thou Son of David*. But her earnestness alone would not have upheld her under the ordeal through which she was called to pass. It would have given way if she had not had the believing conviction that Christ could heal her daughter, and that he would do so.

Her humility also helped her greatly. Had she been a proud woman, she would have stood upon her dignity when she was called a dog; but humility came to her help, and she did not resent even the harsh word the Lord used, but still pleaded for her poor child. Now, parental love and earnestness and humility are good things, but they are not enough to enable a soul to cling to Christ and never let him go. Something more is needed.

This Canaanite was a very sensible woman, wise and prudent. She knew how to turn the hard words of Christ into arguments in her own favor. She would not be put back. If he had not answered her, she would have pleaded with him again. When he did answer her, and said that it was not proper to give the children's bread to dogs, she found even in that dry bone some little marrow on which to feed her heart. But wise as she was, and prudent as she was, she would not have held out to the end, and obtained the blessing she desired for her daughter, if it had not been for her faith.

We may be quite sure that the one thing especially noteworthy in this woman's case was her faith – first, because *we have Christ's word for it.* He said unto her, *O woman, great is thy faith.* He did not say, "Great is your love for your child," or "Great is your earnestness," or "Great is your urgency"; but he put his finger on the power that had urged her forward, and he said, *O woman, great is thy faith.* And not in this case alone did Christ trace the blessing to faith, but in nearly every instance where a pleader obtained favor from him, faith was the medium of securing the mercy. Faith is mightier than all other available forces.

Besides this, *we know that faith supports the other graces.* If other graces can help a soul to plead with Christ, they all owe their power to faith. If it had not been for the faith which she had to support it, parental love would not have helped this woman much. If it had not been for faith, she would not have been earnest and compelling. Faith supplies the strength of the other graces; and whatever they do, it is faith that works through them. Faith is the master-power. Faith hangs on to Christ in the dark, it holds to a silent Christ, it holds to a refusing Christ, it holds to a rebuking Christ, and it will not let him go. Faith is the great holdfast that hooks a soul on to the Savior.

Faith is thus powerful because of its effects. *Faith enlightens, enlivens, and strengthens.* It is written of some of old that *they looked unto him, and were lightened.* Faith sheds a light upon many things, and lets us see that even if Christ has a frown on his face, he has love in his heart. Faith looks right into the heart of Christ, and helps us to perceive that he cannot mean anything but mercy to a seeking soul. Faith also enlivens, and when the heart begins to faint, faith brings its smelling bottle and revives it. David said, *I had fainted, unless I had believed.* Believing is the cure for fainting, and you must do one of two things: either believe or faint. Faith is thus a great help to one who is seeking Christ, because it both enlightens and enlivens the soul. Faith also strengthens. It makes the lame take the prey. Beloved, it is because faith thus enlightens and enlivens and strengthens, that it is the grace most useful to a soul that is seeking to lay hold upon Christ, and yet cannot get a comfortable look at his blessed face.

Moreover, *faith lays hold on Christ.* It is like the Greek Antisthenes, who went to a philosopher to learn; but he was a dull scholar, and the philosopher bid him go away. The next time the class met, Antisthenes returned, and the philosopher therefore sent for a man with a club to drive the stupid scholar away; but he was overcome by his scholar, for Antisthenes said, "There is no club that was ever made that is heavy enough to drive me away from you. Here I mean to stay, and learn whatever you can teach me." Oh, may we have a faith like that, a faith that will say to Christ, "I will not go away from you. There is no threatening in your Book that can drive me from you. I can but perish if I stay with you, and if I go from you, I must perish; therefore, I will abide with you evermore, and learn all that you will teach me!"

Faith is like the Greek in the days of Xerxes, who seized the boat with his right hand. When they chopped off the right hand, he seized it with his left hand; when they cut off the left hand also, he laid hold of the boat with his teeth, and did not let go till they had severed his head from his body. Soul, if you can lay hold on Christ with your right hand, or with your left hand, it will be well with you. Cling to Christ, and say to him with that holy boldness that is the result of faith, *I will not let thee go, except thou bless me.* Faith, then, holds on to Christ.

Further, I would say that *faith does this best without help.* How often we try to assist faith! We want faith to have some works, some prayers, something or other of our own to help it. It is as if somebody were to try and help me to walk by giving me a big chair to carry. I should not walk so well with the burden as without it. Have you never heard this parable concerning faith? She had to cross a stream, and the current was strong, and there came one to her who said, "O faith, I will help you! Come with me up the river till we find a place where we can wade across it." Faith said, "No, I was bidden to cross the river here." So another came and said, "I will build a bridge for you, that you may go over the river with ease"; and he laid a few stones, but not much ever came of it. Yet another said, "I will go and find a boat." But there were no boats around; therefore, they asked faith to wait till they built a boat for her. What did she do? She took off her outer garments and plunged into the water. "Thank God," said she, "I can swim"; and so she swam across, and reached the other side without boat, without bridge, and without wading. That is what I should like to see every sinner here do: begin to swim. Do not wait for help. Cast yourself into the stream of everlasting love. Believe in Christ Jesus, and have no more confidence in the flesh, with its bridges and its boats. Commit yourself to the stream of eternal grace, and swim across. Faith can enable you to do it. Nothing else can. Take that lesson home to yourselves, you who are seeking the Savior at this time.

The only thing that will help you to follow after Christ till you find him is faith. All your groaning and moaning will not help you. All your doubting and your trembling will be of no help; your feeling that you are too vile to be saved, and that faith would be presumption in such a sinner as you are, will not aid you. But believe that Christ can save you, and trust his power and love, and he will save you. Come to him as this woman of Canaan came, with her urgent cry, *Have mercy on me, O Lord, thou Son of David*, and he will have mercy on you even as he had upon her. Believe, believe, believe! You will never come into light by doubting and fearing. The way to liberty lies through this one door of faith. Therefore believe and live.

> Believe in Christ Jesus, and have no more confidence in the flesh.

Thus much upon our first remark, that faith alone can keep a soul seeking after Christ under discouragement.

Secondly, *faith is exceedingly delightful to Christ*. What he said to this woman began with an exclamation, as if he was struck with something in her that delighted him. He said, *O woman, great is thy faith*. Notice that he spoke of her faith, and of that alone. He knew about her love, he knew about her earnestness, and he knew about her humility, but he said nothing at all about them. His one word of commendation was for her faith. *O woman, great is thy faith*. That is what my Lord is looking for now. He comes around and looks at you, who are sitting in these pews, to see whether you have faith in him. There are several thoughts suggested by this that should encourage you who are seeking Christ.

He can spy out the beginnings of faith. *If ye have faith as a grain of mustard seed,* he will see it, and he will accept it. If you have only now begun to believe that Jesus is the Christ and to trust him, though your faith be as feeble as a babe that cannot stand but can only cling to its mother's breast, Jesus will see the beginnings of it. He is *the author* as well as the *finisher of our faith*. Be comforted, then, concerning that tiny trust you have in him.

Still, *he is greatly pleased when he sees great faith*. When a great sinner says, "I believe that he is a Savior great enough to save me," it brings joy to the heart of Christ. When an old sinner says, "I believe that his precious blood can take away the sin of seventy or eighty years," the Lord's heart is gladdened. Christ loves a great faith. He deserves great faith, and when he gets it he is highly pleased. *O woman*, said he, *great is thy faith*.

He is so delighted with faith that *he passes by other things for it*. If that woman's ears had been hung with rings, and her neck had been decked with pearls, and her hands had been covered with diamonds, he would not have cared about her ornaments and her beauty. He sees something that he prizes more than any of these things; therefore, he says to her, *O woman, great is thy faith*. He is charmed with that choice decoration of her heart. By that treasure *the king is held in the galleries*. Christ may say of faith, *Thou hast ravished my heart with one of thine eyes*. When we can but look straight to Christ and trust in him, he is charmed and carried away by our faith.

Why does Christ think so much of faith?

One reason is because *faith glorifies him*. He thinks much of it because it thinks so much of him. Faith believes him, faith trusts him, and faith lives upon him. He is *the chiefest among ten thousand* and the *altogether lovely* one to faith. Therefore, because faith highly esteems Christ, Christ highly esteems faith.

Next, he loves faith because it is *God's appointed way* in which we are to receive blessings. God might have appointed ordinances as the vehicle of grace, but instead, he has made faith to be the means of salvation. If you believe, you shall be saved. He that by faith lays hold on Christ has laid hold on eternal life. *He that believeth and is baptized shall be saved*. To the awakened sinner our word is still, *Believe on the Lord Jesus Christ, and thou shalt be saved*. Since God has put faith into so eminent a place, our Lord Jesus Christ loves to see it; he takes delight in that which pleases his Father.

Another reason why he loves it is because *faith is the signal which permits the train of mercy to come to us*. Whenever unbelief holds up its arms, the train of almighty grace stands still. Of a certain place it is said, *He did not many mighty works there because of their unbelief.* Their doubt blocked the way. But when faith lowers the signal, the great Driver of heaven's express says, "That road is clear," and he delights to see it, and drives right ahead. Oh, if you can but let that signal go down, showing that the line is clear of all obstructions, Christ will surely come to you! He is glad to come wherever he can bring a blessing, and he rejoices when faith reveals to him a clear road.

Besides, *faith has open arms for embracing Christ.* When he comes to our door and finds it locked, he stands there till his bitter lament is, *My head is filled with dew, and my locks with the drops of the night.* But when he comes and the door is open, the poor sinner is so taken up with his beauty that he never thinks of shutting him out. "Oh," says the seeking soul, "if the Lord would but come in!" And as surely as Christ finds the door thus open, he comes in, and dwells there, and makes that heart and that house happy with his divine presence. Christ loves faith because faith gives him a hearty welcome, faith receives him, and faith embraces him.

Oh, I wish to God you would think of this and exercise faith in the Lord Jesus! May you see that nothing delights Christ like a sinner believing in him, that nothing gives him more joy than to have a saint resting completely upon him without doubt or fear!

Thus have we considered two points: first, that the only way to keep a soul seeking Christ from discouragement is by faith; and secondly, that nothing pleases Christ like believing on his name.

The third point is that *faith will, before long, get a kind answer from the Lord Jesus.* This poor woman at first received no reply to her petition, *Have mercy on me, O Lord, thou Son of David.* Then, when Christ did speak to her, he gave her what seemed to be a rough answer. But after a while, these notes of heavenly music sounded in her ear: *O woman, great is thy faith: be it unto thee even as thou wilt.*

Now, someone here probably says, "I have been praying ever so long, and I have received no cheering reply." Well, if you believe in Jesus, you shall have a good reply before long. If you can but hold on to Christ, determined to plead with him till he answers you, he will answer you kindly before long. But keep on believing that he can and will give you what you need, and you shall not be disappointed. "Oh," says one, "you do not know who I am! I am an outcast." So was this woman. She was a Canaanite woman, yet she obtained a blessing from Christ; and you shall get one too, if you follow her in her faith. "Oh, but I do not think that I am fit!" Did Christ ever say to you that you were a dog? He did as good as tell this woman that, yet she held on to him by faith, and prevailed. "Oh, but I have prayed in vain for such a long time!" So did she. She prayed, and for a while she received no answer. "Oh, but I feel worse after I have prayed!" So did she; for instead of getting a comfortable answer, she heard Christ say, *It is not meet to take the children's bread, and to cast it to dogs.*

You cannot be in a worse plight than she was. "But the devil troubles me," you add. The devil also troubled her. She pleaded for her daughter, who was possessed with a devil; and she kept on pleading and believing. She meant to have Christ. I exhort you to come to the same holy determination. Oh, that almighty grace might help you to do so; for in so doing you will surely get an answer of peace! You will get a comfortable answer before very long, probably much earlier than you have reckoned upon.

Remember that *Christ delays in order to increase your faith.* Your faith will grow by exercise; therefore, he tests it so that you may use it, and that thus it may become stronger.

Christ delays in order to increase the blessing itself. While we wait, the blessing becomes bigger, and our hands become stronger to hold it when it does come. You may be sure that our blessed Lord will give you a comfortable answer; for do you not know that he has been sustaining you while you have been pleading and as yet have received no answer? Did you ever notice, when Joseph's brothers went down into Egypt, that he made himself as a stranger to them, and spoke to them roughly, and put them in prison? But in spite of that, there was one thing he did: when they went back to Jacob, he filled their sacks for them. He would not smile upon them, but he would not starve them; and at last, it is said, *Joseph could not refrain himself,* and he *made himself known unto his brethren.* He was obliged to show his love at last; but even before he did that, he filled their sacks for them. Christ will deal with you in like manner: while you are waiting, he will not let you die.

Oh, in what wonderful ways did the Lord support me when, through weary years, I was seeking his face! I could not say that I had any comfort that I dared to call my own, and yet there flowed into my soul, somehow, a secret power that enabled me still to hope, and still to hold on; for that I now desire to bless his name, and I tell it for the encouragement of any who may be in soul-trouble as I was. Keep on seeking his grace, dear friend. Believe still, for he must give you a comfortable answer one of these days.

Consider well that *it is contrary to his nature to refuse to bless.* He is full to the brim with love; and if he does put a sinner back for a while, it is only because it is right and kind and wise to do so. But his heart yearns over every seeking sinner. He wants you more than you want him. He longs for you. He desires to bless you. He must do so, it is his nature to do so.

He must give you a comfortable reply before long, again, for *it is contrary to his glory to refuse.* If he allowed a seeking sinner to die, where would his truth be? Has he not said, *Him that cometh to me I will in no wise cast out*? Our friend Dr. Barnardo announces that in his refuges no homeless boy will ever be rejected, no destitute child shall ever be turned away. Suppose somebody could prove – which, of course, they cannot do – that scores of destitute children were turned away, then all confidence in him would be destroyed. And if it could be proved that Christ ever cast out a single soul that came to him, it would take away his honor and his glory. We could never believe him anymore. Perish the thought of such a thing!

It is contrary to his word to refuse any seeker, and Christ will keep his word. *Come unto me,* says he, *all ye that labour and are heavy laden, and I will give you rest.* If Christ does not give you rest when you come to him, what is his promise worth? My friend Dr. Pierson sent me the other day an imitation of an American banknote, which they call a "greenback" over there, and on one side of it were these words: *My God shall supply all your need according to his riches in glory by Christ Jesus.* A splendid note that was! It had our friend's name on the back, "Arthur T. Pierson," and he said to me when he sent it, "If the Lord does not pay you, I will, for I have endorsed the note." I shall never have to look my

> **He wants you more than you want him.**

brother Pierson up, and tell him that the note he endorsed is of no value. There it stands, and stands forever. God will keep his word. I know it, and I want you poor sinners to know it too. He cannot run back from his own promise. His word is his bond. To every honest man it is so; but to the threefold holy God his oath and his promise bind him eternally.

Let me add that if Christ does not give a comfortable answer to you who believingly seek him, *it is contrary to his practice.* Here are many of us who have known our Lord now for forty years, and we can say that his practice is to hear our prayers, and according to our faith, so is it unto us. Come along, you blackest sinner out of hell! Come, and wash in the fountain filled with blood, and you shall be cleansed, as surely as ever Christ died! Come along, you lowest, meanest, most self-abhorred, most self-condemned of humankind! Come you, and look to him, and trust in him; and if you do not find peace at once, be sure that you shall have it before long. *The morning cometh.* It is not for long that Christ's mercy can be restrained. He must break forth, like Joseph, weeping over his brothers. He must manifest himself to you in love, and tenderness, and kindness. I will be bound for him any day that it shall be so.

Lastly, we come to a very glorious thought: *faith getting Christ's word has all things.* Listen to the text again: *Jesus answered and said unto her, O woman, great is thy faith: be it unto thee even as thou wilt. And her daughter was made whole from that very hour.*

Christ's word was *a comforting word.* How the look on this woman's face must have altered when Christ talked to her so! When he at first answered her not a word, she doubtless had a long and sorrowful face, and probably big tears stood in her eyes; but now that he began to talk in another strain, how happy she felt! The woman was sad no more. So it is even today. One word from Christ can comfort you, even if they talk about putting you into an asylum because you are so miserable. One word from my Master shall be as the balm of Gilead to your wounds. He will bind up your broken heart. He will comfort you, and speak peace to you, as he did to her. It was a comforting word.

It was also *a commending word. O woman, great is thy faith.* She had never been praised like that before. I have no doubt that her husband had praised her. What good husband is there who does not praise his wife, even as it is written of the virtuous woman, *Her husband also, and he praiseth her*, but his praise has never been so sweet as this word from the Lord Jesus. I have no doubt that her daughter had called her all the sweet names she could think of; for she loved her child, and it is only natural to believe that her child loved her. But now, when Christ looks her in the face and says, *O woman, great*— "Ah!" she may have thought, "he is going to say, 'Great is your sin,' or else, 'Great is your noise.'" What astonishment must have been hers when he said, *Great is thy faith*. He gave her a gold medal for her faith, yes, something even better than that: she was put in the class called "highly commended." *O woman, great is thy faith*. It was a commending word, and she needed it.

Next, it was *a commanding word*. Notice that well. Listen to it: *Be it unto thee*. He speaks like a king. And if the Lord today speaks his gracious word with power, as I pray that he may, he will say, "Minister, comfort that woman who puts her trust in me." He will say, "Ordinances, comfort those weary ones. Bread and wine, be sweet to the taste of those poor troubled ones." He will say, "Prayer meetings, be a joy to those poor tested ones." It is a commanding voice with which the Lord of Hosts speaks, when he says, *Comfort ye, comfort ye, my people, saith your God. Speak ye comfortably to Jerusalem, and cry unto her, that her warfare is accomplished, that her iniquity is pardoned.*

In addition to being a commanding word, it was *a creating word*. Why, it was the very word that God himself used when he made the light! He said, *Let there **be** light* (emphasis added). He said to the earth, "Be," and it was. He said to the heavens, "Be," and they were. The word is a *fiat* – a decree. In the Latin it is precisely that, a *fiat*. So here, that same mighty voice says, *Be it unto thee. Be it unto thee*. O God, send forth a fiat at this moment to some poor weary heart! Create light, create joy, create peace. He can create all of these in your heart now. Oh, that he might do it by the power of his almighty grace! The faith of this poor Canaanite thus obtained for its reward a creative fiat from the lips of Christ.

For her, it was *a complying word*. You see all these adjectives begin with the same letter: it was a comforting word, a commending word, a commanding word, a creating word, and a complying word. "*Be it unto thee even as thou wilt* – just as you please, whatever you wish for, and in the way you wish to have it." Christ capitulates to a conquering faith. Nothing ever conquered him but faith. His love is stronger than death. Death could not conquer Christ, nor could all the powers of hell. But here he surrenders at discretion to a soul that can vanquish him by believing. *Be it unto thee even as thou wilt.* Do you want more joy? Do you want full salvation? Do you want perfect rest? Behold, he says to each of you who can and do believe in him, *Be it unto thee even as thou wilt.*

Thus, lastly, this word became *a completing word: her daughter was made whole from that very hour.* From that very hour she was well again. Christ finished that work speedily. He was not a long time in doing it. It does not take so long to save a soul as it does for a lightning flash to be visible. You pass from death to life in an instant. When lost, ruined, and condemned, the man casts himself at Christ's feet, immediately he is saved. It is not the work of hours, or weeks, or years when you trust in the finished work of Christ. All that required time, Christ has accomplished. All that now has to be done, can be done in a moment.

When a man is thirsty, it does not take him long to drink when the water is there. Remember the invitation with which the Scriptures almost conclude: *Let him that is athirst come. And whosoever will, let him take the water of life freely.* The water of life is there, take it. When a man is hungry, it does not take him long to eat when the bread is on the table. God can now give you grace which shall enable you to be made near at once. He can bring you immediately out of the blackness of sin, and make you in an instant whiter than snow. Make David's prayer your own: *Wash me, and I shall be whiter than snow.*

Believe my Lord and Master. Oh, why do you not believe him? Cunning doubts and reasonings cease! I would now take the hammer and the nails, and fasten my unbelief and fear to Christ's cross. Hang there, you thieves, and die! You destroy men's souls, you doubts and reasonings! Come here, simple faith, you who have no wisdom! A mere child you are, but O simple faith, you have the key of the kingdom! Come, and welcome, into my heart. Will all of you not also believe and trust in Christ even now? If you do, you shall be saved. *Be it unto thee even as thou wilt.* God bless you! Amen.

Charles H. Spurgeon – A Brief Biography

Charles Haddon Spurgeon was born on June 19, 1834, in Kelvedon, Essex, England. He was one of seventeen children in his family (nine of whom died in infancy). His father and grandfather were Nonconformist ministers in England. Due to economic difficulties, eighteen-month-old Charles was sent to live with his grandfather, who helped teach Charles the ways of God. Later in life, Charles remembered looking at the pictures in *Pilgrim's Progress* and in *Foxe's Book of Martyrs* as a young boy.

Charles did not have much of a formal education and never went to college. He read much throughout his life though, especially books by Puritan authors.

Even with godly parents and grandparents, young Charles resisted giving in to God. It was not until he was fifteen years old that he was born again. He was on his way to his usual church, but when a heavy snowstorm prevented him from getting there, he turned in at a little Primitive Methodist chapel. Though there were only about fifteen people in attendance, the preacher spoke from Isaiah 45:22: *Look unto me, and be ye saved, all the ends of the earth.* Charles Spurgeon's eyes were opened and the Lord converted his soul.

He began attending a Baptist church and teaching Sunday school. He soon preached his first sermon, and then when he was sixteen years old, he became the pastor of a small Baptist church in Cambridge. The church soon grew to over four hundred people, and Charles Spurgeon, at the age of nineteen, moved on to become the pastor of the New Park Street Church in London. The church grew from a few hundred attenders to a few thousand. They built an addition to the church, but still needed more room to accommodate the congregation. The Metropolitan Tabernacle was built in London in 1861, seating more than 5,000 people. Pastor Spurgeon preached the simple message of the cross, and thereby attracted many people who wanted to hear God's Word preached in the power of the Holy Spirit.

On January 9, 1856, Charles married Susannah Thompson. They had twin boys, Charles and Thomas. Charles and Susannah loved each other deeply, even amidst the difficulties and troubles that they faced in life, including health problems. They helped each other spiritually, and often together read the writings of Jonathan Edwards, Richard Baxter, and other Puritan writers.

Charles Spurgeon was a friend of all Christians, but he stood firmly on the Scriptures, and it didn't please all who heard him. Spurgeon believed in and preached on the sovereignty of God, heaven and hell, repentance, revival, holiness, salvation through Jesus Christ alone, and the infallibility and necessity of the Word of God. He spoke against worldliness and hypocrisy among Christians, and against Roman Catholicism, ritualism, and modernism.

One of the biggest controversies in his life was known as the "Down-Grade Controversy." Charles Spurgeon believed that some pastors of his time were "down-grading" the faith by compromising with the world or the new ideas of the age. He said that some pastors were denying the inspiration of the Bible, salvation by faith alone, and the truth of the Bible in other areas, such as creation. Many pastors who believed what Spurgeon condemned were not happy about this, and Spurgeon eventually resigned from the Baptist Union.

Despite some difficulties, Spurgeon became known as the "Prince of Preachers." He opposed slavery, started a pastors' college, opened an orphanage, led in helping feed and clothe the poor, had a book fund for pastors who could not afford books, and more.

Charles Spurgeon remains one of the most published preachers in history. His sermons were printed each week (even in the newspapers), and then the sermons for the year were re-issued as a book at the end of the year. The first six volumes, from 1855-1860, are known as *The Park Street Pulpit*, while the next fifty-seven volumes, from 1861-1917 (his sermons continued to be published long after his death), are known as *The Metropolitan Tabernacle Pulpit*. He also oversaw a monthly magazine-type publication called *The Sword and the Trowel*, and Spurgeon wrote many books, including *Lectures to My Students, All of Grace, Around the Wicket Gate, Advice for Seekers, John Ploughman's Talks, The Soul Winner, Words of Counsel for Christian Workers, Cheque Book of the Bank of Faith, Morning and Evening*, his autobiography, and more, including some commentaries, such as his twenty-year study on the Psalms – *The Treasury of David*.

Charles Spurgeon often preached ten times a week, preaching to an estimated ten million people during his lifetime. He usually preached from only one page of notes, and often from just an outline. He read about six books each week. During his lifetime, he had read *The Pilgrim's Progress* through more than one hundred times. When he died, his personal library consisted of more than 12,000 books. However, the Bible always remained the most important book to him.

Spurgeon was able to do what he did in the power of God's Holy Spirit because he followed his own advice – he met with God every morning before meeting with others, and he continued in communion with God throughout the day.

Charles Spurgeon suffered from gout, rheumatism, and some depression, among other health problems. He often went to Menton, France, to recuperate and rest. He preached his final sermon at the Metropolitan Tabernacle on June 7, 1891, and died in France on January 31, 1892, at the age of fifty-seven. He was buried in Norwood Cemetery in London.

Charles Haddon Spurgeon lived a life devoted to God. His sermons and writings continue to influence Christians all over the world.

Other Similar Titles

Life in Christ (Vol. 1, 2 & 3),
by Charles H. Spurgeon

Men who were led by the hand or groped their way along the wall to reach Jesus were touched by his finger and went home without a guide, rejoicing that Jesus Christ had opened their eyes. Jesus is still able to perform such miracles. And, with the power of the Holy Spirit, his Word will be expounded and we'll watch for the signs to follow, expecting to see them at once. Why shouldn't those who read this be blessed with the light of heaven? This is my heart's inmost desire.

– Charles H. Spurgeon

Available where books are sold.

***Jesus Came to Save Sinners,* by Charles H. Spurgeon**

This is a heart-level conversation with you, the reader. Every excuse, reason, and roadblock for not coming to Christ is examined and duly dealt with. If you think you may be too bad, or if perhaps you really are bad and you sin either openly or behind closed doors, you will discover that life in Christ is for you too. You can reject the message of salvation by faith, or you can choose to live a life of sin after professing faith in Christ, but you cannot change the truth as it is, either for yourself or for others. As such, it behooves you and your family to embrace truth, claim it for your own, and be genuinely set free for now and eternity. Come and embrace this free gift of God, and live a victorious life for Him.

Available where books are sold.

Words of Warning,
by Charles H. Spurgeon

This book, *Words of Warning*, is an analysis of people and the gospel of Christ. Under inspiration of the Holy Spirit, Charles H. Spurgeon sheds light on the many ways people may refuse to come to Christ, but he also shines a brilliant light on how we can be saved. Unsaved or wavering individuals will be convicted, and if they allow it, they will be led to Christ. Sincere Christians will be happy and blessed as they consider the great salvation with which they have been saved.

Available where books are sold.

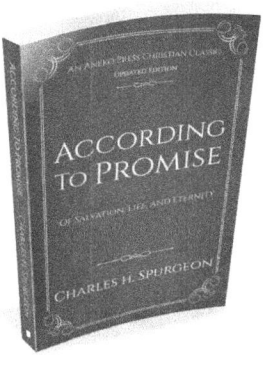

According to Promise,
by Charles H. Spurgeon

The first part of this book is meant to be a sieve to separate the chaff from the wheat. Use it on your own soul. It may be the most profitable and beneficial work you have ever done. He who looked into his accounts and found that his business was losing money was saved from bankruptcy.

The second part of this book examines God's promises to His children. The promises of God not only exceed all precedent, but they also exceed all imitation. No one has been able to compete with God in the language of liberality. The promises of God are as much above all other promises as the heavens are above the earth.

Available where books are sold.

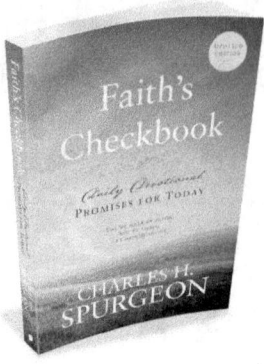

Faith's Checkbook, by Charles H. Spurgeon

Faith's Checkbook is a one-year devotional meant to encourage you to take God at His Word – to take hold of God's promises by faith. Each day you will be presented with a specific promise from the Bible, along with accompanying exhortation by Charles Spurgeon.

This is your "spiritual checkbook," if you will. God's bank account of provision is ample, and it cannot be overdrawn. Every situation you might face is equally met with a promise that, if accepted, will sufficiently see you through.

"God has given no promise that He will not redeem. He does not offer hope that He will not fulfill. To help my brethren believe this, I have prepared this little volume." – Charles H. Spurgeon

Available where books are sold.

***Morning by Morning*, by Charles H. Spurgeon**

Charles H. Spurgeon's devotionals *Morning by Morning* and *Evening by Evening* have inspired, encouraged, and challenged Christians for generations. Spurgeon, with his masterful hand, carefully selected his text from throughout the Bible and covered a broad range of topics, in order to present a well-balanced and fruitful daily devotional for readers both young and old.

Now updated into more-modern English for today's readers, and again separated into two volumes as originally published, with morning devotionals in one volume and evening devotionals in the second. We chose a 11-point font for the sake of legibility, and formatted the devotionals so each fits on a single page.

Available where books are sold.

Faithful to Christ, by Charles H. Spurgeon

I believe that many Christians get into a lot of trouble by not being honest in their convictions. For instance, if a person goes into a workshop, or a soldier into a barracks, and if he does not fly his flag from the beginning, it will be very difficult for him to run it up afterwards. But if he immediately and boldly lets them know, "I am a Christian, and there are certain things that I cannot do to please you, and certain other things that I cannot help doing even though they might displease you" – when that is clearly understood, after a while the peculiarity of the thing will be gone, and the person will be let alone.

However, if he is a little dishonest and thinks that he is going to please the world and please Christ too, he can depend on it that he is in for a rough time. If he tries the way of compromise, his life will be like that of a toad under a harrow or a fox in a dog kennel. That will never do. Come out. Show your colors. Let it be known who you are and what you are. Although your course will not be smooth, it will certainly not be half as rough as if you tried to run with the hare and hunt with the hounds, which is a very difficult piece of business.

Available where books are sold.

Following Christ, by Charles H. Spurgeon

You cannot have Christ if you will not serve Him. If you take Christ, you must take Him in all His qualities. You must not simply take Him as a Friend, but you must also take Him as your Master. If you are to become His disciple, you must also become His servant. God-forbid that anyone fights against that truth. It is certainly one of our greatest delights on earth to serve our Lord, and this is to be our joyful vocation even in heaven itself: *His servants shall serve Him: and they shall see His face* (Revelation 22:3-4).

Available where books are sold.

www.ingramcontent.com/pod-product-compliance
Lightning Source LLC
Chambersburg PA
CBHW070131080526
44586CB00015B/1652